THE NORTON SERIES ON INTERPERSONAL NEUROBIOLOGY

Allan N. Schore, PhD, Series Editor
Daniel J. Siegel, MD, Founding Editor

The field of mental health is in a tremendously exciting period of growth and conceptual reorganization. Independent findings from a variety of scientific endeavors are converging in an interdisciplinary view of the mind and mental well-being. An interpersonal neurobiology of human development enables us to understand that the structure and function of the mind and brain are shaped by experiences, especially those involving emotional relationships.

The Norton Series on Interpersonal Neurobiology will provide cutting-edge, multidisciplinary views that further our understanding of the complex neurobiology of the human mind. By drawing on a wide range of traditionally independent fields of research—such as neurobiology, genetics, memory, attachment, complex systems, anthropology, and evolutionary psychology—these texts will offer mental health professionals a review and synthesis of scientific findings often inaccessible to clinicians. These books aim to advance our understanding of human experience by finding the unity of knowledge, or consilience, that emerges with the translation of findings from numerous domains of study into a common language and conceptual framework. The series will integrate the best of modern science with the healing art of psychotherapy.

A NORTON PROFESSIONAL BOOK

LOVE AND WAR IN
INTIMATE RELATIONSHIPS

LOVE AND WAR IN INTIMATE RELATIONSHIPS

*Connection, Disconnection,
and Mutual Regulation
in Couple Therapy*

MARION SOLOMON
STAN TATKIN

Foreword by Daniel J. Siegel

W. W. Norton & Company

New York • London

For information about special discounts for bulk purchases, please contact
W. W. Norton Special Sales at specialsales@wwnorton.com or 800-233-4830

Manufacturing by RR Donnelley, Bloomsburg
Book design by Bytheway Publishing Services
Production manager: Leeann Graham

Library of Congress Cataloging-in-Publication Data

Solomon, Marion Fried.
  Love and war in intimate relationships : connection, disconnection, and
mutual regulation in couple therapy / Marion Solomon and Stan Tatkin ;
foreword by Daniel J. Siegel.
      p. cm. — (The Norton series on interpersonal neurobiology) (A Norton
professional book)
  Includes bibliographical references and index.
  ISBN 978-0-393-70575-1 (hardcover)
  1. Intimacy (Psychology)   2. Interpersonal relations—Psychological
aspects.   3. Marriage—Psychological aspects.   I. Tatkin, Stan.   II. Title.
  BF575.I5S65 2011
  616.89'1562—dc22   2010037721

ISBN: 978-0-393-70575-1

W. W. Norton & Company, Inc., 500 Fifth Avenue, New York, N.Y. 10110
www.wwnorton.com
W. W. Norton & Company Ltd., Castle House, 75/76 Wells Street, London
W1T 3QT
1 2 3 4 5 6 7 8 9 0

To Matthew, who facilitates my life's journey, and our children,
Bonnie and Glenn, who accompany us on our path.
—Marion

To my wife, Tracey, and my daughter, Joanna,
without whom none of this would be possible.
—Stan

CONTENTS

Contents

FOREWORD

Daniel J. Siegel

Within these pages you will find a fascinating presentation of basic principles that can transform how you understand and carry out couple therapy. Combining the creative minds of two leaders in the field of helping relationships heal, *Love and War in Intimate Relationships* carries us into this new way of thinking by drawing on two important bodies of knowledge: attachment research and neuroscience. As a part of the Norton Series on Interpersonal Neurobiology, this text also draws on the initial emphasis of its two editors. Allan Schore has made seminal contributions to our understanding of attachment and the development of self-regulation within dyadic communication. I have focused my initial clinical and theoretical writings on the power of the Adult Attachment Interview and developmental neurobiology to illuminate the nature of the mind and mental health. Similarly, Solomon and Tatkin have brought these two emphases on regulation and narrative into an exciting blend that brings us to new understandings of how to help couples overcome profound and previously mysterious obstacles to their union.

At the heart of Interpersonal Neurobiology as a field is the concept of integration—the linkage of differentiated parts. In this wonderful book, you will find that the voices of the two authors remain differentiated. Their insightful case examples illustrating the concepts in each chapter are naturally from their separate clinical practices. But the linkage of their independent voices becomes clear in the melding of the central notion of attachment and regulation. You will learn, in a deep and practical way, how to apply to couples' work a modified version of the important research instrument developed by Mary

Main and Eric Hesse and their colleagues, the Adult Attachment Interview. You will also discover how to be a "pscyhobiologically informed" therapist, attuning to the subtle non-verbal cues and interactions within a couple's moment-to-moment experience that can transform both your view and your strategies for intervention.

Not for the faint-of-heart, this book will give you direct access to the guts of the neural underpinnings of interpersonal relations. As mammals, we have a nervous system that requires the attunement with our caregivers early in life for our brain to develop well its circuits of regulation. We learn to regulate our bodily functions, our mental lives, and our interpersonal connections by way of these early attachment experiences. As we leave home, we carry the synaptic shadows of these early experiences forward in ways that are often beneath the radar of conscious awareness. Yet these subtle—and sometimes not so subtle—echoes of the past can entrap us in becoming lost in familiar places as we re-create and inflict past wounds.

On top of these basic physiological regulation patterns, we as humans also have a deeply organizing cortical process called narrative. How we come to tell the story of our life is directly related to our early attachment history as well. These more elaborate synaptic shadows cast their effects on our sense of self and the way we see the importance of relationships in our lives. Narrative also shapes how we construct the future. Attachment research reveals, too, that the best predictor of how a child will become attached to the parent is that parent's Adult Attachment Interview finding of coherence—or the parent has made sense of the impact of early life experience on his or her development. Within Interpersonal Neurobiology, we examine these two ends of our human legacy to be mammalian in our need for regulation shaped by our interactions with others and to be "homo narrativatas"—the story-telling species—in how we shape our lives through making sense of the world through the stories we tell ourselves and others.

So what can be done if our basic regulation and our narrative structures are both shaped by the past? Are we doomed to just recreate our life patterns relentlessly? How can we learn a new way of calming our internal storms, of using our partner to help with such dyadic regulation, and to open up to a new way of defining who we are and who we can become? Neuroplasticity is the pathway to change. This plasticity is the way the brain continues to change in response to experience throughout the lifespan. When we learn the ways to offer experiences to promote more integration in the insecurely attached individual's non-integrated nervous system, we can deeply change the ability to have effective self- and other-directed regulation as well as enable a narrative to emerge that makes sense of a person's life—one that is called coherent and is a part of an earned form of security. In other words, as therapists we can help create new experiences that inspire them to create energy and information flow through the clients' brains that help them change in helpful and lasting ways. But how can these neuroplastic changes be encouraged?

Enter, the informed therapist. Armed now with this important new perspective and with these helpful and creative strategies of intervention, you will have an effective approach that can finally get beneath words and help catalyze transformation even in the most challenging of couples. Knowing how to change the brain in the clinical setting is a basic tool for therapy to be effective. The case histories that the authors provide illuminate a new path that is likely to be rewarding for many couples that before may have found therapeutic efforts ineffective. Read on, soak these ideas in, try it out, and let us know how it goes!

INTRODUCTION

The Context

The last decade has seen extraordinary advances in our understanding of psychobiological processes and the reciprocity between early interaction and the developing brain. Attachment theory and the underlying neuroscience of emotional connection inform modern clinical treatment. The paradigm-changing synthesis of the two in the psychobiological approach to couple therapy brings a new lens to the relational sequences that create problems between intimate partners, offers new ways to effect change, and promises new possibilities for transformation.

At the earliest point in the development of a theory of intimate relations, there was no understanding of the processes by which the brain and the mind affect the dynamics of attachment, and little knowledge of how the earliest such dynamics, between infant and caretaker, are recreated in later relationships. Until the middle of the last century, behaviorists held that babies clung to their mothers, not for affection or attachment needs, but because mothers provided food and rewards, and psychoanalysts believed that dysfunctional development was due to internal fantasy rather than to real relationships between human beings.

Two original thinkers challenged those limiting assumptions. Harry Harlow (Harlow & Woolsey, 1958) found that baby monkeys chose the nurturing contact of a soft, cloth-covered wire-mesh doll (symbolizing *mother*) over the nourishment of food, indicating that the comfort of connection played a crucial role in development. John Bowlby (1979a, 1982) identified the desire of vulnerable human infants to maintain proximity to their caregivers as an adaptive response to real or perceived stress or dangers, and he posited secure mother–infant bonds as the linchpin of security throughout life.

Bowlby went on to theorize that individuals develop *internal working models* (1969) of self and other through repeated daily transactions with their caregivers—models that lead to expectations about future encounters and guide cognition and behavior in subsequent relationships (Main & Solomon, 1990). He further postulated a strong causal relationship between an individual's experiences with his or her parents and later capacity to engage in affectional bonds (Bowlby, 1979b, p. 135), specifically noting romantic relationships.

Bowlby's conceptualization of attachment led to a major revision in our understanding of how people learn to relate. The focus shifted away from the internal fantasy world of the child to the recognition of the impact of actual events with important primary figures. Moreover, the growing acceptance of Bowlby's work launched a giant revisioning of mature development. The early idea that indicators of maturity were based on the ability to separate/individuate (Mahler et al., 1975) was supplanted by a recognition of the importance of the capacity for connection in relationships with others (Schore, 1994, 2001c; Siegel, 1999, 2010a, 2010b). Increasingly this new thinking has become the basis of the clinical treatment of couples.

Subsequent research has confirmed the significant influence of early working models on romantic relationships, and this confirmation has coincided with the shift in focus from the individual to the couple as a unit (e.g., Berlin, Cassidy, & Shaver, 1999; Cowan & McHale, 1996; Hazan & Shaver, 1987). Recent work in couple therapy draws on that research to understand and treat relationship problems in keeping with the premise that seeking and maintaining emotional contact with significant others is an innate motivating principle across the lifespan (Bader & Pearson, 2000; Gottman, 1999; Johnson, 2004).

We now understand the role of secure attachment in the promotion of mature development, self-confidence, and autonomy (Feeney, 2007), the origin and the impact of insecure attachment orientations, and the importance of both to intimate partnerships. And we now know that the lack of secure attachment bonds early in life does not condemn one to a lifetime of unhappy relationships (Byng-Hall 1999); it is possible to *earn security* over time via new, reparative relationships (Main, 2003).

The psychobiological approach to couple therapy described in this book is less about individual attachment than about the quality of attachment in the couple system. Informed by research on affective and interpersonal neuroscience (Damasio, 1994; LeDoux, 1998; Panksepp, 2005; Porges, 2003) that has been masterfully integrated by Allan Schore (1994, 1997, 2000, 2001a, 2001b, 2001c, 2002a, 2002b, 2002c, 2002d) and Dan Siegel (1999, 2006, 2009), this approach identifies the influence of specific neurobiological systems on partners' attachment-driven behavior, and targets the mutually reinforcing association between insecure attachment and dysregulated arousal. Stressful clinical enactments are staged to expose and resolve challenges to partners' capacities to act as a coregulatory team that enjoys mutually amplified positives and mutually attenuated negatives.

OVERVIEW

The psychobiological model, developed by Stan Tatkin, is rooted in the perception introduced by Marion Solomon 15 years ago (*Lean on Me: The Power of Positive Dependence in Intimate Relationships*) that each partner in an adult primary attachment relationship must learn to be the other's *secure base* (Solomon, 1989, 1994).

Part I of this book describes the dynamics of attachment and the integrative value of mindsight (Siegel, 2010a). The case of a single couple followed over 3 years shows how insecure attachment patterns evident even in the glow of a new relationship can turn love into war. Key moments of emotional disconnection spark negative cycles that take over the partners' behavior and communication.

Part II explores the psychobiological approach to treatment. An extended teaching case demonstrates the use of techniques for addressing both attachment and arousal on the levels of assessment, intervention, and regulation, and includes an interview protocol and movement exercises.

Part III navigates through the theoretical universe, profiling the avoidant and angry-resistant incarnations of insecure attachment and zooming in on the dynamics of arousal regulation and dysregulation.

Part IV illustrates the theory in practice, with the therapist assuming the roles of participant and observer in four separate cases highlighting and deconstructing the power of therapeutic enactment and interdependence. A final case study illustrates how taking care of each other strengthens both members of a couple.

In an Epilogue, we apply the principle, discussed throughout this book to the self of the therapist, and consider a number of ways to facilitate therapist self-care.

Appendix A is designed as a systems glossary to reveal the linkage among the scientific components of the psychobiological approach to couple therapy, in addition to supplying working definitions of all terms.

Appendix B presents the Adult Attachment Interview and recent research on its applications to adult romantic relationships.

AUTHORS' REFLECTIONS

Marion Solomon

In the 1960s and 70s I was a young wife and mother and a budding psychotherapist, looking for answers to what makes marriage work. I was invited to coordinate a series of mental health conferences for the University of California's extension division, which would offer cutting-edge knowledge to mental health professionals. In the early years our conferences included such eminent presenters as Erik Erikson, Virginia Satir, Otto Kernberg, James Masterson, John Bowlby, and Heinz Kohut. We looked closely at what they were teaching in their various clinical settings about what happens in the relationship between patient and therapist. We explored the roots of psychopathology and ways to treat various clinical diagnoses. Psychodynamically oriented presenters did not explore other important relationships in patients' lives. Family therapists looked at ways to protect children from what was often found to be several generations of dysfunctional family dynamics.

Marriage and couples' relationships were not on the radar of most American clinical training facilities. And almost nothing in the professional literature focused on relationships between intimate partners (Harville Hendrix, *Getting The Love You Want* [1986], written for a general audience, was the only book I could find on the subject). Nevertheless, I found in Heinz Kohut's self psychology a path toward a model of couple therapy where he described the mutual selfobject functions that partners in a successful marriage provide for each other. "A good marriage," he said, "is one in which each partner rises to the challenge of providing the selfobject functions that the other's temporarily impaired self needs at a particular moment." Further, "who can potentially respond with more accurate empathic resonance than a spouse?" (personal communication, 1980).[1] Similarly, "Who . . . can traumatize a person more than a wife or husband who . . . responds with flawed understanding or, feeling overburdened, fails to respond at all?" (Kohut, 1984, p. 220).

Kohut's quest to find ways to help patients with narcissistic or self disorders (1971, 1977) gave me some important insights into why intimate relationships often fail and what is necessary to make them work. I applied those insights to my work with couples and to a book (*Narcissism and Intimacy*, 1989) on treating partners with a range of problems.

Until the late 1980s there was little to connect adult relationships to the unfinished business of childhood. But by then I'd been working with couples for two decades and I knew that their problems were often recreations of childhood issues; the focus in England on how early object relations impacted adult experience (Balant, 1956, 1964; Guntrip, 1961; Klein, 1955; Winnicott, 1965, 1969) lured me to investigate. What I learned from the training with Dr. John Bowlby about early attachment, separation, and loss created a sea change in my thinking. Importantly, it still fit with what Kohut said about people needing selfobjects throughout life in times of stress.

I realized that partners tend to play out their respective old attachment patterns, bent on repairing whatever was painful or traumatic. They are always testing their relationship: "If I show you my true self, can I be sure that you won't shame me, attack me, or leave me?" Partners need to do for each other what "good enough" (Winnicott, 1957, p. 135) parents do for their children, and if mates take care of each other, old wounds can heal (Solomon, 1994).

In search of ways to help partners make changes in how they relate to each other, I observed videotapes of the work of short-term therapists who focus on the reactions that occur in the body when emotions come up (Fosha, 2000; Kay, 2003; McCullough, 1997; Ne-

---

1. A fuller version of what he said around the planning for our 1980 UCLA conference appears in a footnote of Kohut's 1984 book *How Does Analysis Cure?*

borsky, 2001). I moved on to explore sensorimotor psychotherapy (Ogden et al., 2006), which integrates verbal techniques with body-centered interventions in the treatment of trauma and developmental issues and allows patient and therapist to reach core emotions at the intersection of the mind–body connection. I've found sensorimotor psychotherapy and mindfulness to be gentle and respectful ways to raise awareness in a couple session, and it is easy to incorporate with such other techniques as the mindful tracking of micromovements. Attending to fluctuating sensations and their connection to emotions is an entirely different way to focus on moment-to-moment interactions between partners and a welcome alternative to responding to the presenting problem of the therapy session.

In the 1990s an invitation from Dan Siegel to join a small study group on the brain put me in close touch with the explosion of neuroscience research. What I learned confirmed Bowlby's message that patterns of relating created by attachment, separation, and loss during the first few years of life become fixed and impact all future relationships. It also confirmed that couples' narratives (i.e., their presenting problems) are the logical products of the cortex playing catch-up with the emotional part of the brain. The limbic system reacts almost instantaneously. This understanding supports the view that couple therapy should concentrate not on the espoused content of the partners' conflict but rather on their underlying core dynamics.

That view frames one area of overlap between Stan Tatkin and myself when it comes to treatment. Our styles are different, betokening the unique experiences we each bring to the clinical table. Just as Mary Main's background in linguistics contributed to her development of a new perspective on attachment theory, so Stan Tatkin's background in music and psychodrama and his extraordinary creative use of video technology have enabled him to add a new dimension to working with couples—as, of course, has his immersion in the study of neurobiology with Allan Schore. His psychobiological model harnesses his fluency in that cutting-edge field to his understanding of attachment theory, his appreciation for the mechanisms and management of arousal regulation, and his inventive approach to therapeutic enactment. In addition to an intense professional curiosity about how to apply the material derived from Main's Adult Attachment Interview to couple therapy, Stan and I share a foundational vision of partnership and a powerful commitment to making change happen.

No ideas can claim to be completely new and independent. We learn from our mentors; we learn in dialogue with peers; we learn from the people with whom we live. My interest in treating the couple as the patient rather than treating two individuals who happen to be in a relationship dates back to Harville Hendrix's groundbreaking ideas. I thank Harville for his great insight and constant supportiveness as I studied how past and present are interwoven, and how relationship wounds can be healed through repair in a current intimate relationship.

When I began teaching the application of psychodynamic couple therapy twenty-five years ago, I found a kindred spirit, Dr. Walter Brackelmanns, who was developing his own integration of couple therapy. I thank him for the support that he gave to the new idea that the focus of the work is the relationship, not the growth of the individual self of each partner.

I thank Mary Main, my Adult Attachment Interview (AAI) mentor. Through many discussions in the course of organizing a series of immersion courses with Mary Main and Erik Hesse, I came to understand not only the validity of the AAI, but also the family therapy model of transfer of character traits from one generation to another.

Dan Siegel is ever at the forefront of neuroscience and I am proud to call him a friend and colleague. His invitation to join with distinguished colleagues such as Allan Schore and Louis Cozolino, in joint study of the emerging research in this field was key to new understandings that greatly enhanced this book. Siegel's focus on integration was quite simply transformational.

Since 1990 I have had the good fortune to work with Dr. Judith Anderson in co-coordinating a series of "Anatomy of Intimacy" conferences at the University of California, Irvine. Through the people I met in helping to organize these conferences, I had the opportunity to participate in dialogue with many of the leading couple therapists of the 21st century, including Dr. John Gottman, to whom I am indebted for teaching me ways to study a taped couple interview to identify partners who are likely to succeed or fail in their relationship.

I further wish to thank clinician–researcher Dr. Susan Johnson, who has done a masterful job of applying attachment therapy to work with couples. Her insights in opening new paths to treating relationships have been greatly beneficial as have the many experiences we shared together.

I wish to express my gratitude to those who have given special time and attention to assist me in this project. Collegiate friends Harold Delchamps, Fanya Carter, Pearl Brown, Robin Kay, William Bower, and Judy Miller devoted many hours to discussing and reading early versions of this book as I attempted to integrate psychodynamic self psychology and attachment theory with Stan Tatkin's developing psychobiological approach to couples.

No book could be done without the help of editors at the publishing house. A special thanks to Deborah Malmud and Vani Kannan at W. W. Norton for going above and beyond normal expectations to facilitate the integration of the many ideas in this book.

The help of editors Jessica Ruvinsky and Cindy Hyden was invaluable in integrating what seemed at some points two different volumes. A particular thanks to my daughter and colleague, and much more, Bonnie Mark-Goldstein, whose integration of her work as a child psychologist with my focus on couple therapy has resulted in valuable dialogues about the effect of healing marriages on children and families. Special thanks to the men in my life, son Glenn, who freely shares the unique joys and dilemmas that modern marriage presents, and husband Matthew. Matthew performs a labor of love each time I immerse myself in a new book or project. He gives me feedback as I seek his sage advise on new ideas, helps me stay calm through the pressure of deadlines, and encourages the kind of two-way healing attachments about which I write.

Stan Tatkin

There are no new ideas—just new ways of interpreting and integrating them. It was while I was teaching graduate-level infant, child, and adult development courses that I gravitated toward Bowlby and Ainsworth's attachment model. Here I came up with the notion of doing prevention treatment with mother–infant pairs instead of reconstructive therapy with adults.

I was still treating disorders of the self as an object relations therapist when I first began giving talks on integrating infant attachment with affect regulation and neuroscience, and I had begun to attract a growing number of couples to my practice. The similarities between infant–caregiver attachment and adult romantic attachment became increasingly undeniable—as did my suspicion that arousal regulation played a critical role in marital satisfaction and outcome.

As I continued to write and speak about early prevention work with infant–caregiver dyads, I started applying the same theoretical elements toward adult primary attachments. In a 2003b paper ("Marriage and the Mother–Infant Dyad: Relational Trauma and Its Effects on the Success and Failure of Both"), I made a stronger shift toward adult attachment. The earliest incarnation of a psychobiological approach to marital therapy was published as "Turning Toward and Turning Away: The Psychobiology of Adult Primary Relationships." Once refined to incorporate the four components that define it today—attachment, arousal, neuroscience, and therapeutic enactment—the Psychobiological Approach to Couple Therapy® was launched, online and in print (Tatkin, 2006a).

Our work as couple therapists begins after nature has done the pair bonding: Courtship itself is a rigorous weeding-out process. The psychobiological approach does not focus on changing individual personality structure or attachment organization. Rather, it seeks to make the adult primary attachment relationship more secure by working directly with preparatory and reactive neurobiological systems toward optimizing/enhancing the core elements of safety and security; everything else is optional. Thus the adult primary attachment relationship is defined by its qualities of mutual dependency (Solomon, 1994), not by its romantic or sexual qualities. The fact that adult primary attachment relationships are commonplace is the constant. The safety and security of those relationships, however, are the true variables. It is these variables that are at issue in this book and this treatment approach. I hope the reader will get a taste of how powerful and even enjoyable this multilayered approach can be for both the clinician and the couple.

My earliest training at the Southern California Counseling Center inaugurated my identity as a psychotherapist. The structural and strategic family systems approach delivered there is an indelible part of my work today. Equally influential are the psychodramatic tools I acquired along the way from Dorothy Baldwin Satten and Mort Satten, Kip Flock, and John Bradshaw, the exotic Zen-like worlds of two fabulous Japanese psychotherapies Morita and Naikan, and Vipassana meditation (mindfulness practice) introduced to me by David Reynolds and Stephen Young (a.k.a. Shinzen Young), respectively.

James Masterson and his developmental object relations approach to disorders of the self became a key influence early in my career. Thanks to John Gottman and Paul Ekman for inspiring me and many others to appreciate the biology of romantic coupling. Elisabeth Muir and her work on the Watch, Wait, and Wonder Program in Toronto opened doors for me to so many others in the universe of attachment and neuroscience, including Beatrice Beebe, Mary Main, Alan Sroufe, Jaak Panksepp, Stephen Porges, and Allan Schore, my mentor and friend.

I admired Marion Solomon's work with couples from afar for many years. When we met and began to exchange ideas, I found her to be a kindred spirit: She loves to learn and is passionate about couples. Marion encouraged me to think by providing a never-ending chain of dilemmas for me to resolve. She challenged me when my ideas were not thought through and didn't make sense.

Our shared philosophical belief in secure attachment and interdependence brought us together, and our common concern about partnership and commitment in our modern age has transcended the difference in our backgrounds and approaches to couple therapy.

Marion wrote *Lean on Me* when Americans were still in love with autonomy, separateness, and preservation of the self; she was ahead of her time. We both hope people are now ready for a more reasoned, purposeful, and less lonely approach to partnering and commitment.

Allan Schore continues to be my intellectual guide. Were it not for him, I would not have developed this psychobiological approach to couple therapy. It was through his teaching that I learned to appreciate the inextricable links between personality, attachment, and developmental, affective neuroscience.

I couldn't have translated the psychobiological approach to couple therapy into book form without the support and encouragement of professional colleagues and dear friends (listed alphabetically): Ellyn Bader and Peter Pearson, Jude Berman, Malcolm Cunningham, Karen Dean Fritts and John Schwope, Leslie and Bob Godwin, Cindy Hyden, Edward Kassman, Bonnie Mark-Goldstein, Pat Ogden, Jessica Ruvinsky, Judith Schore, Janet Smith, Paula Thomson and Maurice Godin, and my students and readers.

Finally and most important, I could not have done what I did or continue to do what I do without the unwavering love of my daughter, Joanna, and my wife, Tracey, who is my go-to partner. The real foundation of my attitude toward attachment and relationship is my late parents' constant love and regard for one another—and Tracey, who exemplifies, every day, all that is right and good about a secure primary attachment relationship. She is and will always be my hero and inspiration.

LOVE AND WAR IN
INTIMATE RELATIONSHIPS

PART I

How Love Turns to War

Chapter 1

CONNECTION AND DISCONNECTION

It is no accident that of all the possible people to choose from, often the person we select to become the center of our world turns out to have an uncanny resemblance to a person who raised us. We recreate, in our intimate bonds, patterns of interaction that were scripted in our relationships with our primary caregiver(s), whether good or bad. These interactional patterns, once wired into the brain, tend to recreate themselves in each subsequent relationship throughout life. How often have we seen someone divorce, only to marry a person just like the partner left behind?

The good news is that committed partners with early attachment histories that are problematic can repair the past together—they can make their couple system secure. From recent advances in attachment theory and affective neuroscience, we now understand that patterns of relating alter, and continue to be altered by, partners' individual brains and their collective nervous system (explained below). The transformational model informed by this perspective draws on the power of the couple relationship to enhance attachment and promote change.

Each of us is psychobiologically wired to attach to another. In its most positive form attachment provides a safe harbor, a haven from small and large storms outside. In childhood it is played out in the primary bond between infant and caretaker. As adults, we experience it most powerfully in the relationship between two intimate partners (Dicks, 1967; Shaver et al., 2000).

From our primary other person we derive the energy to brave the outer world of strange people and things. We depend on this same person to breathe life back into us when we are hurt, exhausted, or discouraged by happenings outside ourselves. We hold hands when in unknown territory and we watch each other's backs. How well we steward the relationship is directly connected to our survival and well-being. Christopher Lasch (1977, p. 3) described this as a "haven in a heartless world."

Each member in an adult primary partnership occupies a kind of "office" that represents the position once held by the earliest caregiver, and performs Kohut's (1971) selfobject functions (perceiving the other as part of the self). This office activates the neural networks in the brain that are established in the years after birth and shaped by the nature of our early attachment relationships.

Neuroscience research of the past two decades (e.g., Schore, 2000, 2001c; Siegel, 1999, 2010a, 2010b; Trevarthen, 2001) confirms that attachment, separation, and loss during our formative years profoundly affect lifelong patterns of relating and that these relational blueprints correspond to structural and functional development of the brain, nervous system, and neuroendocrine system (there will be more on this topic in Part III). This wiring is manifest in well-worn neural network pathways, which are stimulated by triggers that remind us, implicitly, of childhood experience—our wounds, triumphs and longed-for experiences.

The bonds of intimacy bring up the very same needs, yearnings, disappointments, and protective defenses that occurred in the primary bonds of infancy and childhood. For this reason, adult primary attachment partners have a unique power to hurt or to heal, to weaken or augment resources of the other. In fact, once the members of a couple have stopped "auditioning" to get the gig and each agrees that the other is "good enough" (Winnicott, 1957, p. 135), adult partners are in the best position to shore up each other's early childhood attachment wounds. The power of this position outweighs that of any other, including a therapist.

Over the years as a psychodynamically oriented couple therapist, I (M.S.) have had opportunities to do premarital counseling with couples newly in love. I've met with long-married couples complaining about disappointments and betrayal, couples frustrated and feeling unloved, and couples who seem to be doing their best to destroy each other. The question has long been on my mind, "What turns two people who feel a beautiful sense of merger and the excitement of being together into two people who are filled with rage toward each other?"

The brain in love produces a wonderful sense of timelessness and euphoria that involves little thought but intense emotion. Millions of neural networks are activated and the brain centers that mediate emotions, sexuality, and the self begin to expand and reorganize (Bartels & Zeki, 2000; Fisher, 2004). Romantic love releases surges of the neurotransmitters dopamine and norepinephrine and activates brain regions that drive the reward system in a way that is similar to addiction (Fisher, 2004). New lovers talk endlessly, intertwine themselves incessantly (often to the discomfort of those around them), call each other baby names—and are convinced that this state will last forever. However, when two people fall in love, the seeds of their later conflicts are already present. Both carry their personal history wired into their brains, and these neural networks are waiting to be activated by reminders of early attachment failures.

The case of Richard and Christine depicts a couple that experienced both sides of the loving–warring relationship over the course of 3 years. The clinical work and the thinking behind this case illustrate psychodynamic treatment informed by, and embodying, our growing understanding of principles of interpersonal neurobiology. The integrative approach in this case can be seen as a bridge from mindful awareness and mutual attunement to Tatkin's psychobiological approach in the cases to come, which feature attention to problems of mutual regulation and intervention by means of therapeutic enactment.

Richard and Christine first contacted me (M.S.) with a request for premarital counseling. Each saw the other as perfect, the answer to a lifetime search for a secure love bond, someone on whom to depend. By the time we met again 2½ years later, each saw the other as the problem. Changing the other will not fix a relationship, however. Once partners become intimately connected, both play out old attachment patterns, responding to their wired-in expectations of a primary other.

5

The work of couple therapy is (1) to help both partners understand why each behaves in ways that seem to create problems, clarifying with them how what is happening in the here and now is caused by a recreation of the past in the present moment; and (2) to use a mindsight lens to facilitate their ability to be present and attuned to the emotions of each other, encouraging them to discover ways to recognize and then calm the angst and pain (Siegel, 2010a). In this way couple therapy has the potential to heal not only the present, but also to help restructure limiting beliefs from the past and establish new neuronal connections in the brain.

RICHARD AND CHRISTINE

Richard and Christine walk into the office holding hands and head toward the love seat without asking the questions couples often ask about where to sit. Their nonverbal, body-to-body communication reflects their current feelings of being "in love." They are here for 3 weeks of premarital sessions, at Richard's behest. He says friends suggested the sessions as a gift they should give themselves in preparation for their forthcoming wedding.

"We know ourselves pretty well," Richard says. "And we don't have any real problems. But we both had bad experiences in our first marriages. So it seemed like a good idea to make sure that there are no danger signals to watch out for. I want to head off any issues that might come up and get the tools to handle them when they do. That's what I do in my business, and this relationship is more important than any business deal."

Richard's declaration prompts me to wonder straightaway if he has a serious need to maintain control. As he spoke, he sat a little taller, his chin lifted, and his voice was confident and authoritative. Couple therapy can be anxiety-provoking, especially for people who have experienced childhood attachment wounds; they often fear being shamed and/or blamed by the partner and the therapist. Seizing control may have proven to be a reliable approach to overcoming difficult life situations for Richard. It could also be a negative way of managing the reemergence of old fears.

At this point I speak to the positive side of the need to maintain control and make a mental note to observe what emerges in the session. "That sounds like a very wise decision," I reply. "But why did you specify three sessions?"

"I'm a value investor," he answers, again with confidence and authority. "I figured that if we have limited time, we will get to the important things right away. And I don't want to get in the habit of seeing a therapist regularly, like some of my friends do. I like to figure things out myself and solve my own problems."

Genograms and Attachment Interviews: Getting an Overview

We begin the extended first session with a short genogram (McGoldrick, 1995). This process identifies family patterns, marriages and divorces, births and deaths, and extended separations and their causes on both sides of the family, going back several generations. I notice common patterns in Richard's and Christine's family histories. I learn that each is the oldest child of divorced parents. Both have mothers and two younger siblings who currently depend on them for much of their support.

I look particularly for traumatic attachments, separations, and losses, anticipating amplification in the longer, targeted, attachment interviews that come next. I want to learn about Richard's and Christine's respective attachment experiences when they were very young, and the procedural tendencies that reflect these relationships. The way they respond somatically to each other, in posture, expression, and movement, especially when under stress are rich with relevant information. I introduce the questions about their memories of relationships with each of their parents and other important people in their childhoods by explaining that their recollections will help me get to know how each of their brains got set up early on for relationships. The questions are derived from the Adult Attachment Interview (AAI) developed by Carol George, Nancy Kaplan and Mary Main (George, Kaplan, & Main, 1984, 1985, 1996; Main, 2000) in their research on the connection between adult attachment patterns and toddler attachment patterns.

The first exploration of the neurobiology of the AAI was by Daniel Siegel in *The Developing Mind* (1999).

Each person develops a complex network of memories, emotions, and beliefs that shape present and future attachment behavior. The questions and follow-up probes I use are designed to reveal the workings of individual partners' models for experiencing the world, experiencing themselves with others, and anticipating how others will respond to them. Both the content of their respective narratives and the ways in which they answer the prompts tell a lot about how their brains are wired, how secure or insecure their attachment styles are, and how they communicate about elements that are stressful.

I continue with them: "People tend to select mates with some similarity to past attachment figures in their lives in hopes of filling important emotional needs. I am interested in seeing the places where you fit well together, the traits that signal to each of you, outside of conscious awareness, that the other is *The One.*"

I also watch their bodily responses as they speak of their parents because these implicit procedural tendencies elucidate their early relationships, sometimes more clearly than the words. Do they sit a little taller, or do they slump in their chairs? Do they tighten up and constrict their breath, or do they relax and breathe deeply?

Getting started with the Adult Attachment Interview,[1] I ask Richard for "five adjectives that describe your relationship with your father when you were under 12 years old." He replies, "*uninvolved, preoccupied, absent . . . ,*" and then says he has no more.

I ask for examples of each of the adjectives. "Give me a memory of when you found him to be uninvolved."

"Dad always seemed resentful that Mom was not keeping us quiet enough so that he could read his paper in peace." For the adjectives "preoccupied" and "absent," Richard's verbal and nonverbal responses convey his sadness and anger that his father was busy with his work or kept his nose in his newspaper and showed no interest in the kids or their mom.

"Anything more?"

"No, nothing," he said, matter-of-factly, masking any emotion.

I then ask him for "five adjectives that describe your relationship with your mother when you were under 12."

1. Although the instrument was designed solely for research purposes, it has practical applications in couple therapy both as a history-taking instrument and as an intervention, as we will discuss.

"Loving . . . caring . . . supportive . . . affirming . . . strong," he replies, his face brightening and his breath deepening. Richard's entire body seemed to come alive at the mention of his mother.

"Now give me an example of each of the adjectives. Give me a memory of when your mother was loving." We went through each of the adjectives in which he described his relationship to his mother. All memories were of exchanges that occurred when he was less than 6 years old.

After Richard does so, I go on to ask a series of other questions drawn from the AAI.

"When you were a very young child, to whom did you run when you hurt yourself?" And, "When you were a child, and you were sick, who took care of you?" He answers, emphatically, "Mom."

"Give me a memory of when you were sick as a child and your mother took care of you."

"I was 5 and had chicken pox. Mom stayed home from work and brought me soup. I couldn't swallow anything. She sat on my bed and put her hand on my head. I remember her reading to me."

In each of his memories he describes turning to his mother when he needed comfort as a small child. He says she did everything for her children and very little for herself.

I learn that Richard's father abandoned the family when Richard was 6 and that his mother worked very hard to support her three children. "Sometimes there wasn't enough money to buy food for all of us, and she'd say she wasn't hungry. That's why I send her money and gifts now. I sent her to Hawaii last year and Europe this year. And I just bought a condo for her to live in comfortably. She deserves it because of all she gave up to care for us."

I pay particular attention to the coherence of his childhood attachment memories, however, and notice that Richard's original glowing description of how his mother related to him as a very young child changed when he came up with examples from later in life. As he spoke, his body seemed to sag and his voice became quieter.

A few minutes later, when I ask, "Was there something you wanted from either of your parents that you did not get?" I observe the muscles in Richard's face tighten as he tries to hold back tears. He seems to stop breathing.

"It looks like something really painful is coming up for you," I say softly.

The tears, he whispers, are not about what he wanted from his father, "who was missing in action my whole life—but about what's been missing from Mom."

After her husband left the family, Richard's mother turned to her son as the "man of the house"; she called him "my little man." At 13, he took a job delivering food from a local market and turned over all his earnings to her to supplement her income as a tailor's assistant. He came to recognize that his mother did not know how to manage money, recalling that when he was 15 his sisters got new shoes but there was nothing left to buy shoes for him.

Throughout his teenage years (a time when adolescents declare autonomy), Richard found himself taking increasing responsibility for his siblings and mother so that they could survive financially. The closeness he and his mother had shared when he was a young child seemed to ebb, however. And he had no idea as to why.

When he won a basketball scholarship to a prestigious college 3,000 miles away, he hesitated to accept it, worried about how his family would manage without him. By that time, without conscious awareness, Richard had come to believe that providing financial support gave him a level of power in his family. He was surprised and excited when his mother encouraged him to go, assuring him that she could handle things at home with the girls; he was also disappointed that he was no longer needed—or perhaps even wanted.

The examples Richard offers in response to questions on the attachment interview reveal not sustained affirmation from his mother but his growing sense of emotional disconnection from her as he grew up. He tells, for instance, of how she recently found a packet of cards he had sent to her over the years—birthday cards, Christmas cards, postcards from his travels. "She thought I'd be happy to see that she saved all my cards. But you know, she never acknowledged receiving them. Never a thank-you when I sent them." The more he tried to help her, the greater the distance he felt from her, and as he spoke of this, his pain was visible in the helplessness and anger in his voice and the tension in his body. It appears not to have occurred to Richard that his mother might have experienced the way he offered financial support and advice as controlling.

I ask a final question. "Is there any particular thing that you feel you learned, above all, from your childhood experiences? I'm thinking here of something you feel you might have gained from the kind of childhood you had."

Using this question drawn from the Adult Attachment Interview evokes mindful reflection of present experience while connecting to past memories. Often the linking of past, present, and future adds a new awareness of early-formed beliefs about self and other, and recognition of how these beliefs may emerge in current interactions. Certain questions from the Adult Attachment Interview protocol bring up explicit memories about a person's history, and a way of understanding patterns of attachment that have been kept out of conscious awareness. Sometimes the questions and probes feel quite painful. For clinical purposes it is best to alternate the AAI probes with questions that can be answered in a positive way. Another possible question is, "What would you hope your child will have learned from his/her experience of being parented by you?" (George, C. Kaplan, N. and Main, 1996). It is then possible to probe more deeply into how attachment history reemerges in the present moment.

Richard says, with a hint of pride in his voice: "It made me stronger. I've worked since I was 13, and picked up skills at whatever I was doing. I learned to make myself successful by working very hard. I guess what I gained was the assurance that I can take care of myself and my family." After a short pause, he added, "I also learned not to do what my father did to us. I know that I will never walk out on my family, no matter what. It's too devastating to those left behind."

"And how does your childhood affect you in this moment?" I ask, noting his fingers forming into a fist as he talks.

"I'm tense; I get anxious when I try to understand what happened with my mom. But it reminds me that I am strong and can take care of myself."

As Richard discusses the dual messages he got from his mother, it becomes clear that his seizing of the caretaking role has had a price—the "loss" of his mother as he knew her, and her distancing from the warm connection they had shared. She adored him as a child, saw him as the one who would make it in the world, and seemed to depend on his doing so. But as she got over the shock of her husband's abandonment and managed to survive on her own with three young children, she began to regain her strength—to the point that she encouraged Richard to accept the faraway college scholarship.

Richard's early experience of his mother led to a belief that women were weak and that he needed to be strong to to take care of those he loved. That perception would blind him to his mother's growing sense of empowerment: He continued to see the vulnerable woman of his childhood and could not understand why his attempts to help were met with such chilliness. The same behavior would later significantly affect his relationship with Christine. He could take care of himself and the women he loved, denying his own needs for nurture and caretaking. His mind and his body held two opposing messages.

Moving to address the same series of attachment questions to Christine, I say, "Give me five adjectives that would describe your relationship with your mother when you were a child."

"No *there* there," she responds, rather plaintively, with a deep sigh, and then adds, "*sad . . . depressed . . . needy . . . demanding.*"

"Give me an example of "No *there* there."

"I wasn't the only one who couldn't get her attention," Christine says. "No one could. She was usually high on something. Occasionally she kicked it, but that never lasted. At least that's what I remember from before I went off with my uncle." Christine's voice was sad, not angry, and she sounded childlike. Her body visibly seemed to shrink into the sofa.

I learn that Christine was raised from the time she was 8 by her father's brother, Uncle Ted, a talent agent who took her on as his ward. She had been recognized as a musical prodigy from the age of 4, when she walked over to the piano at her nursery school and reproduced what the teacher had just played. Uncle Ted first got her singing roles in the companies of big shows, touring the country; later she played a child in a popular musical on Broadway. She also composed songs on her own, and he helped her get a contract to record them.

To my request for adjectives describing her relationship with her father, Christine offers "*uninterested, not there, sometimes playful, sad, untrustworthy.*" When I ask for an example of *"uninterested,"* she says: "I loved to play the piano. Daddy complained that I was making noise when he wanted to sleep—at 4:00 in the afternoon!" Here, she sounded indignant, her chin lifted in defiance.

Mainly, Christine's memories of her early relationships with both her mother and father are foggy. "They were hippies and mostly tuned out. There were lots of drugs; strange people showed up in our house for days or weeks at a time. Mom was like a shadow in the background. Dad was 'the little man who wasn't there.'"

She isn't sure how her parents made the arrangements to give her to her uncle—maybe some money was exchanged or maybe they just welcomed having one less mouth to feed—but she remembers liking him and not missing them very much. She especially recalls how she loved to curl up on the couch next to him and listen to tales of all his travels and stories about the famous people he knew from his work. When Christine spoke of her uncle, her demeanor changed—her eyes lit up, and her body softened, signs of security she had felt with him.

For a while Christine became quite successful, with three of her records making the pop charts. When she was 16, her uncle took her back to her mother's home (her parents were again living apart) and "temporarily" left her there. He wasn't feeling too well, he told her, and would come back for her when he was better. But he didn't come back; he died 2 months later. As she speaks of this, there is a downward turn of her chin and slump of her shoulders, slightly less than might be expected as she describes the loss of her one solid attachment figure.

She missed him a lot and sometimes fantasized that if she had been with him, he would still be alive. She was not happy with her mother, or with her father, who moved back home when she returned. "They were better than they used to be," she recalls, "but still using pot and still disorganized." Neither had a steady job. Their income was supplemented by one or another family member.

Christine soon came to understand that mismanagement of money had been a serious problem for both her mother and father over the years, and one cause of their on-again/off-again relationship. They had no idea of how to keep a budget; when money occasionally came to them (e.g., a gift from her grandmother, a couple of small inheritances), it seemed to vanish quickly.

Shortly after she rejoined her parents, they began talking about expenses and asked her to help support the household. Uncle Ted had invested most of Christine's earnings for her so she was a fairly wealthy young woman at the age of 16. Christine was thus thrust into a similar position as Richard, supporting the family. However, because of the way Uncle Ted had created a trust for her, she had only limited access to her income until she turned 21. She helped to the extent her trust would allow it.

When I ask questions about family, Christine looks at me blankly. The only sense of family she knew was herself and her uncle, traveling around the country living in hotels and short-term apartment rentals, and finally in an apartment in New York City. Her parents' only connection to their own families was financial: Money, rather than love, had always been the means of exchange between them. Christine followed the pattern: Her money bought their approval and kept them from being angry with her.

At age 18 she married for the first time, a short-lived and unhappy experience that ended when her husband stole from one of her accounts. Although not educated about money, Christine learned to protect what she had. She found an accountant, who taught her to balance her checkbook, guided her on financial decisions, and let her know what she could afford. She bought the home in which she and Richard now live when she was 21.

Christine sees both of her parents often. She also talks to her mother on the phone several times a week, although she says she would rather not, because her mom is like a child, always needing something. Yet Christine keeps giving her mother and also her sister whatever they ask for—to avoid having arguments with them, she says.

I ask her a final attachment question: "Is there any particular thing you feel you learned, above all, from your own childhood experiences? Something you feel you might have gained from the kind of childhood you had?"

Christine answers, "I learned to be a good girl and to do what other people wanted me to do. But I realize now that that is not good for me. I need to find out who I am and what I want to do. Richard is wonderful; he helps me—when my mom and sister become too intrusive, he helps me think clearly about things. I am so lucky to have Richard in my life."

Exploring the Current Issue

New love is like magic: Each partner has a fantasy that the other will fill in everything that is missing. Christine and Richard are not asking whether they should marry, as some couples do, but how to make sure that their relationship thrives. In the two remaining pre-marital sessions, we discuss their living arrangements, plans for a family, issues around money, and goals for the future. We also talk about ways to handle problems that develop. I ask them about the kinds of problems that come up and suggest that they think of a specific issue: "Are there any issues that haven't been talked about that we might explore together now?"

"The only issue," says Richard, "is the one about our difference in religion. Christine first promised to convert and raise our children Catholic. I was disappointed that she changed her mind."

"How did you try to resolve it?" I asked.

"Well, neither of us is that religious," Richard responds. But I do want my children baptized and brought up Catholic. I don't understand why she changed her mind on it. I wonder if she even knows why she is now reneging on her promise? And if so," Richard turns toward Christine, "how do I know I can trust you about other promises?" Under the surface was the boy who felt betrayed by his mother's withdrawal of her adoration. But his rising anger triggers Christine.

Christine sinks into the couch, and her body seems to contract. She appears getting smaller every moment. I comment on the shift in her body and demeanor and ask Richard if he notices it also. "I notice it a lot. When I try to talk about serious things, Christine seems to go somewhere else."

I ask Christine to take some time to stay focused on her body in this moment and see if there are any sensations, images, or memories that come up. I want to access the early experiences that are playing out in her relationship with Richard in the present.

The memory that emerges, Christine says, is of her uncle, and how frightened she felt when he was angry with her.

"Give me an example," I say.

"I got knots in my stomach when he got upset at my wanting to play, or do anything else instead of practice." When she begins to talk about it, a memory arises, and she freezes. In the face of her uncle's past (and her fiancé's present) anger, Christine's arousal spikes and she is no longer in her "window of tolerance."

The window of tolerance (Siegel, 1999) is a band of arousal within which a person functions well. Inside it, we can feel and think at the same time, or "hold the elements of our internal world in awareness" (Siegel, 2010a, p. 138). Outside the window, when new experiences reactivate neural networks established when we were young, intense emotions may shut down the "higher" cognitive functions. The person may then behave in the current relationship as they did in the past. Rational thought becomes impossible, and integration is impaired.

Christine's window of tolerance is narrow. Her strength, however, is her internal observer, which emerges at times and enables her to look clearly at herself, recognize when she "zones out," and use the information to shift direction. This self-awareness is a positive sign that this couple may be able to learn ways to recalibrate after problems arise and to develop new solutions together.

After a few minutes, Christine is again able to both think about what she is experiencing and process her emotions at the same time. She responds to Richard on the religion issue with clarity and insight.

"In the past, I always agreed to do what other people wanted—my uncle, my parents, my first husband. I never went to school or had a real education. I've always been afraid I'm not smart enough. I have to change that. I have to decide what I want separate from what other people want me to do. Richard, I need you to understand that about me."

Christine goes on, her voice gaining confidence and her body looking less childlike. "I'm not reneging on a promise; I'm growing. We can raise the children as you wish. That's fine with me. But I don't want to give up the religion of my grandparents and great-grandparents. I have enough trouble holding on to my identity, knowing who I am."

Richard seems to accept that and turns toward her. "I want you to grow. I'll help you," he says. "And I'm glad you have no objections to bringing up our children in the Catholic religion. You know how important it is to me."

Religion, like money, sex, and childrearing, can become the battleground for loving–warring couples. Richard and Christine avoided a major problem. Each felt that an important message was heard, accepted, and responded to by the other.

I reflect on what I have learned about Richard and Christine, their histories and attachment patterns, their needs, yearnings, and defenses. Both were seen by their caretakers as unusually gifted, and both achieved the success that was expected of them, but neither has been able to translate achievement and financial abundance into sustained love. Both had parents who were unavailable emotionally, and both have felt used and misused by important people in their lives. They each yearn for connection, but both have become accustomed to insecure patterns of interaction.

While their relationship is new, Christine and Richard are reveling in the certainty that they have found someone to love who loves them back, and in the tacit assurance that their individual histories have been overcome. But they, like all of us, are likely to bring their old relational patterns to any partnership. They are unconsciously connecting around the fit they experience with Richard's being a supportive partner and Christine remaining dependent and trying to please him, while at the same time, attempting to grow.

Richard takes the role of caretaker, and in the process of playing it out, vicariously experiences the nurturing that he craves, as he did with his mother when he was small. His feelings of being loved and appreciated make him work very hard to keep Christine happy and close to him. As long as he is in control, he feels like he is doing his job well.

Christine wants to learn from Richard, as she did from her uncle. When he occasionally points out her mistakes and tells her how she might think about things, she responds positively, as her wish is that he will help her grow and become more independent. At this point, she sees Richard as an ally in her self-actualizing process.

Their unspoken contract works for them—at this time. I summarize my take on their relationship. "You both have the capacity to encourage the strengths of each other. To make your relationship deeper, Richard, you need to allow Christine's learning, growing, and becoming autonomous. Christine, you need to know Richard beyond his outward self of strength, to know that inside there is an abandoned little boy who is as vulnerable as your abandoned little girl. If you attune to each other and encourage each other's dreams, you will grow together in a partnership of trust and security."

Richard and Christine marry a few weeks after our three sessions end. I know there will be times of misattunement between them, and serious questions: "Will he be there when I need him? Will she accept me if she knows how vulnerable I am? Do I have to hide my true self to be loved?" I wonder whether they will find the path to healing their respective attachment wounds without additional help. Will they go in the direction of attunement to each other's internal state, responding to the other's needs and strivings—or will they get mired in a cycle of unmet needs, anger, defense, avoidance, and disconnection? I have the opportunity to revisit these questions two and a half years later, when Christine and Richard return to therapy.

Chapter 2

THE BATTLEFIELD

Happiness can be ephemeral. Six months after they send me a card with a picture of their newborn daughter, Christine calls for an appointment. When they come in, their seating choices are different and indicate a relational shift. Richard heads toward the love seat. Christine sits catty-corner on one of the rolling chairs. She brings out pictures of their daughter, Emily, in whom they both clearly delight. When I ask how things have changed since Emily was born, Richard replies that he has been working even harder to make sure that the family is well provided for, no matter what happens. His voice sounds slightly accusatory, his body stiff. Christine says, "Richard is trying to teach me how to handle money. I've learned a lot from him, but sometimes we end up arguing."

As couples move from the euphoria of new love to a committed partner-ship, the patterns of interaction they learned from their first attachment figures begin to emerge. Those with a history of secure attachments may not notice minor misattunements within the intersubjective field, or may quickly correct and repair them. As specific problems surface, such partners stay connected, deal with the issues, and talk things through. Those with a history of insecure attachments, however, will begin to test each other, particularly under conditions of stress. They are predisposed to expect that this relationship, too, will disappoint, and to respond with criticism, contempt, stonewalling, and a variety of other defenses (Gottman, 1999). Such well-established negative behaviors by one partner are likely to provoke reciprocal negative responses in the other, setting up entrenched patterns between them.

Richard expands on what he sees as the problem. "Chrissie has always had her own money that she made with her music. We've kept our money separate, which we both want, and we keep one joint account for household expenses. But I just don't understand some of her spending. She pays her accountant thousands of dollars every year and I don't think that he's doing the right things for her. Before we were married if she asked him whether she could afford a new car or a new house, he always told her there was plenty of money and that if she needed more, all she'd have to do is go back to work. So she spent whatever she wanted. She even had a dog walker three days a week. But now when I tell Christine that since she's home with Emily, she should find time during the day to walk the dogs herself, she tells me that maybe she should go back to work." He speaks directly to me, as if speaking about a recalcitrant child.

Christine begins talking about an offer she got to do a show beginning in a few months, sounding excited, but also defensive. Like Richard, she speaks only to me.

"I haven't taken any jobs since Emily was born, and I feel ready to work again. Besides, I want to know that I can afford the things that I think are important," she says with a mixture of firmness and trepidation in her voice. Clearly she is not used to standing up for herself and wants my support.

Looking toward Richard, I say that I know how important it has been to Christine to be able to make important decisions on her own, just as I recognize his attempts to convey to her the message of financial caution.

This energizes Richard to go into advisory mode. He recalls what it is like for a family to not have money for food, and goes into his autopilot response of protecting the family against financial ruin.

"I'm just trying to understand why you won't listen to my suggestions about saving money," Richard says. "People pay me thousands of dollars for these kinds of suggestions."

"I try to talk with you," Christine says, pulling back slightly. "But whenever I make decisions about what I want to do for the house, or for Emily, you always begin talking about how much it will cost. When you say you don't understand, you mean that *I shouldn't do it*. There are things that I want to do and can afford to do."

"That may be," Richard interrupts, "But I keep asking to go over the budget with you and we never seem to get to it. Help me understand why we need a dog walker."

Christine looks at the bookshelf behind us in the room and does not respond.

"And help me understand why we need a housekeeper full time, plus a nanny five days a week?"

Christine sits very still and expressionless, looking frozen.

At this point Richard becomes very angry. "Right now I'm trying to talk to you, and it's like . . . you're gone. I try to understand, but it doesn't make sense to me."

Richard looks at her and then away. I point out what I see and ask if they know what their bodies are communicating to each other. They look confused and to clarify, I add, "I wonder if you know what you are saying to each other nonverbally?" Richard says, "Well, if she's not interested, there's nothing to talk about." I say, "Maybe not in words, but there is a whole lot of communication going on here. It may be a good start to recognize that you are looking to Christine for some sign of connection and she looks like a deer in headlights."

I want to focus not on their description of what's going wrong, but on the layers underneath, the unmet needs that cause an emotional and somatic reaction. The first step is to make sure that the reaction itself is picked up—by me, if not by them—at the beginning. Sometimes nonjudgmentally modeling the way to read each other's somatic responses teaches them how to attune to each other's underlying, unspoken messages.

"Christine" I say, "I see you tuning out. Is that what happens at home?"

Christine nods, and replies quietly, "something happens inside me when he gets angry. He goes at me and I can't stop him. So I walk away."

"Right now you are not physically walking away; you are sitting here next to Richard, but you are gone," I say. "Maybe I can help you just look at what happens inside that's scary and together we can find the words for you to tell Richard what's going on."

After a few moments, Christine starts talking quietly, not knowing how to say what she feels. I ask her to look at Richard and to Richard I say, "Don't say anything. Try to just hear."

Soon Christine finds her voice. Her chin lifts and she says, "It's always about money for you. That's why I don't talk to you about it. We have two big dogs. They need someone to walk them. And I have a relationship with Margie, who has walked the dogs for five years. She needs the work; the dogs need walking. I don't want to cut it out. I don't need to."

Presenting problems such as their earlier issue around religion, or now, money and work, are generally the "tip of the iceberg," covering many layers of underlying issues. They are like nested Russian dolls (Neborsky & Solomon, 2001; Solomon, 1994), with the outer doll representing the presenting problems, and each inner doll representing ever deeper yearnings and fears.

This is how the rumbles of war begin—with the issue of the day: What's worth spending for? Who makes the money? Who walks the dog? Failure to identify and resolve underlying issues keeps partners stuck in repetitious arguments—and is the reason that their initial loving relationship may turn into a battlefield.

Even if partners listen to each other on this surface level, they are not getting to the recognition and repair of core needs and feelings that could open the channels to earned secure attachment (Main, 2002). Old, well-established neural networks are activated, threatening reenactment of old wounds, but also providing the opportunity for healing. Here is the place for the therapist's intervention to open the channels in a way that is not shaming or blaming.

Being Present in the Moment

I ask Richard and Christine if they are willing to try an exercise that may help redirect their focus from their habitual communication patterns and toward attunement to themselves and each other. I explain that simply becoming aware of the sensations, emotions, or thoughts that come up as they breathe deeply right now, in this office, in this moment, will help provide a sense of safety so that we can access some of the things that may underlie the issues the two of them are dealing with.

When they agree, I suggest that they move over to the love seat in my office. "What I will ask you to do now is simply focus your attention on your breathing. You can begin with your eyes open or closed. Breathe deeply, feeling the air enter your nose, go down past your throat into your chest, or perhaps even deeper into your belly. Notice the breath going in and out, and if anything comes up . . . any image, emotion, thought, sensation . . . notice it, and then return your attention to your breathing. There is no need to judge, analyze, or figure things out, no right or wrong in this exercise. Just let yourself be aware of the breath, of the air going into and out of your nostrils . . . your chest . . . your belly. When your focus wanders to thoughts, memories, or anything else, gently bring it back to the breath. If you are having any difficulty, it's OK. Just be aware of that. Exercising attention is like exercising a muscle. We flex and relax, focus and refocus our attention when it wanders, mindfully going back to the breath."

This monitoring of awareness and intention is at the heart of a mindfulness orientation to clinical practice. It can be a powerful tool to help move the dialogue toward integration and a new experience of being together. Mindsight (Siegel, 2010a), or practicing self-observation in a nonjudgmental way, opens a space for new awareness and can widen the window of tolerance within which psychological work can be done. By expanding the range of emotions that do not throw clients into chaos or rigidity, we expand their capacity to heal (Siegel, 2010b).

I now take them through a body scan (Siegel, 2010a, 2010b; Stahl & Goldstein, 2010), modified for couples to do together. "Start by sitting side by side, but only as close as feels natural and comfortable to you. Be aware of how close you are and what it feels like in your body. Before going on, correct for any discomfort." When they both indicated it was fine, I said, "Take a few deep breaths and as you breathe deeply, let your body relax. Feel the sensations of your back against the back of the couch, buttocks on the seat. Now gently shift your awareness to the bottom of your feet on or near the floor.

Sense what is being felt; the heel, ball, and soles of the feet. Now notice your toes, and now the top of your feet, slowly shifting awareness up to your ankles."

"Still taking your awareness slowly, move to your calf and shin on each leg, and moving upward, feel the connection to the knees."

"As you go up to the thighs and beyond to the hips, remember to be mindfully present. Be aware of any tension in your feet, your legs, thighs, or hips. Notice whether there is a sense of relaxation as you scan your lower body. Keep your breathing even."

I continue to direct their awareness slowly to each part of their bodies: the pelvic region; the organs of elimination, sexuality, and reproduction; the abdomen and the belly, the lower, middle, and upper back; the chest, heart and lungs, rib cage and breasts; the fingertips, fingers, palms, back of the hands, and up into the wrists; the forearm, elbow, and upper arm, shoulders and armpits, neck and throat; the jaw, teeth, tongue, mouth and lips, the cheeks, and the sinuses; the eyes, eyelids, and muscles around the eyes; the forehead and temples; the top and back of the head; the ears and the passages that lead to hearing; and the brain itself.

We take our time, doing this slowly. The exercise takes about 15 to 30 minutes, depending on what is happening in their bodies. At each stage I remind them to be mindfully aware of the particular part of the body, to notice the sensations in each part of the body as they focus on it, and to be aware of any tension.

"Note any sensations in your body right now. Expand your awareness to the whole body: head, toes, hands, and fingertips, experiencing your body as a whole organism, with all its physical sensations, thoughts and emotions. Stay with this wholeness without focusing on any one part. Breathe in and feel the whole body rising. Now feel your breath upon exhalation."

"Continue for a few more breaths, being mindful of your presence. If you find yourself drifting into thoughts or memories, remember that we will have time to talk about them later. For now, just stay with your breath, keeping your mind in the present without memory, thought, or desire."

Asking both to tune in to where they are in the moment—not the argument they had last week or last night or on the way to the session—is often the fastest way to go from the content of their narratives right into what their bodies are saying about the emotions underneath.

Mindfulness exercises a part of the brain just behind the forehead, the prefrontal cortex, that links together the otherwise separate regions of the brain that think, feel, and connect to the body. Integrating these parts by focusing attention on the present moment paves the way for attuned communication, emotional balance, empathy, and insight (Siegel, 2010a, 2010b).

After a few minutes of silence, I say softly, "Can you turn toward each other and talk about what is happening for you right now?"

Richard says, "At first I noticed a lot of knots in my stomach, then tension in my back and neck. It feels very familiar. But when I began to breathe deeply, I started to relax."

Christine looks down, fidgeting with her fingers, but says nothing.

"I see a lot of emotion, but it's hard to talk right now, huh," I say.

Tears come to her eyes. I wait. Richard looks at me, but not at her.

Then Christine begins to cry. Richard turns toward her and asks, "What's wrong?" .

"I don't know," Christine says. "I just feel so sad."

"That makes me sad," he interjects. "I don't know what to do when you get like this."

I help him move away from his natural inclination to problem-solve and bring him back to mindful attunement. "Perhaps just tuning in to her feelings will help," I say. "You don't need to do anything but be present with her. See if you can make contact without words." Richard reaches over and takes her hand. He does not look relaxed. Nor does Christine.

After another silence, Christine says, "I try so hard to please you, and then you tell me that that I'm doing it wrong. All my life people have been telling me what to do, where to live, how to dress, when to practice. I have grown up a lot since my uncle died, and I've been managing my own money and making decisions about my career. I'm trying so hard to take care of myself. It seems like you don't trust me to be able to make good decisions."

Richard looks uncomfortable and shakes his head as though he doesn't understand her. "But I've always wanted you to be able to grow up," Richard says. "I've always tried to help you be the responsible adult you want to be."

"I depend on your advice, Richard. You're the smartest person I know," Christine says. "I love being with you. You're funny, you've read everything, you want what is best for us and for Emily. I love your desire to help. But I really want to have you see me as a person who can make my own decisions. I would love to have your input, as long as I don't feel that I must do exactly what you say."

"We're in this together," Richard says, "and if that's what you need, we can talk about it, and then you can decide and do as you wish."

Christine's body visibly changes She takes a deep breath, reaches over to take both of Richard's hands, and says, "Oh, that would be so good." They sit together in silence for a moment and Christine adds, "I love you so much." Richard puts his arms around her, and pulls her close. His body seems to relax.

At this moment each of them has the experience of feeling felt by the other. They know that the mind and body of the other experiences them accurately, and they are able to let down their guard.

Our time was about up and I said we would continue this next week.

It would be wonderful if such interpersonal attunement and insight led to a change in underlying dynamics, but that is often not what happens. It takes repeated, small healing experiences of feeling understood, safe, and comforted to begin to change relational blueprints.

Christine starts the next session by saying, "We were trying to talk to each other during the week, but we didn't get very far. Can we talk about it here?" She looks directly at Richard. His body tensing up, he hesitantly says, "Of course."

"Well, then, let's talk about my taking that part I've been offered. You can be home with Emily while I work in the evenings."

Richard and Christine have made their way back into their presenting problem, about money and work; this time the spiral grows to encompass an issue that was on his mind.

"You would also have two matinees, and you wouldn't be home on Sundays, when we are supposed to have family time."

I hear in his emphasis frustration and anger. His body language reveals both his irritation and his need—his chest collapses ever so slightly, but his voice bristles. I do not yet know all the specifics, but I recognize his desperate yearning to have more family connections and a more secure attachment. Yet as he responds to her need for autonomy, his bid for connection comes out as a complaint.

Christine replies, "I know. It will be hard on me also. I hate to leave Em; she will miss me too much."

Her response does not soothe his sense of being forgotten or address his underlying need for her positive attention. She's focused on making her own decisions about using her time and money to meet her own needs. They are each speaking in a code not understood by the other. Richard continues the miscommunication by asking a question rather than saying what he is feeling.

"Then, help me understand, why are you thinking of taking this job? You have plenty of money," Richard says. "I spend nothing of your investments. I'm very careful to save what I earn. Why do you need to work?"

Christine looks down at the floor. I note her hesitation and recognize a pattern. His questions invite no answers; they are closer to injunctions. What Richard wants from Christine has nothing to do with her earning, or even spending, money. There is a deeper agenda. On his part, issues of control overlie a craving for nurturing; when his mother went to work, he was bereft, and when he tried to help her, his efforts were rebuffed. On Christine's part, her fight for an autonomous identity is an attempt to supplant her codependent[1] responsiveness to others' demands; she is afraid that if she allows herself to need Richard's help, she will be trapped in an old pattern that began during the years when she lived with her uncle.

I note to myself that both Richard and Christine act as though he is the strong one and she has limited capacity to function. That myth—however belied by her professional success—seems to be playing around the edges of their relationship. She feels powerfully her lack of formal education. He still carries the belief from his childhood experiences that his mother cannot function without his help and support.

1. The difference between codependence and positive dependence is what is being enabled. Codependent people stay in relationships in which they enable those who abuse alcohol, drugs, or family members. Happy couples enable the positive aspects of one another.

I mentally review what I see as the impasse that we need to break, the place to intervene. Each learned ways to shield him- or herself with protective defenses when experiencing the pain of emotional disconnection. Richard's protective defense is to be in control. As long as he is in charge, he can make sure that everyone is taken care of—except for that vulnerable part of himself, which he suppresses. He has a deep fear, hidden from everyone including himself, that if he is not in charge, things will fall apart, as his family did when he was a child. Christine initially welcomed his take-charge style from the child place in her that needed guidance, but now she experiences it as an attempt to quash her own disposition and choices, and diminish her capacity to function autonomously. Rather than recognize Richard's controlling behavior as a core security issue for him, she thinks it reflects his desire to control *her*.

Christine's protective defense is to withdraw from contact, as she did when she was a child. Perhaps because he continues to feel his mother's emotional distancing from him as a tremendous loss, Richard reads Christine's withdrawal not as her way to cope with the insecure residue of her developmental traumas, but as her ignoring or dismissing him. Each partner's defenses activate the other's wounds.

Richard and Christine need to attune to each other on an emotional level and be able to resonate with the other's internal experience. I ask if they are willing to try another exercise. When they agree, I suggest that they can get another perspective if they get up and go to the other side of the room, where I have two barrel chairs on wheels. "The exercise," I explain, "requires only that you sit down and turn the chairs toward each other. Then look at each other's eyes and sit for a few minutes in silence."[2]

After a moment I add, speaking quite slowly, "I want each of you to imagine that you can see very deeply through the lenses of the eyes, into the core of the other. Imagine you are going to paint the eye. What would you look at? Look at the different parts of the eye. The whites, the pupil, the iris. Are there lines in them? Note the color of each eye, any differences between them, the shade, the darkness of the pupil. See if you can capture the expression of what's behind the eyes at this moment. Get ready to paint it in your mind."

2. Sometimes I ask partners to look only at each other's left eye. The goal here is finding a direct route to the right brain (Kawashima et al., 1999; Nicholls et al., 1999).

Eye-to-eye contact is, along with skin contact, among the most funda-
mental ways that humans connect. Without such contact, at any time
in life, both mind and body are negatively affected. Bowlby's (1969)
landmark attachment research included observations of children in
hospitals who were separated from their parents; their responses go
from protest to withdrawal to detachment over time. Adults who were
not held as children, or who feel a lack of connection in their current
lives, go through a similar protest–withdrawal–detachment cycle,
sometimes with a lot of demonstrable emotion in the protest stage.

"When you have finished painting the eyes in your mind," I say,
"you can begin to address the other important need of all human
beings, to be gently stroked by a loving other. Continue being the
artist, this time painting the other's whole face using your index and
middle fingers as your brush. We'll do this one at a time. Who would
like to start?" Christine volunteers.

"With the tips of your fingers, gently paint the outline of the
face. Include the neck. Stroke the eyes. Now paint around the
eyes, the eyebrows, the nose, the cheeks, the outlines of the
mouth. Paint the lips, the chin, the ears, and if you wish you may
go to the top of the head, and back to the face. Do this in silence.
Now, ask if there's something else that he would like—heavier,
lighter, more than two fingers—and try the face painting once
again."

When she is done, I say, "Now, without talking, pay attention to
the feelings around touching and being touched. For the moment,
just hold the feelings. See where they are held in the body. Take as
much time as you need."

"Now switch roles, with Richard being the artist." I give the face
painting instructions again, and watch their bodies to see signs of
relaxation or tension.

After several minutes I suggest that they stop and again concentrate on how they feel in the moment. The effect of this exercise
varies. It may bring up laughter and playfulness, expressions of extreme discomfort, or a desire for more, often with sadness.

The gentle contact of skin-to-skin touch often has a powerful effect on
people. It is a reminder of the most basic human contact, that of child
and caretaker, and often brings up strong emotion.

The responses of Richard and Christine relate to the yearning for contact that is safe and nourishing. Richard responds first by saying how good it is to feel connected with Christine. "She really seemed to see me." And then suddenly, he stiffens. "It's so rare."

Richard turns to Christine, longing in his eyes. He says plaintively, "So many times I try to talk with you, but it's like your lights go out. You're gone. I don't understand where you go, and I'm afraid you won't come back for days. . . . Sometimes you don't."

"And what happens in you when Christine seems to withdraw?" I ask.

"I become anxious, and frustrated . . . I try not to get angry because I know that pushes her away further."

"Does this remind you of any other time in your life when you had these kinds of feelings?"

Richard starts to talk about his memories of his absent father and distant mother, and what it felt like to be alone, believing that he had to take care of both his mother and his sisters. I can see the tears welling up, and then he suppresses them. Richard coughs, clears his throat, and remains silent.

"Painful, huh?" I say, quietly.

With what seems to be a deep sadness, and a quietness that I felt resonating within me at that moment, Richard says, "I really was all alone." After a moment of silence, he continues. "My father wasn't there even when he lived with us. But after he left us, mom, who always treated me special, wasn't there anymore either. She had to work to support us and sometimes worked two jobs. But when she was home she was with my sisters, taking care of the house. I was so lonely."

I feel very connected to the little boy in the room, and say, "You've been trying hard to ward off that alone feeling that keeps coming to remind you that if no one is there you must care of everything yourself." He nods, choked up, and I say "All the feelings are caught right here," pointing to my throat.

Christine, looking directly at Richard, says, "When I saw the way your mom acted towards you last week, what you've gone through became pretty clear. She really is not letting you have a close relationship with her."

"Can you tell me a bit about what's been happening?" I ask.

Richard explains that he moved his mother from her home on

the East Coast to a condo near their home in California six months ago.

"My sisters came to town for a visit," Richard reports. "They all [his sisters and their husbands] got together at the condo I bought for Mom. But they didn't invite *me*." His disappointment, frustration, and feeling of being unappreciated are obvious.

"I bought her a place near the ocean. I want to make sure that she has a really good life with no worries. She never even says 'thank you.' I just don't understand it. I know she loves me, but I don't understand why she is so distant. It didn't used to be like that."

Richard is beginning to sound like a child and his face and posture take on a younger quality. I tell him that I can see how painful it is when he talks about this deep yearning to recapture his mother's love. I ask him to stay with his feelings right now, and to see where he holds them in his body. He points to his chest, his throat; I see tears forming in his eyes. Christine reaches over, takes his hand, and squeezes it.

I ask, "What's coming up for you right now?" Either of them can respond. It offers Christine a chance to connect to core affect that impacts the feelings coming up in her relationship with Richard. It offers an opportunity for Richard to access early formative memories and their corresponding neural pathways—those that are impacting his relationship with Christine.

Both sit quietly for a minute. Christine listens while Richard begins relating a memory. "I can picture my mom sitting and reading to me when I had chicken pox. She had so much patience."

I go with Richard's memories and images of a time with his mom reading to him.

"Stay with the image," I suggest, speaking quietly, as if to a child. "Can you see that little boy, Richard? Can you recall the scene, the room, the color of the walls . . . the furniture, how her voice sounded, what she looked like, any sensations you felt?" For a moment Richard speaks as if he were there with her.

"It feels good to have her with me. She is so loving. And I love it when she just sits near me and reads to me."

"Can you just stay with the little boy and see him with all his feelings?" I ask quietly.

"Yes," he whispers, and then he falls silent and tears begin to flow.

"I don't know what happened to her. I seem to have lost her. No matter what I do, it's like she doesn't keep me on her mind."

I turn toward Christine, but I'm giving the message to both of them. "I think we have an idea of what Richard may want in his relationship with you—an experience of repair. Whatever went wrong between him and his mom in the growing-up years, he lost a very important relationship. As his wife, you are the closest counterpart to the bonds between Richard and his mother. He wants you to be the adult equivalent of the loving, caring, nurturing figure who reads to him adoringly. He wants your love when he feels upset or under stress. Just as you want the child in you to grow and become fully adult, and he wants the adult you to love the child in him."

Christine puts her arm on his knee and speaks directly to Richard. "It was hard to understand all of your complaints when she was so nice to me. But when I saw your mother's recent behavior toward you, I felt terrible. She really avoids any close contact with you. No wonder you get so upset. I'm going to see that this doesn't happen anymore. I just know she can't treat you like this."

Christine at this point feels strong enough to not only understand Richard, but to support him. Here she can be the adult who comforts and nurtures, which not only gives Richard the sense connection he craves, but also helps Christine overcome her lifelong sense of dependency and obeying a powerful male figure.

"Your mom and I are planning to get together for lunch to talk about how she can help with Emily if I decide to take the part in that musical. Why don't you join us at lunch, Richard? I know your mom loves you; she always tells me how proud she is of you. But I also see that she avoids being with you a lot of times. We've got to figure out what is going on with her." Richard hesitates, but from the way his body perks up, she can see that he wants to be invited. Christine repeats, "Please come, Richard."

He reaches out for her hand and edges closer to her.

"I guess it will give me the chance to talk with her," Richard says, adding, "I'm not sure why I have put it off. Thanks for suggesting it." Clearly he is appreciative of Christine's attunement to his feelings.

Richard and Christine are sharing a rare experience of "feeling felt" by one another. Richard's tight face loosens, and Christine's eyes soften a bit, as if she has just discovered something hidden and important. For the moment each is attuned to his or her own internal feelings, and the partners maintain contact through physical touch, smiles, and glances. Right now, they seem to resonate with each other.

The resonance circuits of the brain (Siegel, 2010a, 2010b) include those fibers that are stimulated by mindful awareness to integrate thought, feeling, and body sensation. The very process of attuning to another can help each partner become more balanced and regulated within themselves.

As Christine and Richard begin to understand and respect each other's internal experiences, they have a sensation of being accepted by someone who knows them deeply. Each feels the other responding to needs beyond words. They have begun to understand each other's ways of operating, as well as what each might do to advance the other's sense of security.

In relationships that work, partners are able to hold and contain the vulnerable underbelly that yearns for a warm hand and loving heart. Once partners are able to stay with each other through the process of uncovering and unblocking core emotion, as well as listen to each other's messages, the inevitable problems of living together as part of a family can be discussed and resolved. Repair involves a step-by-step resolution of issues, a process that can bind two individuals together as an intimately attached couple.

Chapter 3

HEALING WOUNDS

Repair takes place over time, peeling off layer upon layer of defenses erected to protect against deep wounds long buried. Where there have been early attachment wounds, partners are predisposed to expect pain in the face of perceived injury, regardless of whether or not the mate has intended to do harm. Healing these wounds requires that partners recognize each other's vulnerabilities and respond to deep emotions when such encounters occur.

Deep vulnerabilities and old wounds manifested relationally when Richard came home from a business trip with a respiratory tract infection. Christine scheduled an initial appointment with Richard's internist, and when his doctor called on a Saturday morning to suggest follow-up tests, Richard asked when he should schedule these. The doctor replied "Why not have them today?" As Richard's anxiety grew, he told Christine he was going to the emergency room to have the tests done.

Now, in session, he's angrily repeating her response. "You said, 'we have friends coming over with their daughter this afternoon. Can't the tests wait until Monday?' It felt as though you didn't care. Your friends were more important than my health."

"I didn't know why you would go to the emergency room for tests. I thought you should get them on Monday," she replies.

"The doctor told me to get the tests that day." His voice is even angrier. "He must have thought it was important, but you didn't."

"I was wrong," she says, contritely, but his anger does not abate.

"I stayed in the hospital for 7 hours; I was alone. You were home with your friends who were visiting. You forgot about me. I don't feel very important to you."

"I called you, but you didn't answer your cell phone. I thought you were angry at me and that's why you didn't answer. You were just getting some tests, and you were mad at me." Christine obviously did not understand the depth of Richard's wound triggered by her absence at the hospital.

"The calls didn't come through in the downstairs lab at the hospital. If you wanted to reach me, why didn't you come to the hospital to talk?"

"I thought you were mad at me, and it got me upset."

Richard gets up from the couch they've been sharing and moves to the barrel chair on the other side of the room. From his body language it is clear that he is fuming.

"See, this is what always happens," Christine said, turning to me. "We go for weeks with everything fine. I'm starting to think we're over the worst, and I do one thing wrong and Richard hates me. That's what happens every time." Clearly exasperated, she throws up her hands in a helpless gesture.

"This isn't *every time*," Richard retorts. "I was in the goddamn hospital. And you weren't there."

"I had Emily to take care of."

"You should have found a way to be with me."

"You were there for tests. If you were sick, I would have called someone to watch Em and gone right to the hospital," she replied. Christine sounds sincere, really trying to make him understand her, but his emotions are too volatile—he simply can't hear her.

"Oh, so if I'm dying, you might have tried to get there before I'm dead. I was there in the emergency room, all alone, and didn't even know why my doctor told me to go right away to get the tests."

"I'm sorry. If I had realized, I would have been there."

"That's what I'm afraid of: Something will be wrong, you won't think it's serious, and I'll die all alone."

"I can't do this," she said, talking neither to me nor to Richard. "I know there are things you need from me. We've talked about it, and I try to be there for you. But it's never enough. One time I don't understand and do it wrong, and we're back to square one. I failed." Christine is very still, appearing to lose hope.

"You don't like it when I get upset," Richard acknowledged, "but even when I tried to explain it the other day without being angry, you got distant."

"I could tell when you were angry."

"Then I'm in a box. No matter what I do, you can't hear how important this is for me. You're preoccupied with yourself."

"You don't know how often I do things that I know you want. Whether it's the food you like to eat or the way we make love, I try to be there for you the way you want."

"Sure, it's like a checklist: dinner, check; sex, another check." Richard moves his hand and his fingers to demonstrate. "I want someone who wants to be with me, who cares if I'm sick, and not because it's something you have to check off."

"I took care of you when you had the flu. I called the doctor to make an appointment for you."

"You didn't go to the doctor with me." Richard then lists examples of sick friends whose wives watched over them, went to every doctor's appointment, monitored their medications.

Christine cries as he goes through this litany. I say to her, "I may be wrong, but right now as I watch you, I have a sense of you asking, 'Why be in this relationship where I'm always bound to fail?'"

"Yes," she responds, "I can't bear all his anger."

"You're both in a lot of pain right now. You were afraid of what was happening to you, Richard, when the doctor told you to get the tests right away. You felt so alone."

"I still do," he replies.

"And Christine, right now, from the way you are holding your arms around yourself, you look as though you have just been punched in the stomach. I can see that you're hurting a lot. But I also see that you're feeling your feelings instead of numbing yourself completely. That's important for you." After a short wait, I ask her, "Can you talk about what is coming up for you right now?" offering Christine the opportunity to get in touch with the repetition of her early history in her reaction to this situation with Richard. Are there any images or memories, any emotions or thoughts?

"I remember when I was little, maybe 8 or 9, I didn't want to memorize my lines; I wanted to play. My uncle got really mad and smacked me. He said I was ruining everything. He said I was such an ungrateful child after all he did for me. I wanted to run away but I didn't know where to go. So I went inside myself. After that I listened to him, and he was nicer to me."

"So you listen to Richard, but it doesn't work like learning a new song. You can't always figure out what he wants. Then you get afraid that if you don't figure out what he wants, he'll rage at you, and you'll want to get away. The problem is that Richard wants you to be with him because you want to, not because he wants you to or because you have to."

Richard, sarcastically, says, "It shouldn't be hard for her to figure out that when her husband is in the emergency room, she should be there."

"That was an awful experience for you, Richard. In fact, it may have touched on one of your worst fears, and we should talk about that. But it is important that Christine be able to hear and understand what you were going through—and your anger may be making her disconnect from a message that is very core for you."

After letting Christine and Richard know that I am attuned to what's going on somewhere deeper than words can convey, I ask them both to stay with the emotion in their bodies. No one spoke for what seemed an interminable time. I felt like breaking the silence and asking a question, but I also knew that to do that would be an enactment of my own uncomfortable feeling.

Finally Richard began to weep, with deep gasping noises. He was having trouble crying and breathing at the same time.

"My father died all alone. . . . My mother got a call from his girlfriend that she had taken him to the hospital. . . . I went over as soon as I got the message, but he had died before I got there. His girlfriend had left him there, I didn't make it on time. He was only 45 years old, and he died alone. I think of what that must have felt like for him. What it must be like to be dying and all alone. I don't want that to happen to me. But I'm afraid it will."

Christine, now crying with him, says over and over again, "How awful," and "I didn't understand." Through a series of understanding reparative responses, the brain's plasticity can result in changes in early imprints. They are each experiencing something different, the beginning of a reorganization.

"Do you see Christine's response to what you are feeling?" I ask him, wanting to make this reorganization conscious.

As Richard looked up, his rage still apparent but tightly bound, he says to Christine, "My father died at 45; I don't know how long I'll live. I'm trying to live the life that I want, and to protect you, Em, my family. But I have dreams about dying; I dream that I'm trying to tell you, but you don't hear me, and I'm dying and I'm all alone, just like my father was. You're with your parents, or your sister, or your friends. . . . And you'll be sorry afterward because you didn't notice that I was really dying."

"That fear and the guilt of not being with your father when he died alone has weighed heavily on you, Richard," I comment. "You've talked about being angry with your father for leaving the family, and you've said that you would never leave yours—no matter what. But I can tell from what you are saying today that there is much more than anger."

"I never really got to know him," Richard said. "I didn't see him for a long time after he left Mom and us. But when I got into basketball, he started coming to my games. We really had some good talks—about why he left, what he was looking for, what I wanted to do with my life. But we had only a little time before his heart attack. . . . I just wanted a family, a dad and a mom. I felt so alone when he died."

As Richard continues, tears flowing heavily, Christine seems to grow in her understanding that all his rage came from his deep painful core and was not really about her. As they leave the session, she reaches her hand out to him, and he grasps it tightly.

"Can we come in later this week?" he asks me.

At the next session several days later, something has clearly changed. The reorganization of brain, body, and mind that began in the last session seems to have taken hold. They walk in seeming more relaxed and sit close together.

Christine begins. "Last time, when we went outside, Richard gave me a hug. I was surprised because he was so angry the whole hour in your office."

"I told you what I was feeling, and I was finished," he says. Richard had tapped into core emotion, and Christine did not withdraw as she had in the past. Her tears were for him, and he seemed to sense her presence differently at the end of the session. The repair was palpable to both of them, repair longed for in childhood but often not provided.

The problem they had been having for the past 2 years was one of having no way to let each other understand what was happening deep inside. Every time one tried to let the other know of his or her anxieties, fears, core pain—things they barely let themselves know—it touched a hurt spot in the other. They kept closing each other out, leaving a residue of hurt, anger, and numbness, along with the belief that the other was the cause of the problem.

Each has needed the other to hear, understand, and do something that could reduce the pain. Christine's reaching out a hand when Richard was experiencing so much painful emotion and Richard's reaching out to hug her after the difficult session helped them experience each other differently, at least for that moment. There was a beginning of a connection at that core level of emotional arousal that each has always defended against, and possibly a reorganization that can be a big step toward deep relational security for both of them.

"It's so important that you found a way to repair a serious rift quickly rather than letting it fester," I comment. "Richard has been saying he needs to know that you love and want to be with him and that you are capable of taking care of him in an emergency. Christine has been wanting to prove that she is capable of taking care of things that are important to her."

"Look, I knew you could take care of yourself when I first met you," Richard said. "Look at all you accomplished before most people even graduate from high school. Nobody bothered to see that you got an education, and yet, you have read more books than anybody has, more than I have. I've never had a doubt that you would keep growing. Sometimes I worried about how long it would be before you grew right out of this marriage."

"Maybe that's why you didn't want me to take any jobs."

"I wanted to be the one to support you."

I say firmly, "There are lots of kinds of support."

Toward the end of this session, I ask them to look at each other again and alternate starting some sentences with the words, *I want.* "See what comes up."

CHRISTINE: I want to see more of the you that has needs and feelings, not just anger.

RICHARD: I want you to promise to be with me, and not disconnect from me, when I get upset.

CHRISTINE: I want to be able to make my own decisions.

RICHARD: I want you to know how much I love and respect you.

CHRISTINE: I want to be there for you.

RICHARD: I want your help to talk to my mom. She listens to you.

CHRISTINE: I want us to have another child.

RICHARD: I want us to have a happy family.

The conversation then becomes playful, and sexual, their body language much more open to each other. For the time being, the war is over. Their brains, bodies, and minds are not repeating the wounds of the past; instead, they have grown and changed from the repair of their deep-seated conflict. There will be other scuffles and skirmishes, but they know no one will get killed. Richard and Christine are learning that they can survive without resorting to auto-pilot defenses. They are learning that there is someone who is a witness to their emotions, one who cares about and accepts them, who is interested in knowing those deep vulnerable parts that nobody else knows. They are learning that they can be friends.

Each married the other with certain expectations and then felt disappointed. They did not get all that they wanted. For a time both thought they'd picked the wrong partner. But they didn't. They had the right partner to get what they needed, someone who could meet them on an unconscious common ground, who could help them repair their attachment injuries of the past.

The treatment focused on fostering reciprocity in meeting each other's core needs (Solomon, 1994). There was a strong emphasis on educating them to tune into their bodies during stressful interactions and stay with the emotions that arose without piling on shame or blame.

By coming to understand the attachment injuries that were being superimposed on the relationship, and learning to recognize when they were reacting automatically and where those reactions came from, Richard and Christine could begin to change their behavior.

In the next few chapters you will see other ways to reveal, and directly influence, couples' nonconscious patterns. Stan Tatkin's psychobiological approach focuses on evoking experience, using poses, movement, and therapeutic enactment to shape brand-new automatic reactions that support a vision of the couple as each other's primary ally and go-to person.

PART II

The Psychobiological Approach

Chapter 4

THE PSYCHOBIOLOGICAL
IMPERATIVE

Emerging neurobiological evidence shows that our earliest experiences around safety and security are archived in implicit regions of the brain and generate a kind of somatic "knowing" that is different from thinking (Cohen & Shaver, 2004; Henry, 1997; Nelson & Panksepp, 1998; Schore, 2002a, 2002b, 2002c). These earliest experiences include the formative attachment strategies that generate both our internal working models (Bowlby, 1969) and the sources of our reactions to approach–avoidance impulses and tolerances. The developing child's repeated encounters with primary attachment figures accumulate—like the action sequences required to ride a bike or drive a car—as stored procedural memories. These memories direct automatic psychobiological motor reflexes toward or away from a primary attachment figure. Before we "know" what has happened, autonomic arousal processes have readied us for action and reaction.

Whereas traditional therapies privilege insight or the development of a conscious mindset to alter a behavioral pattern, the psychobiological approach described here respects and relies on the primacy of implicit mechanisms—nonverbal, nonconscious, procedural, and somatic processes as found in the autonomic nervous system, limbic circuit, and right hemisphere. These fast-acting implicit mechanisms, rather than cognition, are the driving force behind actions and reactions when people are under threat—and they run the show in primary attachment relationships.

The trust, safety, and security that we do or do not experience during our most critical periods of early development alter the parts of the brain that interpret our need to take action. These include the neuroendocrine and autonomic nervous systems, which prepare us for action, and the somatic nervous system, which carries out that action. Our actions then express our histories in real time with real people, through our patterns of arousal regulation.

The success, security, and stability of a partnership hinges on the partners' capacity to regulate various internal bodily, emotional, and mental states in real time, separately and together. Accordingly, unlike many clinicians who tune into content to identify areas of conflict, the psychobiologically oriented therapist attends to mostly nonverbal communications to discover individual and collective deficits in the couple's social–emotional capacity for interactive regulation. Working dyadically with social–emotional deficits, including self-regulatory problems, the therapist provides each partner with an opportunity to push development forward.

TREATING THE COLLECTIVE

In this book the couple, rather than the individual, is the focus of attention. Intimate partners constitute a protected dyadic system, a sealed-off entity that can interact with the external world as easily as it can shut it out. "Home" becomes understood not as a physical place but as the couple system itself, two best friends celebrating profound companionship while maturing and growing together.

In this vision a two-person system supersedes the one-person psychologies that dominated the theoretical landscape from Freud's intrapsychic analysis through Maslow's glorification of self-actualization. A two-person psychological system triangulates self-interest with mutual interests in a way that leads to novel, jointly developed and jointly enhancing products, such as courage, self-esteem, healing, intellectual development, professional success, and creativity. In other words, individual assets are parlayed into mutual assets that would be otherwise unavailable. In such a two-person system, the well-being of each rests in devotion to the well-being of the other. Thus, it is in the best interest of each person holding the office of "primary attachment figure" to ensure the other's comfort, safety, and security at all times.

Secure partners demonstrate knowledge and understanding of the vulnerabilities encoded within the implicit memory system of the other during early attachment formation and reinforced later in childhood via trauma or loss. Those vulnerabilities are often exquisitely available to both attack and repair, and each partner knows how and when he or she becomes activated by external events and how to regulate them quickly and effectively in public and in private. As in secure mother–infant attachment, secure adult romantic partners tend to maximize positive moments through mutual amplification and tend to defuse (not dismiss) negative moments through mutual attenuation of painful affects.

In contrast, partners who are identified as insecure on the AAI are surprised and mystified when these areas of vulnerability are struck inadvertently as well as when attempts to please or comfort fall flat. Such partners can be together for years without ever really knowing one another. They need to create owners' manuals for each other, whereby they are equipped with knowledge of what works and what doesn't work. That mandate directs the couple toward secure attachment and interactive regulation by placing emphasis on real empathic understanding and protection of one another as a two-person psychological system.

In all intimate partnerships, people make both pro-relationship and non-pro-relationship behavioral choices. Pro-relationship choices tend to be experienced as loving (and, as such, increase the perception of security), whereas non-pro-relationship choices tend to be experienced as unloving (and, as such, decrease the sense of security). It is not the intention of the giver but the experience of the receiver that determines the effectiveness of actions that are intended to be pro-relationship. This is a very important concept. What counts is not whether one partner claims to value attachment and put the relationship first, but rather how the other partner experiences his or her efforts. It's the "if a tree falls in the forest . . ." quandary: Is an act loving if the appointed receiver doesn't experience it that way? In terms of intimate attachment, the answer is emphatically no.

Pro-relationship values put attachment security ahead of other values. That isn't to say that pro-relationship values are better than non-pro-relationship values; they are not—except in the primary attachment relationship, where they ultimately make or break stability and satisfaction. The primary attachment partnership operates under very different rules than any other relationship. In outside arenas where a sufficient level of self-interest must reign to facilitate survival, not to mention success, pro-relationship values may be inappropriate. In a primary attachment relationship, however, self-interests are served by partners' dependency and devotion; both surviving and thriving depend on true mutuality.

Where true mutuality prevails, each partner is the other's go-to person and serves as witness, minister, cheerleader, and facilitator of the other's life journey. We fare much better in the hand of another who is willing, interested, and able to partner with us. Internal processes, such as mental and emotional states, become more manageable under secure partnership conditions. From our very beginning and throughout our lifespan, we experience ourselves in connection with others. We learn about ourselves while in the close company of important others. Our deep wish, if we are to trust current research about secure attachment, is to be able to hold hands with our important others while in heaven and in hell, in high states and in low states, in positive emotion and in negative emotion, and to do this without fear of dismissal, abandonment, or punishment (Bowlby, 1988).

FROM CONTENT TO IMPLICIT PROCESSES

In the psychobiological approach to couple therapy, treatment moves quickly to help partners identify underlying core needs, patterns, and defenses; to educate partners about how to move past issues that block their ability to meet each other's needs; and to model new ways of working collaboratively to provide safety and security for one another. The therapist works solely with the couple because the premise is that growth and change happen through the dyadic encounters between partners, not between patient and therapist. Because individual therapy attempts to recreate the primary attachment relationship, it should not compete with or unseat a patient's ongoing adult primary attachment relationship. The question of concomitant individual and couple therapy should be examined carefully, especially if the former is to be considered a supplement to the latter. Individual therapists who understand the nature of primary attachment relationships will likely remain respectful and supportive of existing primary relationships. Real dangers arise if the individual therapist, allying with the patient's internal representational world, unwittingly supports insecure strategies that contravene existing relationship fidelity. From that standpoint, individual therapy can coexist with couple therapy so long as it does not compete with or undermine fidelity to the relationship.

Additionally, however, the psychobiological approach mandates that partners are responsible for one another's care and must be experts in the care and treatment of the other. Partners should bear witness to one another's mental and emotional therapeutic experience. The soundness of this principle can be tested against the backdrop of the caregiver–child relationship: Interventions that include the parent(s) are more effective than those that do not—because children live with their parents, not with their therapists. Partners likewise live with one another.

It is the couple's collective nervous system on which we focus, understanding that the problem cannot be found in content; that is, in the couple's narratives when early attachment issues permeate the relationship. Compelling as narratives can often be, they are mostly red herrings, which, if pursued, can lead the couple therapist down a circuitous, endless, and ultimately fruitless trail. To use another metaphor: Our interest is primarily in the music, not the lyrics. A psychobiological approach shifts the attention of partners away from content and toward implicit processes, encouraging moment-to-moment awareness of each other's faces, voices, bodies, and so on. Narratives can be used, however, as behavioral markers that point to patterns of non-content-related, nervous-system to nervous-system misattunement. Ultimately, it is the rapid misattunement–error-correction process that, if faulty, leads couples down a path of misappraisals, mutual dysregulation, biological threat, systemic avoidance, and eventual dissolution of the safety and security system.

In a psychobiological approach, each partner in an intimate relationship inherits and occupies the office of primary attachment figure. Transference of early attachment relationships between partners is to be expected and should not be considered pathological. It has become a cultural convention that partners should not project on one another or expect one another to take responsibility for injuries incurred by past attachments. In point of fact, in an APAR partners naturally project past needs and injuries, and the current person is the only one in position to repair the wounds.

The old song "I Want a Girl Just Like the Girl Who Married Dear Old Dad" is transference in its positive form. A child brought up with a secure attachment to both parents is likely to want to recreate what worked. In the same way, a child who grows up with an insecure attachment is just as likely to find someone who will replay the old dynamics in an attempt to repair what didn't work. The therapy should prepare partners for the likelihood that each of them is likely to "dump" such material on the other. Defensive attempts by partners to parse out who did what and when as a way of avoiding the projection of past attachments onto them may actually make a bad situation worse. It is better that partners take a stance of readiness to minister to one another, even when (as is likely) it seems that one is not the original offender.

The ability to work with a couple in areas involving both attachment and arousal is vital. The two theoretical tracks influence one another, and the clinical typologies overlap: Secure couples are skillful at interactive regulation, whereas insecure couples manifest *regulatory deficits*. Awareness of shifts in arousal is the "royal road" to awareness of implicit systems—and implicit systems, which are noncognitive and nonverbal, can quickly make the difference between love and war. Therefore, a psychobiologically oriented therapist must work with these systems to circumvent problems that arise moment by moment. Because implicit systems include extremely fast-acting, survival-oriented, and nonverbal biological mechanisms, a psychobiological approach to couple therapy centers on *experience* via therapeutic provocations and conflict enactments, social cues, movement exercises, and other psychodramatic techniques. The therapist focuses on real-time interaction in order to reenact the interpersonal stress that leads partners into dysregulation. For example, the therapist, in the service of exposing attachment and regulation problems in real time, can ask partners to face each other to discuss areas of importance or conflict and also can ask them to move around the room as a way of triggering nervous system reactions to proximity, contact, and approach. Sufficient time is required to allow partners to cycle through various states of arousal inside the therapeutic milieu, just as they do outside it. Accordingly, the psychobiological model supports the scheduling of long sessions (2–4 hours or even more) to safely stage dysregulating enactments that can then be repaired. The therapist must maintain focus on moment-by-moment shifts in partner arousal and affect and seize upon the awareness of these shifts above all other matters.

In the initial phase of work the therapist often serves as the external regulator for both partners, establishing conditions of safety and security. This means that the therapist must be able to help move partners up or down the arousal scale, toward sympathetic (fight–flight–freeze) or parasympathetic (withdraw) arousal, as needed. The therapist may also need to help a partner "hold" a previously unregulated state in awareness long enough to develop tolerance. Eventually the therapist becomes more of a "coach" who can quickly intervene and guide partners while in problematic states. These interventions are aimed at evoking rapid state changes that allow for novel and contingent (rather than fixed) and often reparative interactions to take place. In short, the psychobiologically informed therapist focuses on changing experience, sometimes by assisting a new experience to occur.

TOOLS OF THE PSYCHOBIOLOGICAL THERAPIST

Psychobiological tools include top-down and bottom-up, left-right and right-left interventions, all of which can be highly provocative and evocative. These tools can accelerate our appreciation and grasp of the psychobiological underpinnings of our everyday behavior. The terms top-down, bottom-up, left-right, and right-left refer to conceptualizations of brain/body information flow in colloquial terms.

49

Top-down refers to general processes that begin with high left and right hemispheres and move downward toward the body. This term often implies a cognitive-first approach to mental processing (or psychotherapy), rather than beginning with body sensation or core affect. If someone very close to me, for example, my mother, is hospitalized with a grave illness, I am likely to talk about it in my next therapy session. My therapist asks me how I'm reacting to her hospitalization. I respond that she is likely to get better soon as long as I stay on top of the physicians in charge of her care. My first reaction is a top-down thought about how to handle the situation rather than allowing myself to recognize all the emotion that is likely to be going on internally. My therapist makes an interpretation that it seems I think I can control her survivability by staying on top of everything. He or she then helps by focusing on awareness of my body and my deep feelings, as we talk about her hospitalization.

Left-right refers to processes that begin with the more explicit, verbal, and linear left hemisphere and cross to the more implicit, non-verbal, and non-linear right hemisphere via the corpus callosum. The process goes from left (explicit/language) to right (implicit/experience).

For instance, my therapist asks me how I'm feeling about my mother's illness. I answer that I'm not doing very well, and I begin to look and feel depressed. My therapist then asks "What does it mean when you say you're not doing very well?" The first question addresses my feeling state on a verbal, declarative level (left) and triggers a mental picture of my mother looking sickly (right). The follow-up question focuses first on the declarative meaning of "not doing well" (left) as a means to explore the more autobiographical meaning of the phrase (right).

Right-left refers to processing that begins in the implicit, non-linear, nonverbal regions of the right hemisphere and moves to more explicit, linear, and verbal regions of the left hemisphere. For example, my therapist asks me if I could "see" my mother's pained face when I last visited her in the hospital. The therapist's suggestion activates a vivid memory of this emotional event, and the feelings evoked from this memory drive my narrative about the experience.

Bottom-up refers to processes that begin as body memory and sensation and move "up" toward the brain, evoking emotional experi-

ence, awareness, integration, and perhaps but not necessarily inter-
pretative cognition. For example, my therapist notices that I have
stopped breathing, my eyes have glazed over, and I've suddenly become quiet. In response I take a deep breath and put my hand on
my chest and notice that it feels tight and my hands are clammy. As
I focus on these sensations, I begin to explain that I am feeling very
anxious for some reason. And then I "remember" that I will be visiting my mother in the hospital following the session. I realize how
much I am reacting as I anticipate this visit.

In the next two chapters I (S.T.) present a case study that illustrates some of the tools I use in the psychobiological approach, notably the Adult Attachment Interview. Originally devised as a research
rather than a clinical instrument (George, Kaplan, & Main, 1985;
Main, 2000), the Adult Attachment Interview has been found to
"surprise the unconscious" (George et al., 1985) and connect individuals to core affects in a relatively short time (see Siegel, 1999,
2010a, 2010b). It can be conceptualized as partly top-down and
left-right, and as a therapeutic intervention, right-left and even bottom-up.

Chapter 6 discusses directed movements and physical poses—
often amplified by short, emotionally relevant verbal declaratives
and commands—which are bottom-up (body-to-brain), noncognitive, experience-first means of capturing glimpses of attachment organization that start within implicit systems in the body. These attachment patterns often involve touch and can have a powerful
regulatory or dysregulatory effect, which can be processed as it sur-
faces during a session. We can directly observe partner split-second
reactions to physical proximity, whether they are in movement toward or away from each other or fixed in one spot (like statues).
Partners cannot conceal their macro and micro reactions to these
movements or poses because they are reflexive. These reactions can
be replicated and are therefore stable reflections of, among other
things, attachment defenses. For instance, each of the following exercises involves the near senses (touch, taste, smell, and vision):
partners make eye contact in close proximity over an extended period of time; one partner breathes strongly into the other partner's
face; partners hold an embrace for several moments. Each of these
exercises can reveal attachment patterns by arousing procedural,
body memory, and activating neurobiological anticipatory systems—

the outward manifestation of which is visible to the naked eye and most certainly to video frame analysis.

These tools are three-pronged: each is an intervention in that it provokes awareness and change; each is diagnostic in that it reveals information that either confirms or refutes the therapist's hypotheses about attachment, arousal regulation, or social–emotional deficits; and each has a regulatory purpose or consequence in that it intentionally leads to, or unintentionally causes, either an increase or decrease in arousal.

Chapter 5

THE PARTNER INTERVIEW

This chapter offers strategies for using the Adult Attachment Interview (AAI) in clinical practice with couples. The interview was devised in Mary Main's laboratory at the University of California, Berkeley, and consists of both an interview protocol (George, Kaplan, & Main, 1984, 1985, 1996) and an accompanying scoring and classification system (e.g., Main & Goldwyn, 1985; Main, Goldwyn, & Hesse, 2003). The interview as used for research consists of 20 questions and set probes; usually takes about an hour to administer; and is often transcribed verbatim so that trained coders can apply the accompanying scoring and classification system (see Hesse & Main, 2000; Main, 2000; Main, Hesse, & Goldwyn, 2008; and Steele & Steele, 2008, for a review of some of the different ways of speaking identified in this interview context).

The analysis of this interview by Main and her colleagues relies upon a cognitive–linguistic model of inquiry, in which speakers whose interview responses are relatively coherent and signify that they are collaboratively engaged in the process are considered "secure-autonomous." Although the interview often asks speakers to describe early interactions with parents and their effects, it cannot be presumed that the interactions described are accurate. Rather, the reader looks to see whether the "memories" described are consistent with the remainder of the text and the interviewee's current behavior. A person's way of speaking during this interview has been found to be predictive of interactions with his or her child, a finding which has been replicated many times worldwide in research contexts. The AAI can also be used in the clinical context (see especially Steele & Steele, 2008a), who have edited a volume regarding its clinical use), and in this chapter I (S.T.) describe the ways in which I have used some of the interview questions in the context of couple therapy.

Recognizing that intimate partners often unconsciously experience each other as incarnations of their early primary attachment figures, I seek to introduce that awareness into the equation early on. The AAI conducted in the presence of both members of the couple opens a window into their respective attachment histories, allowing the therapist to estimate where each partner falls on the attachment spectrum and also, not incidentally, to form an alliance with the less forthcoming one. Furthermore, the AAI draws attention to the (quite possibly buried) early life experiences of each partner. It can help reveal the role of their attachment injuries in generating the encoded behavior patterns that affect arousal regulation. The AAI can be used for couples as a history-taking instrument, an intervention, and a memory stress test. See Appendix B for an overview of the AAI itself, as well as a review of some of the findings emerging from its use in studying couple interactions.

AN ATTACHMENT-BASED
HISTORY-TAKING INSTRUMENT

Unlike conventional history-taking protocols, this one seeks to collect specific information relevant to early attachment experiences. The clinician utilizes the content to connect early relationships with primary attachment figures to the current primary attachment relationship. Because both partners are interviewed together, at one sitting, the data are cross-correlated between past and present, here and not-here, literal and mythological, with the clinician looking for fractals and similarities in the partners' histories. *What is said* and *how it is said* are equally important.

The combined content becomes the compote out of which the clinician can generate a coherent corporate narrative. The evidential outcome of this "docudramatic" process should support the clinician's premise that partners are more alike than not and that their union makes historic sense, in keeping with the conviction that people enter into intimate relationships to heal old wounds and meet important attachment needs. The clinician returns to the AAI data throughout treatment to explain both what is happening within the couple system and what to do about it. From the perspective of the attachment aspect of the psychobiological approach, the AAI is essential to the therapeutic compass.

The AAI may reveal many similarities between partners that were previously unknown. The couple system often pushes partners to opposite sides of insecure attachment in a behavioral manner—but we have found that, despite how individuals initially appear to present within a couple system, there seems to be more avoidant–avoidant and angry-resistant–angry-resistant partnerships than opposite types. Structurally, the clinician may be surprised to find that partners are most often alike.

A MEMORY STRESS TEST

The AAI is a highly stressful process of autobiographical memory recall and integration that alternates between episodic and semantic forms of declarative or explicit memory. Episodic memories are stored in autoassociative neural networks and later (it is believed) in semantic memory (Schacter, 2000; Tulving, 2001, 2005). The semantic version of the memory resides in the brain's left hemisphere, whereas the episodic and implicit version resides in both hemispheres (Daselaar et al., 2007). Sometimes there is a sharp difference between what we remember as ideas and what we actually remember as experience. (Memory as experience shares both explicit and implicit forms of knowing: One may "remember" sitting on Mother's lap from having viewed a photograph of the event but may not be able to remember the actual experience.)

AAI questions focus on early attachment experiences (before approximately the age of 12) with primary caregivers. The clinician-interviewer follows a disciplined line of inquiry about childhood relational events that first elicits the autobiographical/semantic response ("To whom did you run when injured as a child?"; "My mother") and then asks for the supporting autobiographical/episodic response that recalls the actual experience ("Give me a memory of when you were injured as a child and you ran to your mother"). For many, the call for a supporting memory (proof that it happened) may result in mismatch ("It was a neighbor"), distortion ("My friend told my mother"), vagueness ("I always went to her"), lack of detail ("She took me to the doctor"), or no recall ("I don't know").

The clinician-interviewer pushes for accurate, detailed memory despite the characteristic behaviors evidenced by *avoidant* and *angry-resistant* partners (see Chapter 7), whose attachment styles are represented by Tim and Caroline, respectively, below.

Avoidant partners' memories of themselves and their families of origin tend to be superficial and most often idealized, focused on *ideas* of themselves and of their caregivers rather than actual experience. Their autobiographical narratives commonly lack detail, freshness, and complexity; their responses are generally overly terse and absent of emotional expressiveness. "I don't remember" is a frequent refrain. Typically they have difficulty connecting their current adult relationship challenges with their early attachment experiences.

Angry-resistant partners tend to be overly verbal, overly expressive emotionally, and digressive in speaking style. Their inductive approach to answering questions can sometimes be frustrating, as they will "bury the lead" and lose their listeners. Their narratives often contain flares of anger toward spouses, children, and other family members, past and present.

AN INTERVENTION

Using this interview toward the beginning of treatment inspires "buy-in" by the more avoidant or therapy-resistant partner. This intervention can sometimes shift the avoidant partner's distancing or dismissive defenses from ego-syntonic to ego-dystonic. In general, the interview is useful with partners who have insecure attachment and who tend to rely on defenses that effectively protect them from experiencing distress.

TIM AND CAROLINE

In their first session Tim asserts the belief to me (S.T.) that Caroline, his wife of 12 years, is "wildly hormonal" and that her emotional outbursts should be treated medically, by her physician or by a psychiatrist. Caroline, who insisted that Tim come with her to couple therapy, has become increasingly unhappy with Tim's devotion to his work and his golfing buddies and with his need for solitude. She is also angry that he dismisses his behavior as having nothing to do with her distress. He complains that she is always angry and that she pushes him away when he wants sex.

During initial history-taking, both Tim and Caroline describe his childhood as "perfect" and her childhood as "dysfunctional." This sharp disparity between their reported childhoods prompts the decision to conduct a AAI. What follows is an abbreviated version of what is most often at least a 2-hour process, during which the clinician interviews both partners within the same session, together but one at a time, beginning with the apparently more avoidant person.

Tim

"I'm going to ask you a few questions you've probably never been asked before," I say to Tim. "They may not make sense at first, but I will explain everything to both of you when I'm done." Caroline sits next to Tim, listening intently and holding his hand. "It's very important that you, Caroline, don't try to help him out at all during this interview. When I finish with him, I'll ask you the same questions, okay?"

"Okay," says Caroline.

"Tim, when you were a child and you were injured, to whom did you run?" Tim answers quickly, "My mother."

"Give me a specific memory of when you were injured and you ran to your mother," I say. Tim thinks for a moment and says, "I don't know, I can't really think of any time I was hurt."

"But you said that when you were injured as a child, you ran to your mother, didn't you?"

"Right . . . I just assumed that she would be the one. I didn't think you'd ask me specifics," says Tim with a chuckle.

"Okay. Fair enough. But you say you don't remember being injured as a child, is that right?"

"Not really," he says.

"Well," I say, "children always get injured in some way, whether it's a scrape on the knee, falling off a bicycle, tripping—you know, that sort of thing."

"Right," says Tim. "I know that, but for some reason I just can't remember."

"Okay," I continue. "When you were a child and you were sick, who took care of you?" Tim thinks again for a moment and then says, "I think my mother."

"You *think*?" I ask.

With a burst of nervous laughter, Tim says, "Well, she always took care of us when we were sick."

"Okay, but what about just you? When you were sick, did she take care of you?"

"Yeah," says Tim, "I know she did. She would bring us soup and take our temperature."

I interrupt him, "Right, remember this is just *you* we're talking about, not your siblings."

"Okay. She would bring me soup," says Tim. "I don't remember getting very sick. I was always out and about playing with my friends or building some model in my room."

"Well," I ask further, "what do you remember about being sick as a child? Your mother would bring you soup and take your tempera-ture."

"Yeah," Tim says, "I remember her taking my temperature and she would bring the soup."

"What kind of soup?" I ask.

Tim looks over to Caroline, who shrugs. "I don't know," she says. "I wasn't there."

"Ah . . . chicken noodle soup!" Tim shouts out, smiling.

"What brand?" I ask.

"Oh, man! I don't know," he says impatiently. "What's the damn difference? Soup is soup, isn't it? It had broth, noodles, and probably chicken in it."

Caroline puts her smiling face down into her hands, shaking her head in response to Tim. "Even I remember what soup my mom made for me, and she hardly ever made food for us at all."

"Hold on, Caroline." I turn to Tim to explain. "I'm asking because I'm trying to understand if her caring for you while you were sick was meaningful for you, and since you said she brought you soup, I would imagine that meant something special to you."

"I don't know, man. It was just soup, you know. What can I say?"

Details: *We remember things meant just for us, good and bad. Powerful loving or unloving events between ourselves and our most important caregivers become encoded in long-term autobiographical memory along with details of those events. Reports of being read to, sung to, and even fed during sickness or injury should be checked for details. If the memory was of a meaningful attachment experience—that is, meant just for us—we should be able to remember the book, the song, or the food.*

"When you were sick," I continue, "would she spend time with you? You know, lie down with you, stroke your head, rub your back, or read to you?"

Tim pauses to think. "No, I don't remember anything about that, I just remember watching TV by myself in bed, and she would come in every now and then to check on me." After a short pause, he adds, "She was always there, my mother, she was always there."

"Your mother was a stay-at-home mom?" I ask.

"Yes," Tim says.

"When you were child, did anybody hug you, hold you, kiss you, or rock you?"

"My parents were warm, affectionate people."

"Give me a memory from your childhood when either parent hugged, held, or rocked you."

There's a long pause. "I'm sure they did. I just can't remember anything in particular."

"Just give me one memory."

At this point Tim's eyes begin to water.

"Are you okay?" I ask him.

"Yeah," says Tim. "I just don't understand why I'm not remembering anything."

"That's okay," I say, "this is a stressful interview. And, again, I'll explain why I'm doing this after we're done."

"When you were a child," I continue, "who put you to bed at night?"[1]

Turns out he put himself to bed at night. He cannot remember a

---

1. This question was added to the interview by Stan Tatkin because it offers a rapid entré to early transition rituals and parent–child interactions.

nighttime ritual involving his parents. No one read to him, sang to him, or talked to him about his day. If he had nightmares, he didn't call out to anyone and he didn't go to his parents' bed for comfort.

Bedtime rituals: *Bedtime is an important event for all children. It is a time of transitioning from full wakefulness and activity to unconsciousness and inactivity. Some children have the benefit of caregivers who listen to them as they debrief their day, allowing their minds to empty before going to sleep. Caregivers may read or sing to them, or children may read to their caregivers. Many people who did not have good sleep hygiene as children exhibit similar problems in adulthood with their primary adult partners.*

"When you were upset as a child, what would happen?" I ask.

"I remember that I would throw tantrums," he says.

"And what would happen?" I ask.

"Nothing," he says shrugging his shoulders. "I don't remember anything happening. I just remember throwing tantrums."

"I take it that nobody stopped you when you would have a tantrum as a child. Did anyone say, 'You can't do that' or 'Just stop it right now!'"?

"No," Tim says, "nobody did that."

"How did you calm down, then?" I ask.

"I don't know, I don't remember. I think I just calmed down by myself."

"What about when you were sad as a child and you cried? Did anybody come to comfort you?"

"My mother."

Following up, I ask, "On a scale of 1–10, *1* being really bad and *10* being great, how good was your mother at comforting you?"

"I'd say about an *8*."

"Give me a memory from your childhood that would support your answer that your mother was an *8*."

He pauses. "I can't."

"So how do you know she was an *8*?"

"I guess she was a lot less than that."

Looking into Tim's eyes, I ask, "When you were a child, did anybody look at you with a gleam in the eye that suggested 'Gosh, I really love you' or 'You're such a great kid' or anything like that?"

Tim says, "No."

Tim begins to get more tearful and defensive. "I don't want you to get the wrong idea here. My parents were good parents. I think Caroline would agree with me." He looks over at Caroline, who doesn't look back at him. She presses her lips together and tilts her head slightly from side to side as if to say, "Sort of."

Tim, becoming more defensive, explains how popular his parents were in the neighborhood and how well they treated other children. Nonetheless he is unable to come up with specific memories of loving parental behavior meant just for him.

"What are five adjectives that would describe your relationship with your mother when you were a child," I ask.

"Five adjectives. . . ." Tim mutters to himself while tapping his chin with the fingers of his right hand. "Five adjectives . . . she was *beautiful, intelligent, popular. . . .*"

Tim misunderstands the question even though I repeat it several times. He wants to describe her and not *his relationship* with her. I eventually get him on the right track.

"Five adjectives that describe our relationship: *Loving* . . . uh . . . *generous* . . . *supportive* . . . *loving. . . .*"

"You already said *loving.*"

"Oh, yeah. This is really hard. Why is this really hard?" Tim asks himself. "That's all I can think of."

After much prodding, Tim is unable to come up with any other adjectives. I start with his first word and try to get an autobiographical memory that supports his assertion.

"Okay, give me a memory that would support the word *loving,* that your relationship was *loving.*"

"She would always throw parties for the whole cul-de-sac, and she would make cupcakes for all of my friends."

"But what about loving between just you and her?"

"She would always take me and my brother for ice cream. Does that count?"

As Tim struggles with each adjective, his arousal and distress levels begin to increase. He is unable to come up with any specific memories that support the words he used to describe his relationship with his mother. He blames his poor memory.

"Let's move on," I say. "Give me a memory from your childhood that would support that the relationship was *generous*."

Tim's face begins to redden as he holds his head in his hands. Caroline sees this and begins to rub his back. Her acknowledgment of his growing distress pushes Tim over the edge, and he begins to sob. Several minutes go by as Tim cries silently, unable to speak. He eventually recovers and says, "What was your question again?"

He breaks out laughing, as does Caroline. "What just happened?" I ask.

"I don't know," he admits. "I feel really bad that I can't remember anything specific. I know I should be able to do that, but I just can't. I can remember loving things that she did for the neighborhood kids, but I can't remember anything specific with me. I'll probably walk out of here later today and think of it, and it will bother me because I didn't think of it now."

"I'm so sorry to be putting you through this but. . . ."

Tim interrupts, "That's okay . . . that's okay, I'm fine."

"What we're doing here is really important, as I promised to explain. It's relevant to what's going on between you and Caroline, and if it's any comfort, I will be doing the same with her in a few moments."

"That's okay," Tim says again, trying to pull himself together. "Let's continue. I'm perfectly fine."

"Can you come up with a memory that would support the word *generous*?" I ask. "No," Tim answers.

I continue to try to get his supporting autobiographical memories for his adjectives, but to no avail. Several moments go by, with Tim staring at the greenery outside my office windows. He shakes his head at various intervals and finally says, "I can't remember anything specific right now."

"That's okay. Let's go on to something else. Give me five adjectives that would describe your relationship with your father when you were a child."

Tim is able to provide only three adjectives, all of them positive and nearly identical to the ones he used for his mother. Once again, he is unable to support his adjectives with autobiographical memory.

"When you were a child, how did your parents' marriage look to you? Did you see them as affectionate and loving when you were little?"

"Not really. They went out together a lot. They were definitely a couple. They fought a lot . . . my mother fought with my dad a lot over money."

Parents as regulators: *This question is important because the answer sheds light on how the parents did, or did not, regulate one another. Children get most of what they understand about romantic relationships by watching their parents interact. Children are most secure when their parents are good interactive regulators.*

"When your parents fought, who would win between the two of them?" I ask.

"My mother, definitely."

"Did you ever see them make up with each other or apologize to one another?"

"No. I just saw them being together. But I don't remember ever hearing either of them apologize to the other."

"Did either of them ever apologize to you when you were a child?"

"Absolutely not. That was not something my parents did . . . apologize. My father always had to be right, and my mother couldn't stand it if you were angry with her about anything. So I guess she had to be right too."

Injury and repair: *Secure caregivers tend to be attuned to injuries that occur within the intersubjective relational field and also tend to repair those injuries as soon as possible. In contrast, insecure or insensitive caregivers frequently either tune out, ignore, or overlook injuries altogether or fail to repair them when they occur.*

"You said your mother would get angry with your dad. How long would it take her to recover?"

Tim thinks for a moment. "I don't know, maybe a day or two?"

"A day or two?" I say sounding surprised. "That's a long time. It took that long for your mother to recover from being angry?"

I can see Caroline nodding in agreement out of the corner of my

ᴇ. "Caroline seems to agree that it took your mother a long time
ᴛᴏ recover."

They both look at each other in amusement. Tim says, "Yeah,
she's kind of like that still."

"Oh, yeah!" says Caroline, nodding emphatically in wide-eyed
agreement.

"Did your mother get angry with you a lot?" I ask.

"Yeah, she could get pretty angry with me. She would just give
me the silent treatment for hours. I would have to go up to her to
'make nice.'"

"What about your dad? How long did it take for him to calm
down?"

"My dad would explode—and I mean just really explode—but
then it would be over. He didn't hold grudges."

Recovery issues: *Recovery times for both parents matter. Caregivers
who frequently experience high-intensity affects, such as rage, and
maintain intensity over long durations tend to produce relational
trauma in their children.*

"One last question before I move on to Caroline: Did anything in
particular frighten you when you were a child?"

Tim thinks for a moment. "No."

Caroline

"Okay, Caroline, it's your turn." She smiles and nods for me to
continue.

"When you were a child and you were injured, to whom did you
run?"

"Oh, my mother, most definitely."

"Okay, give me a memory when you were injured as a child and
you ran to your mother."

"I was riding my bicycle at the park. I remember this because my
aunt Ethel was there, and my mother and Ethel were really distracted. I was angry with my mom because I wanted her to pay attention to me and see me ride my bike. I kept yelling at her to stop
talking and look at me, and she would look at me for a while and

then she and Ethel would start talking again. I don't remember whether I hit something or what. . . . I probably stuck my tire in one of those cracks where I couldn't get out and then I fell and screamed. My mother ran over to me and I remember the first thing out of her mouth was 'What did you *do*!?' Ethel would say 'Don't be so harsh,' and then my mother would calm down. Aunt Ethel was always sweeter than my mother. Sometimes I used to wish she was my mother. I remember feeling jealous that my cousins had a better mother than I did. They always . . ."

"Let me interrupt you for a moment. I want to keep you focused on your being injured."

"Right, right, sorry about that, right." Caroline thinks for a moment and then says, "I guess that's all there is . . . what I just told you."

"That day when you fell off your bicycle, did your mother hug you or hold you or kiss you? Did she do anything to soothe you that you remember?"

"Oh, yeah, my mother was really, really affectionate with me. We were affectionate with each other. We would hug and kiss each other all the time, really kind of obnoxious, actually."

"I mean, was she calming and soothing to you after you fell off your bicycle?"

"Yeah, she would hold me and rock me . . . and probably said something like 'next time watch where you're going.'"

"So she would be warm and comforting but also kind of harsh, is that right?"

"Yeah, that's right."

"When you were sick as a child, who would take care of you?"

"My mom."

"Okay give me a memory of when you were sick and she took care of you."

"Well, I was home sick a lot. Sometimes I was really sick, but other times I just wanted to stay home and I would fake it. My mom didn't seem to mind. Sometimes she'd be home from work, just lying around and watching TV. I loved being with her, so I would stay home just to be with her." Caroline shrugs her shoulders in a childish fashion. "I really think she knew that I was faking a lot of the time, but she seemed to want me there too."

"Why do you think she would want you to miss school to be with her?"

"Well, I don't know. She was sad a lot and sometimes I'd see her crying and I would comfort her. She and Daddy got into lots of fights when I was young. Sometimes, I remember, after they'd fight she would get into bed with me."

"Was that a common event for you . . . comforting her?"

"Oh, yeah, I was her little baby and her little mommy too. It really got out of hand sometimes, especially later when I got to junior high. She would tell me all sorts of things about Daddy that I really didn't want to hear."

Role reversal: *Caroline is describing role reversal with her mother, who sounds as if she may have needed Caroline to regulate her emotionally. Role reversals commonly begin at around 14 years of age, but sometimes much earlier, and are a marker for the preoccupied parenting style that produces the ambivalent attachment profile that we call angry-resistant.*

One of the things I notice with Caroline is her tendency to digress. She goes off topic very easily and doesn't stay focused. She talks a lot about things that made her angry and still make her angry with her family of origin. This preoccupation and anger with her primary attachment figures give me some clues as to her internal working model.

As I continue the interview I find that Caroline spent a good deal of time with her mother playing games, doing projects, and other fun things. She complains that her mother was sometimes very present for her and at other times preoccupied and angry with her father. When I ask her what happened when she got upset as a child, she says her mother would sometimes cry and then she would have to take care of her.

Caroline had a poor relationship with her father, whom she saw as the perpetrator of her mother's unhappiness and preoccupation. But despite that negative characterization, Caroline says that her father would tuck her in bed at night and read to her; she remembers especially loving *Where the Wild Things Are*. And while she felt that she couldn't get angry at her mother because her mother would then sulk and withdraw, her father was tolerant of her anger (though he had problems with anger himself).

When I ask Caroline to give me five adjectives that would describe her relationship with her mother, she comes up with *loving, immature, funny, fun,* and *frustrating*. She's able to support each with memories of experiences, although again I have to rein her in as she becomes wordy and goes off on tangents, flooding me with material.

When I ask her to give me five adjectives describing her relationship with her father, she comes up with only four—*angry, scary, selfish,* and *unavailable*—and all of them are negative; it is unclear whether her supportive memories belong to her or her mother.

She describes her parents' relationship as "contentious" and "rocky," depicting her mother as easily angered and "going on and on" while chasing her father in and out of rooms. She was witness to their making up several times, her mother taking longer than her father to settle down. Neither parent, she says, admitted being in the wrong, and neither parent apologized to her when she was a child.

Interpretation

At the completion of the interview, I explain the process and how their relationship is unlike any other relationship except perhaps for their earliest attachment relationships. "This is important: Many of the struggles that you are currently having probably existed before you even met and were bound in a way to arise because of your histories. It's normal for attachment insecurities to surface as two people become more committed to one another. It's supposed to happen; it could be no other way."

Keeping an eye on Tim, I turn to Caroline to explain Tim's autobiographical memory problems, feeding back the discovery that his ideas about his early relationship with each parent differed from his real experience and from how alone he actually seemed, and the observation that the reason the interview upset him so much was his own realization that he lacked significant, personal interactions with each parent. I say this to Caroline for two main reasons: (1) Tim is in *her* care, so it is appropriate to tell her, and (2) directing my comments to her lessens the opportunity for Tim to become defensive. If what I say is disagreeable to Tim, I should be able to pick it up through verbal and nonverbal cues out of the corner of my eye and then adjust my narrative.

"I think one of the reasons Tim appears so self-sufficient and so averse to needing anything from you is because he learned very early not to depend on anyone. To him, being needy is simply shameful and must mean that there is something wrong with him. His independence isn't really independence at all but an adaptation to neglect by his parents. He spent too much time alone, stimulating and soothing himself, because the most important persons in his life valued attachment and relationships less than other things. This isn't to say he wasn't loved. He was, but not in a way that cultivated mutuality. Did you know this about him?"

"No," Caroline responds, "he always acts like he doesn't need anything, like he's normal and I'm sick. But now that you mention it . . ." (*she turns to Tim*) "now I understand why you never want to visit your parents and why you always want to be alone so much."

I elaborate. "He wants to be alone because being with others is difficult, especially those he would depend on, like you. He also likes to be alone because it's what he's always done to take care of himself. Being alone is safer for him, and most of the time he doesn't even realize he's doing it. He naturally drifts into being alone as a default state of mind. He probably barks at you if you approach him when he's in that state."

They look at one another and laugh. Tim, still looking at Caroline, admits, "She's always complaining that I'd rather be alone than be with her, and I feel terrible because when I'm working or reading the paper, I get annoyed when she interrupts me. I don't know why I do that. I love being with her." I motion to Tim to turn to Caroline and speak to her directly. "I really do love being with you. But then I have this other thing . . . "

I say to them both, "That's because you're wired to regulate yourself. You are accustomed, from a very early age, to turn to yourself for stimulation and soothing. It happens automatically without your thinking about it. When Caroline approaches you, she is interfering with your self-care, which is generally stress-free. As if waking you from a dream, her intrusion shocks you and increases your stress. In addition, I think you believe, on a body level, that she is wanting or needing something from you, and that you have to comply."

"Absolutely!" Tim replies.

"That's what it feels like to me," Caroline agrees.

"Okay," I say. "Tim, now I'm going to tell you about Caroline. She had a different experience from you. She described more loving interactions, especially with her mother; however, she also described her mother as being rather intrusive and at times childlike. Additionally, she implied moments of role reversal wherein her mother became the child and made her the adult. Her descriptions of her parents feature ambivalence and preoccupation: Often her mother was there for her, but at other times she was inattentive and rejecting. Caroline's adjectives describing her relationship with her father were all negative, yet she admitted that he often played a loving role with her.

"Further, it seems as if she never had the opportunity to see her parents manage one another very well. Her father didn't seem to know how to manage her mother, and vice versa."

I can see Caroline nodding in agreement from the corner of my eye.

Parent coregulation modeling: *How do children know how to manage relationships with each parent? They learn by seeing each through the other parent's eyes. That is, the child learns how to relate to the father by watching how the mother relates to him, and how to relate to the mother by watching how the father relates to her. This social–emotional learning function whereby we look to a known person to get a sense of a lesser known person is called* social *referencing. A child looks to a parent for social referencing when a stranger approaches: The stranger is either safe or unsafe through the eyes of the parent.*

An easygoing parent can be vilified, feared, or avoided by children because the other parent does not know how to manage his or her partner. Likewise, a hard-to-get-along-with parent may be easily approached by children because the other parent manages that partner very well. By manages *here I mean that one partner regulates the autonomic nervous system of the other partner.*

Secure partners are master coregulators of each other's nervous systems. Arguably, witnessing a good coregulated parental team is every bit as important as, if not more so than, the individual relationships a child has with each parent. Ideally that parental unit should emulate a secure attachment that embodies true mutuality—high mutually amplified positives, low mutually attenuated negatives, and evidence of repair.

"I think the two of you probably don't know how to manage one another as well. Tim, would you say that you're an expert on Caroline?"

"No," says Tim.

"Would you, Caroline, say that you're an expert on Tim?"

"No."

Owner's manual: It's reasonable to expect that each partner should be equipped with the knowledge of what works and what doesn't work with the other—that each, in other words, should have an owner's manual on the other. What are the three or four things that he or she needs to hear or have reinforced to make him or her feel good? What are the three or four things to which he or she has remained vulnerable since childhood? What is the quickest way to calm him or her down? What is the quickest way to excite or stimulate him or her? What are some of the surefire ways to bring tears to his or her eyes? What are some of the surefire ways to bring a true smile to his or her face? In secure attachment relationships, partners are able to perform these tasks and quickly minister to one another in ways that others cannot.

I continue feeding back information from the attachment interview. Current issues come up: Caroline complains that Tim is neglectful, avoidant, and distant; Tim complains that Caroline is angry, accusatory, and rejecting, especially with regard to sex. I decide I will gather more information about their attachment orientations next time but in a completely different manner.

Conclusion

The AAI is but one method of garnering information about a couple's attachment dynamics. It operates primarily as a top-down (high cortical to subcortical), left–right (explicit to implicit) investigatory instrument. (*Top-down* refers to communication from the upper parts of the brain to the body; *left–right* refers to communication from the left hemisphere, which specializes in speech and language processing, to the right hemisphere, which specializes in nonverbal processing.) For our purposes, the AAI can be an effective tool for uncovering schisms between ideas about early attachment relationships and actual experience. Discoveries during this process can be deeply distressing, especially for insecurely attached individuals who have heretofore denied their dependency needs. The resulting distress can be converted into a therapeutic buy-in or alliance through a skillful, coherent narrative presented by the couple therapist.

For Tim and Caroline, the experience in this one session led to information and insights neither possessed before—about themselves and each other. The inventory altered the couple's narrative about their relationship struggles by providing a larger context and meaning to why they got together, why they stayed together, and even why they should remain together. The AAI, if executed properly, should provide the couple with an expanded sense of continuity, trajectory, and destiny, and of attachment as a process that antedates their relationship. In this case, the AAI resulted in a dramatic shift in Tim's attitude toward his early relationships and his relationship trajectory up to this point in time. It also suggested a not-so-happy future unless he attends to the limitations it revealed. The interpretation of the AAI offered a coherent narrative of this couple's shared history of attachment injuries, fears, and limitations.

Chapter 6

THE IMPORTANCE OF MOVEMENT

The importance of approach and avoidance, separation and reunion, in all primary attachment relationships cannot be overstated, and *movement* is a powerful way to access a kind of evidence—in the form of somatoaffective information—that precedes or bypasses cognition. Movement where possible should be built into the office setting; chairs on wheels that offer a multitude of adjustments and options should be available to therapist and couple. The therapist can have partners move toward and away from one another while sitting in their chairs or on the sofa or love seat or while standing. Given enough space in which to move, exercises and interventions that get partners to go toward and away from each other can dramatically affect both far and near senses. Movement exercises are psychobiologically provocative. Designed to evoke fast-acting, right-hemisphere processes that pop up unexpectedly in the form of moment-by-moment shifts in the body, the face, the eyes, and the breathing pattern, such exercises reveal a great deal about attachment organization and the early hardwiring of approach and avoidance behaviors. The Moving Toward and Away exercise described in this chapter can activate approach and withdrawal behaviors and reactions. Whether physical, psychological, and/or emotional, those behaviors and reactions reflect the very core of attachment security and insecurity both in childhood and throughout the life span.

We might not ordinarily think of the simple act of walking away or avoiding as a "separation" experience, but psychobiologically, it is equivalent. When either partner moves *away* in some perceptible form, we experience a felt sense of leaving, being left, losing, going away, pulling apart, disengaging, or disappearing; conversely, when either partner moves *toward* in some perceptible form, we have a felt sense of approach, being approached, coming together, coming back, becoming joined, or reuniting. Even the subtlest shifts toward or away are registered on a nonconscious, psychobiological level. Indeed, subcortically, a perception of *toward* and *away* need not differentiate between "moving" objects. A train feels like it's moving but turns out to be stationary; it's the adjacent train that's moving and producing a perception that we are moving. Similarly, we can register movement toward or away from a primary figure and not know exactly who is actually moving. For instance, one partner may move away from the other, but experience the distance as if created by the other. A partner who initiates a divorce later feels abandoned and is no longer clear about who left whom.

Insecure relationships always reveal problems with separations and reunions, and these problems are as observable and measurable in the adult romantic dyad (Gottman, 1999; Shaver et al., 2000; Waters et al., 2000) as they are in the infant–caregiver dyad (Ainsworth, 1978; Sroufe, 1985). The Moving Toward and Away exercise is, in fact, intended to enact separations and reunions (i.e., Ainsworth's Strange Situation). I (S.T.) decide to use it to gather more information about the attachment orientations of Tim and Caroline.

Moving Toward and Away

"I'd like the two of you to stand up. Tim, I'd like you to stand on one side of the room, and Caroline, I'd like you to stand on the other side of the room facing Tim. I want you to maintain eye contact with each other at all times, even when I'm talking to you. I'm going to ask you both not to talk during this exercise; however, you can laugh all you want as long as you keep eye contact and keep your hands and arms to your sides." (I will have to continue reminding them to maintain eye contact because there is a tendency, when the therapist talks, for one or both partners to direct their gaze away from each other. I want hands and arms free so that I can observe subtle changes in their bodies as well as micromovements in their faces. This is similar to what Pat Ogden [Ogden & Minton, 2000] does in her work with trauma victims.)

"Tim, your job is to just stand there. Caroline, while keeping your eyes on Tim, you are going to slowly walk toward him." (The instruction is for the partner who is approaching to walk very, very slowly; I model this in order to show the right speed.)

"Stop at the point you think you ought to stop." (That instruction is purposely vague.) "Where and why you stop is up to you, based on what you experience in your body and what you see in Tim's face and eyes. Okay? Start walking."

I want to see where the approaching partner stops by watching the face of the partner who is being approached. I keep my eyes on Tim and remain angled so I can view three quarters of his face, favoring the left side.

The brain's right hemisphere is dominant for emotional expressiveness. Due to the contralateral connections of the hemispheres to the body, the left side of the upper part of the face should be more expressive than the right.

Caroline stops and I ask her, "Why there?"
"I think this is as close as he wants me to get."
"How do you know that?" I ask.
"I don't know. He just kind of looks tense in his face."

Most couples seem to stop at a particular point, roughly 2–3 feet from each other. Why? The brain seems to change at around this distance, when we are still using far vision as opposed to near vision. At a distance we cannot see the fine musculature of the face, and we're not looking at the eyes so much because they're too far away. We're looking at the gross anatomy, the gross picture of the body, and making assessments such as safe, not safe, attractive, and not attractive.

There appears to be a radical change in the brain when the details of the other person come into focus (Blakemore & Frith, 2004; Siegel & Varley, 2002; von Grünau & Anston, 1995; Wicker et al., 2003). We are seeing and being seen at this lesser distance. Many partners try to resolve the interpersonal stress that exists in this 2- or 3-foot field by coming together in an embrace that removes the problem of eye contact and goes right to the tactile, which can be calming and soothing.

I ask Tim, "Is that where you wanted her to stop?"

"Uh . . . I don't know. I guess that's okay."

"Caroline, I want you to take a big step toward him."

She moves toward Tim, and they both giggle. Tim leans slightly backward with his neck arched, jaw clenched, and breath held.

I ask Tim, "Is her coming closer like this better, the same, or worse?"

"Uh . . . worse," he replies.

"Okay. Caroline, take a giant step back. Tim, is this better, the same, or worse?"

"Uh . . ." Tim takes too long to respond but his body relaxes.

"Caroline, take another giant step back. Tim, better, the same, or worse?" Tim's body again shows signs of relaxation.

"Uh . . . it's . . . uh . . . I think . . ." Tim begins to laugh uncomfortably, "I think it might be worse. I don't know."

These questions (better, the same, or worse) are much like those the optometrist asks to ascertain which lens is better, number one or number two; most people understand the instruction. Why is Tim having difficulty answering? Is he freezing or locking up with anxiety? Is he out of touch with his body? Is he fearful of hurting Caroline's feelings if he admits he feels better when she moves away?

"Caroline, I want you to turn your back to Tim." Caroline turns and faces the wall. "Tim, is that better, the same, or worse?"

Again Tim stalls. I ask, "Are you afraid of what Caroline might think?"

"Yes," he replies without delay, and then lets out a burst of laughter.

"It's okay," I say to him and then ask Caroline, whose back is still turned away, "Did you know this about Tim, that he feels both relieved and guilty when you move away?"

"Yes," she says with an understanding tone.

"Okay, so Tim," I say, "she already knows this about you." He again lets out an embarrassed laugh.

"Caroline, I want you to leave the room for 3–4 seconds. Leave

the room, close the door, and then come back inside." I watch Tim
as I hear her leave the room and close the door.

"Tim, better, the same, or worse?" I ask.

"Better," he replies, this time without delay and with a more
sober look on his face.

When Caroline reenters the room, I ask her to physically invade
Tim in some way and to sustain the invasion. She approaches Tim
straight on, going toe to toe and nose to nose. I notice that Caroline's
body and face are relaxed as she continues to breathe even in this
close proximity. Tim, however, is noticeably tight throughout his
body and face and seems to be holding his breath. This approach is
enormously provocative for him.

*The discovery of intensely phobic psychobiological reactions to close
physical proximity and eye contact can be especially enlightening to the
couple that has been together many years and has had sexual problems. For some, sustained close physical proximity with a primary
partner can lead to a profound negative effect on the near senses (smell,
taste, touch, sound, and near vision). Given this reactivity, sex would
naturally become problematic.*

I ask them to sustain this position for a moment. Tim's eyes
wildly dart back and forth as he attempts to avert his gaze from her.
They laugh and enjoy a shared moment of amplified positive feelings and sensations when Caroline breaks away briefly to cough.
As she turns her head, Tim takes a deep breath from his chest and
resets himself before Caroline's gaze returns. It is not accidental
that he repeats his down-regulating strategy when Caroline is not
looking.

*It is not uncommon for individuals with avoidant attachment to feel
uncomfortable in the realm of the senses (smell, taste, touch, and near
vision). Some of this discomfort may derive from low-contact caregivers
during early infancy. Margaret Mahler (1968), for example, observed
mothers who were uncomfortable with sustained face-to-face, skin-to-
skin contact with their infants during the symbiotic phase of development, which is a time of fusion and melded bodies and minds that
theoretically forms a psychobiological basis for later romantic and sexual physical contact (Mahler, 1968, 1974). Early lack of contact may*

result in childhood aversions to touch, physical confinement, seeing and being seen, and the smelling and tasting of another. Many avoidant individuals, on a body level, don't like sharing air with another person. Their discomfort lies in the perceived intrusiveness of the other and the fear of intruding on the other.

Tim's psychobiological discomfort is due to his experiencing a kind of interpersonal stress that is predetermined by his attachment organization and dictates his (implicit) rules for safety and security. He cannot be fully himself—cannot reveal his intense sensitivity to invasion—because his internal working model tells him (nonconsciously) that his primary attachment figure would not approve of his impulses to pull or push away; doing so would surely threaten the safety and security of his attachment bonds. Tim must keep all these contradictory feelings and impulses to himself, where they remain shame-bound and incomprehensible.

"Okay," I say to Tim, "correct this if you need to or want to. Correct this in a way that makes you completely relax."

Tim sidesteps Caroline to assume a more comfortable position. The pained look on Caroline's face is palpable as Tim continues to look tense with a fixed grin on his face. Noticing her shift in affect, he awkwardly starts to tickle her belly. She briskly removes his hand and says, "Stop it. You know I don't like that."

"This is completely relaxed?" I ask Tim.

"Yeah," he replies.

"Because you do not look relaxed in the least," I say.

He shrugs his shoulders. Caroline's face is now fallen and forlorn.

"I'd like to see you two embrace for a moment. Can you embrace and hold one another as if reuniting from a long separation?"

Caroline turns to face Tim and begins an embrace. For several moments, Tim's left arm remains straight at his side while his right arm wraps around her. When both arms embrace Caroline, I notice that his eyes are open and staring out the window. I move around to look at Caroline and see her face nestled in Tim's shoulder, her eyes closed. Her body, relaxed and folded into his, appears settled by the embrace. Tim, however, does not look settled or comforted. His gaze appears dissociative and he seems alone, unable to make use of Caroline in a soothing manner.

Directed embracing: *This exercise produces very stable, repeatable results within each couple; behaviors are astonishingly idiosyncratic between different couples. However, two striking behaviors seem to repeat in many avoidant partners, whether male or female. One behavior is the tendency to sidestep the partner on approach just before becoming, or just after being, face to face. The other remarkable behavior is the straight arm while moving into an embrace. (Clinicians who have viewed the Strange Situations have seen this postural reaction in babies during reunion with their mothers.)*

I ask the partners to change positions and start over, this time with Caroline standing still and Tim approaching. Tim moves too quickly, and I ask him to begin again only more slowly. (It is not uncommon for partners who are themselves sensitive to being approached to approach their partners quickly and intrusively.) In his next attempt, Tim stops considerably farther back than did Caroline.

"Why did you stop here?" I ask him.

"I don't know . . . something in her eyes," he replies.

"What did you see in her eyes?"

"They widened a bit."

"Did her pupils become larger?" I ask.

"Maybe, I know her eyes got bigger."

"Caroline, do you have any idea what he saw?"

She pauses for a moment and says, "I just wanted him to come closer. I was feeling excited."

"Is that what you saw, Tim?"

"Yeah," he says smiling. "She gets that look in her eye, like she wants me—it feels clingy."

"And so you stop," I clarify, "because you feel her wanting more . . . ?"

"Yes."

"Almost as if she is approaching you, rather than you approaching her?"

"Yeah. That's right. I never thought of it that way before. It feels like she's coming *at* me."

Pupil dilation: *The eyes are a part of the brain and the windows to the nervous system. The autonomic nervous system plays a large role in love and romance. Open or dilated pupils are a sign of sympathetic arousal. Dilated pupils say, "Come hither." Ordinarily people are drawn to dilated pupils[1] and tend to move away from constricted pupils; this attraction–aversion response is not conscious most of the time. Keep in mind, however, that the avoidant person can find the open eyes of his or her partner threatening. The angry-resistant person may also sometimes react negatively to his or her partner's dilated pupils.*

Caroline was excited by Tim's approach, and it showed in her eyes. Tim, who is sensitive to approach, reacted to her silent beckoning as a threat and thus stopped.

"Okay, let's continue," I say. "Tim, take several steps forward," which he does. "Caroline, is this better, the same, or worse?"

"Better," she responds with no delay.

"Tim, take another giant step forward." He moves much closer to her, and both are smiling. "Caroline, better, the same, or worse?"

"Much better!" she says brightly.

Since I know that Caroline will continue to react positively to approach, I decide to check withdrawal.

"Tim, take a giant step back." As he moves back a noticeable shift occurs in Caroline's face and eyes. Her skin color reddens, the corners of her mouth turn downward, and her eyes begin to fill with tears. "Better, the same, or worse?"

"Worse," she replies, her voice lower and quieter. With each subsequent step back, Caroline's face registers more distress; for milliseconds, her eyes betray a burst of fear.

"Tim, turn your back to Caroline." Her eyes quickly scan his body, head to toe, as her own body leans slightly forward. Her face and neck, now a darker shade of red, appear tense and anguished. "Better, the same, or worse?"

"Definitely worse."

"Tim, leave the room for a few seconds, close the door, and then

1. Cleopatra, who obviously understood the concept of attraction, used belladonna, the modern-day equivalent of atropine, to charm males with her eyes (del Amo & Urtti, 2008). Studies indicate that infants and children are attracted to large eyes and large pupils (Demos et al., 2008; Trevarthen & Aitken, 2001). Highly popular fictional characters such as *ET the Extraterrestrial*™ and the more recent *Wall-E*™ possess enormous eyes. In contrast, some unpopular film characters, such as *Jack Frost*™, have beady eyes. A current teen craze, Japanese manga (comic books) and anime (animation), may be attractive in part due to the medium's hyperfocus on large eyes and pupils.

come back." I hear the door shut behind me as I study Caroline's reaction. She quickly turns to me.

"Wow," she says, tears streaming down her face. Caroline looks to me quickly for external regulation as Tim is now gone and her arousal is up.

Tim reenters the room, and I repeat the instruction for him to invade Caroline's physical boundaries in some way and sustain the invasion. He quickly approaches her and at the last moment, sidesteps and presses his nose against the right side of her face. In a flash, I see a micro-expression of disgust appear and disappear on Caroline's face (Ekman & Friesen, 1984; Ekman & Rosenberg, 2005), which quickly settles into an angry look.

I say, "Your face looks angry."

"I don't like that he goes to the side and doesn't hold me."

"Caroline, change this if you need to or want to so that it feels better to you." With that she turns to him and slips into an embrace, again with her body melded against his, her face tucked into his shoulder, and her eyes closed. Her face and body show no signs of tension. It's as though she is immediately soothed by the embrace. Tim, on the other hand, holds her stiffly, head upright, his gaze again out the window. Caroline is clearly able to make use of the embrace, unlike Tim, who again appears unheld and alone.

Conclusion

The Moving Toward and Away exercise provides evidential experience of Tim's and Caroline's attachment reflexes and impulses. Partners' knee-jerk reactions to approach and withdrawal, separation and reunion, infiltrate and influence daily relational life for any couple. Most partner conflict and dysregulation may actually be attributed to ongoing separation and reunion stress (Haley & Stansbury, 2003; Henry, 1997; Kochanska & Coy, 2002; Rosario et al., 2004).

The body remembers and it does not lie (Perry et al., 2007; Rothschild, 2003). By moving partners together and apart, we can observe their bodily reactions to one another close up, at a distance, in motion toward and away, even when each disappears. By means of close real-time and video observation we can identify attachment strategies through micromovements in body, face, and eyes, and through changes in prosody, skin color, and somatoaffective shifts that arise instantaneously, before thought and before speech.

Partners can explore their experiences as they arise and review them on video immediately afterward. This exercise is reliable and stable and can be repeated several times for skeptical couples; a panoply of other movement-oriented interventions can be undertaken to show the same, otherwise hidden, attachment insecurities and confirm their ubiquity.

The Lovers' Pose

Physical posing is another bottom-up approach that captures attachment insecurities through activation of the autonomic nervous system and somatoaffective neuropathways. The therapist puts partners into a series of poses, such as making statues, whereby they must hold positions that play with physical distance and close proximity. For instance, one partner may be placed on the other partner in a pose that resembles mother–infant cradling with sustained mutual eye gazing.

Terming this position the *lovers' pose* removes the stigma of the mother–infant, or superior–inferior meaning behind this evocative exercise, which can be used with and without words. In the case of Tim and Caroline, the intent is to physically reverse their roles, to have an impact on both their attachment systems and their neurobiology and create an experience that we can explore, expand, and mold. The exercise also has a reparative purpose: I (S.T.) give Caroline specific words to say that target known injuries in Tim.

For this exercise I use my full-length couch and have Caroline sit on the far end of one side with a pillow in her lap. I ask Tim to lie down with his head in her lap, looking upward at Caroline. I look at both partners' bodies for signs of awkwardness or tension and make corrections as necessary. As with any pose I first make certain that they hold eye contact without speaking and observe any shifts or changes that come over their faces or bodies.

I move onto the floor where I can see both Caroline and Tim up close. This position allows me to speak quietly, which in itself focuses both of them. From here I can also observe subtle shifts and changes in their faces. This position subordinates me and superordinates them.

"Tim, has either of you been in this position before?" I ask.

"Nope," says Tim. They both chuckle.

"I like this," remarks Caroline.

"Well, don't get used to it," says Tim in a sweetly sarcastic tone.

After the pose has been struck and held, I amplify the exercise by directing the interjection of attachment-relevant surprise declaratives. I choose these particular words because of what I know so far about Tim and Caroline—through their AAI and other information gleaned throughout the two lengthy sessions. I will also stretch the limits by trying words and phrases that are possibly outside of what I expect to be meaningful. Often neither partner reacts to these words and phrases, but sometimes the results are very powerful.

"Caroline, I want you to say these words exactly to Tim while keeping eye contact with him. '*You can depend on me.*'"

"*You can depend on me,*" Caroline softly repeats to Tim as she slowly strokes his head.

Moments pass and I notice that Tim's skin tone begins to change color. He swallows as his eyes well up with tears, and he quickly ducks his face into Caroline's abdomen. Caroline continues to stroke his head, looking down at him as her eyes begin to mirror his.

"'*I will take care of you,*'" I direct Caroline to say.

"*I will take care of you,*" she repeats to Tim. Caroline reaches for a tissue and begins to dab his eyes lightly to absorb the tears rolling down his cheek.

The therapeutic use of short, emotionally relevant and unexpected verbal declaratives introduces an element of surprise intended to evoke or provoke an immediate somatoaffective experience similar to throwing a rock in a pond ("Ask him [her] to divorce you"). The unexpected event causes an initial splash with subsequent waves; the therapist sustains the moment to observe the aftermath—which is very different from making an interpretation ("It seems that the two of you fear the idea of divorce") or making an inquiry ("I wonder why the two of you avoid the topic of divorce?"). The latter approaches are aimed at thinking, whereas the surprise statement is aimed at evoking an experience *by bypassing slower, defensive, higher cortical processes. The body doesn't lie because it has neither the time nor the ability to confabulate; that is the job of higher cortical brain regions and the left hemisphere.*

"Caroline," I say, "do you notice what's happening in Tim's face and eyes?"

"Um-hmm," she responds softly as she continues to gaze lovingly into Tim's eyes.

"These are words that I think he is unaccustomed to hearing, but they need to be heard at least sometimes," I say to her.

Though I am saying these things to Caroline, I keep an eye on Tim because these interpretations are aimed at him as well.

"This feels good," says Tim.

"Yeah, it feels good to me too," adds Caroline.

Conclusion

The use of poses, as noted, is another psychodramatic tool for assessment, illustration, and intervention. It employs a strategy of posturing and stillness as opposed to movement. Posing can evoke powerful somatoaffective reactions in partners through a juxtaposition of bodies. Structurally, it enables the therapist to check for each partner's ability to read facial cues and perform other near-proximity, interactive regulatory functions.

Bottom-up approaches, of which this is one, go first for experience and then for insight or change. Like other experience-driven tools that directly address fast, primitive, and fundamentally reliable sensorimotor, subcortical operations, using poses bypasses slower, more confabulatory and unreliable verbal/cognitive functions. Since implicit systems continually influence and drive the behavioral minutiae that form our perceptions of safety and security, verbal and cognitive intervention alone will have no appreciable effect on the actual, state-dependent problems all couples encounter in real time.

PART III

The Theoretical Universe

Chapter 7

ATTACHMENT

Research on rodents, primates, pachyderms, cetaceans, and humans affirms that attachment is basic to survival. Starting in the 1950s, compelling research controverted Sigmund Freud's drive theory and John Watson's behaviorist paradigm by validating the superordinate human need to connect, bond, and attach to other humans. Evidence ranges from the findings of Harlow and Woolsey (1958), Harlow and Mears (1979), and Prescott (1975) that rhesus monkeys reared without parental touching, holding, rocking, and playing experienced brain damage and became violent and socially impaired as adults; to Bowlby and Ainsworth (1952) on orphans, Ainsworth (1978) on infant–mother pairs, and the human infant failure-to-thrive cases discovered more recently in the Balto-Slavic region (Carlson et al., 1995; Chisholm et al., 1995; Gunnar et al., 2001; Haradon et al., 1994; Kaler & Freeman, 1994). We are wired psychologically and biologically to need other people (Hofer, 2005, 2006). A relational bond with another person that provides an ongoing, pervasive sense of safety and security provides a *secure base* (Bowlby, 1988; Clulow, 2001; Gillath et al., 2008; Waters & Cummings, 2000)—a safe harbor from existential loneliness and despair and a bioenergetic launching pad from which to brave the outside world. Caregiver enrichment or deprivation over the first 18 months influences the infant's relational trajectory with regard to primary relationships throughout the lifespan (Schore, 2005; Siegel, 2006; Siegel & Hartzell, 2003; Siegel et al., 2006). Thus, kind and degree of attachment security are of vital importance to a psychobiological approach to couple therapy.

OVERVIEW OF ATTACHMENT THEORY

John Bowlby (1988) suggested that during the period from infancy to adolescence, individuals gradually build expectations of attachment figures based on experiences with primary caregivers. These expectations are incorporated into the internal working models that guide their perceptions and behaviors in later relationships. Although his theory emphasized the foundational importance of early bonding patterns, Bowlby (1979a) considered the relevance of attachment principles to adult relationships significant. The nature of the attachment bonds between infants and caregivers involves the seeking of proximity to the attachment figure, resisting and protesting separations, and seeking safe haven by turning to the attachment figure in times of threat.

Attachment formation directly affects the development of structures and functions in the brain and body from infancy throughout life (Schore, 1997, 2000; Siegel, 1999, 2006). According to Allan Schore (2002d, 2005), the right hemisphere, which is believed to develop prior to the left hemisphere, is devoted almost in its entirety to attachment functions and is implicated in social–emotional acuity, implicit memory, stress regulation, intuition, and fundamental human qualities such as empathy and morality. (See Part V for further discussion of the neurobiological aspects of the psychobiological approach.)

Although largely dismissed by the mainstream psychological community during the second half of the 20th century, attachment theory has recently reemerged as a focus of interest for those studying social–emotional development, emotions, and human bonding. Technological advances, particularly in neuroimaging, electroencephalography (EEG), and less invasive video- and audio-frame analysis, have enabled researchers to look into the minds, brains, and bodies of infants and adults with more precision than ever before. These technologies also provide new methods for studying human relationships.

Two "low-tech" methods of viewing and assessing human relationships have garnered increasing respect among scientists and clinicians alike. First was Mary Ainsworth's Strange Situation (1978), developed for use with infants to understand approach and avoidance behavior, especially in reaction to separation and reunion. Later came Mary Main and colleagues' Adult Attachment Interview or AAI (George et al., 1984, 1985, 1996; Hesse, 1999; Main et al., 1985), developed for use with adults for the purposes of assessing parental attachment organization and predicting offspring attachment (but not for diagnostic application in couple therapy). Phil Shaver (1987) has studied the application of Bowlby's attachment theory to research on adult romantic love, focusing on attachment-style differences in defenses or coping strategies and in marital communication. Whereas the AAI is used to make inferences about the defenses associated with an adult's current state of mind regarding childhood relationships with parents, Shaver's self-report questionnaire asks about a person's feelings and behaviors in the context of romantic and other close relationships. All three approaches offer powerful conceptual images and analogs that can assist the psychobiologically oriented couple therapist in assessment, case formulation, and intervention planning.

Ainsworth, building on John Bowlby's theory of attachment by developing classifications for studying infant–mother attachment security (Ainsworth, 1978; Bowlby, 1969, 1979a, 1988), identified two organized, relational forms of attachment: secure and insecure. She divided insecure attachment into *anxious-ambivalent* (fussy, clingy, anxious, angry, and unsettled) and *anxious-avoidant* (distant, apathetic, oppositional, anxious, and sometimes aggressive). Others (Crittenden, 2008; Horowitz et al., 2005; Main & Weston, 1981a) have since termed those classifications *angry-resistant* and *avoidant*.

Ainsworth also used the classification *disorganized-disoriented*. Children who are disorganized-disoriented tend to have at least one primary attachment figure who is disorganized and disoriented, has a history of unresolved loss and/or trauma, and has a parenting style that can be deemed frightening, unpredictable, and psychologically unavailable (Cassidy, 2001; Cassidy & Mohr, 2001; Cassidy & Shaver, 1999; Hesse & Main, 2006; Lyons-Ruth, 2003; Main et al., 1985; Main & Solomon, 1986, 1990; Main & Weston, 1981b; Scaer, 2001; Schore, 2002d; Slade, 2000; Volling et al., 2002; Zimmermann, 1999). Researchers consider disorganization more transient than structural, unlike secure and insecure designations, and therefore view it as a kind of overlay atop secure or insecure internal working models.

Secure attachment, neurologically speaking, may correlate with structural and functional integration of the right hemisphere[1] and frontolimbic circuits. In particular, modulation of the amygdala is achieved by higher cortical areas such as the anterior cingulate, insula, and orbitofrontal cortex (Bechara, 2000; Morris, 1999; Schoenbaum, 2004). In contrast, neuroimaging studies on individuals with borderline personality disorder (which is often associated with extreme forms of angry-resistant attachment and disorganized/disoriented states) show low perfusion in the prefrontal cortex, particularly in the ventromedial region, suggesting poor top-down regulation of amygdalar activation (Driessen, 2004; Kunert, 2003; Tebartz, 2003). Similarly, individuals with attention deficit disorder and impulse control problems tend to test as insecurely attached and have problems with prefrontal cortical activation (Atkinson et al., 2009; Hill & Braungart-Rieker, 2002; Soloff et al., 2003; Volling et al., 2002).

Attachment theory offers an extremely rich and multidimensional therapeutic perspective for understanding human psychological, neurological, biological, and social development. This is especially true in the context of organizing assessment and treatment hypotheses in couple work, partly because—along with arousal regulation theory—attachment theory can help the therapist conceptualize a couple's dynamics without pathologizing partners.

Unlike personality theories, which primarily focus on intrapsychic or intrapersonal cause-and-effect factors, attachment theory privileges the psychobiological reality that is shared in relationships between two or more separate conscious minds—that is, between the inner subjective experiences of two or more individuals. It pertains to the connection, pattern, and exchange of the contents of experience conceived not as the one-way traffic of objective knowledge but as reciprocal communication of responses to experiences. Thus attachment theory, readily applicable as a nonlinear, intersubjective approach, opens doors to expanded conceptualization when it comes to difficult couples or partners who are deemed personality-disordered, whereas other theoretical approaches may hit a dead end.

1. Horizontal integration between the left and right hemisphere is also necessary for the fresh tracking and meta-awareness that is necessary for regulation and a secure state.

Organized forms of moderate to severe insecure attachment look similar to disorders of the self. (In fact there is much overlap. They simply use different psychotherapeutic languages to frame what they are seeing.) Both evolve out of pathological infant object relations, but the former more clearly implicates a disordered two person system. Both lack complexity due to their predictable, rigid adherence to rules of engagement and disengagement with another person. But using the frame of self or personality disorders, rather than seeing partners as people with insecure attachments who can heal through a mutual relationship, might be of little help and may even be defeating to the clinician dealing with couples. The designation "insecurely attached" provides a systems context from which the couple therapist can actually work.

Secure individuals reside within a world of true mutuality, a two-person psychological system in which the well-being of both partners is an ongoing priority. They seek closeness, or proximity, without ambivalence, resistance, or anger; they react to the proximity-seeking of their partner without anger, compliance, withdrawal, or dismissal. We all have some early frustrations and disappointments, of course, but with "good enough" early attachments, we develop in a world of mutual understanding, a two-person system where both feel truly connected.

We focus here primarily on the two insecure types of attachment—avoidant and angry-resistant—because these are the most common presentations in couple therapy. The labels are shorthand, depicting a set of behavioral and psychobiological patterns with a rather large brush. In reality, attachment categories such as secure, avoidant, and angry-resistant represent umbrella classifications under which finer and subtler distinctions exist. (Attachment organization itself represents only one piece of the psychobiological model, coexisting with arousal regulation, whose role is explored below, and nervous system development.)

THE AVOIDANT ATTACHMENT STYLE

Avoidant partners are primarily proximity avoidant and maintain a do-it-myself, "nobody can do it better than I can" orientation. Dependency—their own and others'—is a central issue in their relationships, especially primary attachment relationships. Their early childhood experiences served to consolidate the belief that dependency will yield only disappointment, gross misattunement, insensitivity, emotional pain, and shame.

These individuals, who are often found to be products of dismissive/derogating parenting dominated by neglect or intrusiveness, are themselves dismissive and derogating of attachment values and behaviors. Their early caretakers often avoided or devalued attachment behaviors and may have had a low tolerance for, and difficulty maintaining, physical or emotional proximity. Commonly, individuals who distance themselves from people gravitate toward "things." That gravitation toward things and the reflexive aversion toward a primary attachment figure are also outcomes of parental neglect and dismissal of attachment values and behaviors.

Because avoidant individuals do not depend on a primary attachment figure for stimulation and soothing, they reside in a one-person psychological system that is, by definition, masturbatory. Their need to withdraw from primary attachment objects is sometimes euphemistically referred to as the need for "alone time" (Buchholz & Helbraun, 1999; Tatkin, 2009a, 2009c). Alone time can take different forms, but almost always reflects a return to *autoregulation* for self-stimulation and self-soothing. The metaphoric use of the term *addiction* may be appropriate in that the avoidantly attached individual's adherence to autoregulation is ego-syntonic. Awareness of the downside of this way of living is kept at bay through the individual's aggrandized belief in his or her own autonomy, which is actually an adaptation to childhood neglect or parental unavailability. In actual fact, real autonomy never developed due to the considerable neglect that almost always pervades the history of this attachment profile.

The avoidant person's behavior is mystifying to the more interactive partner. He or she cannot understand how the avoidant counterpart can forget him or her so quickly or suddenly seem so disconnected—engaged one minute and disengaged the next. The partner may feel forgotten. And, in truth, this is exactly what has happened. We could say that the avoidant partner is better off, in some ways, than the angry-resistant partner. The avoidant person maintains a pseudo-secure relationship that is internally based on a fantasy of his or her partner's omnipresence.

Consider, for example, the following couple: he's avoidant, she's angry-resistant, and they are both out for a drive. He is staring straight ahead while his wife struggles with his disengagement. He is without discomfort because he is operating within a one-person psychological system wherein he autoregulates. In other words, he is playing alone in his room with his toys and is unaware he is with another person. She, on the other hand, is painfully aware that she is with another person and feels quite alone and possibly persecuted by the disengagement of her partner. Confronting the problem can produce a salutary reorientation, however, as in the case of an avoidant wife who was shocked to learn that her unexplained bolting away to locate a notebook in the middle of a conversation with her husband caused a momentary breach in the attachment system for him. The severity of the breach was moderated by her surprise at her own behavior. In couple therapy she came to learn that she was in a dissociative state, autoregulating, and she became aware enough to try to switch to a two-person orientation: The next time she decided she wanted note-taking implements during a conversation, she used her husband as her pen and paper and shared her thoughts with him.

For the avoidantly attached individual, the ball naturally rolls in the direction of autoregulation as the relationship evolves. All external disruptions of the autoregulatory state are experienced, to a greater or lesser degree, as a shock to the nervous system. The dissociative aspect of autoregulation screens out minor intrusions, such as bids for connection and interaction. In this way, the avoidant can maintain an unawareness of breaches in the attachment system. However, when the partner approaches physically, a threat response is inadvertently triggered within the avoidant partner, which results in an attempt to withdraw or attack. Depending on how early the neglect, avoidant partners may experience strong reactions to their partners' touch, smell, and taste. A partner's voice (prosody) and appearance can take on negative valences, with near vision evoking feelings of invasion and far vision inducing disgust and aversion.

Because avoidant partners operate within a one-person psychological system, they may not suffer problems during initial dating and courtship. Instead, they easily incorporate the new partner into their fantasy world, where all resemblances to the troublesome primary attachment relationship are as yet out of awareness. This behavior closely resembles the narcissistic characteristics of fusion, one-mindedness, and self-object relating (Kohut, 1977; Masterson, 1981; Solomon, 1989). The avoidant adult is able to maintain a dissociative but stable autoregulatory strategy that depends on an unrealistic image of a partner's presence. This pseudo-secure tactic expresses the avoidant person's need for continual but implicit proximity to the primary attachment figure—minus the problem of explicit proximity, which is experienced as intrusive and disruptive to the autoregulatory strategy. Fears and concerns about dependency, intrusiveness, and inadequacy do arise, however, when the romantic relationship has progressed, and the avoidant person's perception of the relationship's possible permanence increases.

The problem for those with an avoidant attachment style lies in their inability to shift states rapidly, especially when they need to move from a one-person to a two-person psychological orientation. The need of the other to connect may lead to a spike in the avoidant partner's arousal and distancing behavior. If this shift is made, however, interaction can be tolerated fairly well. Nevertheless, after the avoidant person leaves the two-person system again and resettles in an isolated state, he or she finds it very difficult to shift back out. Secure individuals, on the other hand, learn very early in life how to transition smoothly between one- and two-person states, play and nonplay states, alone and interactive states, high and low arousal states, wake and sleep, and so on.

It is possible for the partner to intercede to change the avoidant person's pattern of response. The reparative action on the part of the partner involves modifying his or her voice, forward acceleration, and phraseology to counter the avoidant person's reflexive misappraisal of a bid to reconnect as an aggressive demand to surrender autonomy. At the same time, the avoidant person must counter his or her own avoidant and dismissive behavior through quick and effective repair. He or she also must become proactive and seek out proximity with increasing frequency.

Individuals who distance themselves are acutely sensitive to significant others who are physically or emotionally advancing on them. The advance is automatically viewed as intrusive and accordingly triggers a host of seen and unseen distancing defenses, all of them psychobiologically reflexive and nonconscious. That exquisite reaction to being approached is embedded in the nervous and musculoskeletal systems; its roots are in the earliest attachment relationship.

Avoidant individuals operate outside of a truly interactive dyadic system and primarily rely upon themselves for stimulation and calming via autoregulation. The avoidant adult may wish to depend upon the love object, but skitters away the moment that his or her needs are not met *perfectly* by the other. Often there are complaints about what the other is doing wrong, which result in hurt and distancing. This response confirms the avoidant person's worst fears, of failure when depending on another, and the necessity of autoregulation for safety.

THE ANGRY-RESISTANT ATTACHMENT STYLE

The primary orientation of angry-resistant individuals in relationships is "I can't do it myself," combined with a feeling of helplessness and anger that the partner isn't available. Although they are primarily proximity-seeking, wanting close contact, they have a proximity-avoiding feature that often arises in reaction to reunion, lest it ultimately lead again to painful separation. Their history is a constant reminder, an implicit memory, of failed relationships and the hurt and anger that they always feel when they experience the other as unavailable. In the rare instance when they get exactly what they claim they want—another who always tries to be available—the angry-resistant person finds reasons to end the relationship (often, "It's boring").

Such people tend to move forward up to the point of reunion and then rapidly stiffen or move back. This can be witnessed as a physical moving or pushing away or through other negative behaviors. As a result, partners of angry-resistant individuals often experience them as distancing despite their basic insistence on proximity-seeking. These partners' attempts at repair—at any reunion gestures, in fact—trigger psychobiological anticipation of imminent rejection, impatience, or some other form of withdrawal on the part of the other.

The traits of angry-resistant individuals, like those of avoidant people, have their roots in the original primary relationship. As children, they become fussy and clingy when in the presence of the primary caregiver if the caregiver seems preoccupied. This fussiness, which is their own preoccupation and over time becomes an ingrained interactional style, prevents them from settling and exploring their environment.

Physical separation from the caregiver is met with a lot of signal crying and distress because the child cannot maintain an internal caregiver representation sufficient and constant enough to calm him- or herself. He or she either becomes overstimulated or conserves energy and withdraws, resulting in an inability to explore or interact with the environment. When the caregiver returns, providing obvious signs of meeting the demands of the proximity-seeker, the immediate reaction seems to be one of resistance—which frustrates the caregiver. The child's body fails to fold fully into that of the caregiver, as if to say, ambivalently, "I'm glad to see you—but wait, I just remembered that you weren't here and I don't trust that you're going to be here again, so I'm angry at you!" With this resistance, neither child nor caregiver can adequately calm and recover. Then they do it all over again, cementing the distressed, insecure pattern of attachment.

In adult primary attachment relationships, the angry-resistant individual often responds negatively to approach, particularly upon reunion. The negativity may be either a literal, physical pushing away or a verbal, gestural pushing away, usually with hostility—an angry reaction to separation and to the anticipated rejection and withdrawal by the partner. There may also be guilt deriving from the angry-resistant person's belief that he or she is a burden to the needed other. The negativism is a hardwired response, imprinted by early attachment organization and replayed repeatedly in all significant relationships throughout life. This dynamic is very similar to Fairbairn's (1972) antilibidinal ego that defends against disappointment by sabotaging positive expectations.

The angry-resistant partner, like his or her early caregiver, often tends to be preoccupied and unavailable. This preoccupation, with the self, family members, work, or the primary attachment relationship, often takes an angry, irritable tone. The person makes demands on others to regulate him or her but without reciprocation, and that lack of reciprocity puts a great deal of pressure on the partner, often resulting in a domino effect that creates further distancing with more anger. The outcome is a sense of helplessness and rage and an increase in blaming, with each partner convinced that the other could provide relief but chooses not to.

In couple therapy the opposite partner can come to understand the attachment wound that drives the behavior. Both partners can be helped to see the negative behavior as a psychobiological reflex that, though not subject to conscious control, is amenable to "taming" as feelings are held and contained. The takeaway message for the couple is that this is a team effort: The angry-resistant person cannot heal the attachment wound alone and needs the other's help to change the negative behavior pattern.

Eventually, their interactions can take a different shape. The pivot here is not so much what is said by the opposite partner as what is done. In the face of negativism, the partner must make a counterintuitive move forward to positively override the push away. This move exactly opposes the expectation that drives the angry-resistant pattern, which assumes that the partner will be angry and frustrated by the individual's behavior and withdraw. This expectation of the angry-resistant person is based in real experience with the early caregiver.

The partner's moving forward in the face of negativism must be repeated often, and perhaps forever. If it is done properly, it will produce a positive state shift in the other, which in turn creates a mutually amplified positive moment; thus both partners benefit. As soon as possible, the angry-resistant partner must also take responsibility for his or her own rejecting/punishing behaviors and make things right with the other person.

Chapter 8

AROUSAL REGULATION

In nature we can see and hear the ocean waves as they swell, crest, and crash, rushing forward and then receding backward. An experienced surfer rides the waves and gracefully balances while rising with the swell and crest, and then just as gracefully lands with the wave's denouement. Similarly, we can see and hear trees as they sway back and forth with the wind, and we can feel the wind blowing us this way and that. A hang-glider rides the wind currents, gracefully balancing with and against the forces moving upward and downward.

The ocean waves and blowing wind can be compared to arousal, a force of nature that rises and fades, that pushes us forward or holds us back, or that knocks us over and causes us to lose our balance. As with the surfer and the hang-glider, our ability to manage these forces gracefully and in a balanced manner can make the difference between pleasure and misery. Depending on our ability to regulate arousal, we either joyfully and effortlessly master the forces of arousal, or fly out of control until we crash.

Arousal refers to specific brain–mind–body states that are products of various systems and processes. The *sympathetic* branch of the autonomic nervous system (ANS) influences emotions, produces vitality states, and generates action readiness; it does so in tandem with the neuroendocrine system, in particular, the hypothalamic–pituitary–adrenal (HPA) axis, which churns out adrenaline. The *parasympathetic* branch influences emotions, produces relaxation states, and generates a recovering counterresponse to sympathetic activation. It does so in tandem with the vagal motor complex and the HPA axis, which manufactures corticosteroids (cortisol). (For further details, see Part V.)

When the ANS is functioning optimally, we are able to remain both alert and relaxed at the same time, without creating too much action readiness and subsequent recovery readiness. In other words, a well-running system is economical: It never expends too much unnecessary energy, and so saves us from too much unwanted downtime. A state of optimal arousal in the ANS modulates the neuroendocrine production of adrenaline and corticosteroids, keeping us from spending too much of either substance. Optimal ANS arousal also affects the amount of available oxygen and glucose metabolism in the brain, which in turn determines our availability to process and respond to experience (Beneli, 1997; Burleson et al., 2003; Eagle et al., 2007; Iacoboni et al., 2001).

THE NUTS AND BOLTS OF AROUSAL REGULATION

Arousal regulation is the process of managing our arousal states and the transitions between them. Arousal can be regulated both internally, by automatic (nonconscious) and voluntary (conscious) means, and externally through the intervention of significant others in our environment. All *automatic internal regulatory functions* are performed by subcortical areas. These are the lower limbic structures (e.g., the amygdala, hippocampus, and hypothalamus) as well as the midbrain, brainstem, spinal cord, and dorsal vagal motor pathway. The ANS is responsible for nonconscious arousal regulation (e.g., fainting, falling asleep, waking up; perhaps even turning away from a disturbing person, scene, or sound). *Voluntary internal regulatory functions* are performed by higher cortical areas. These include the frontolimbic structures—the ventromedial prefrontal cortex, orbitofrontal cortex, anterior cingulate, insula, and ventral vagal motor pathway. Without a functioning prefrontal cortex, one would have to rely either on automatic internal controls or on external controls such as another person or medication. Children and adults with attention-deficit problems often depend on psychostimulants such as methylphenidate (Ritalin) or dextroamphetamine (Dexedrine) to activate the frontal lobes, which restore self-regulatory capacities.

Many voluntary regulatory strategies are available to us. We can, for instance, take a deep breath when we get too excited, sending a parasympathetic volley to the heart that helps us calm down by reducing our heart rate and increasing oxygen to the brain. We can use distraction or other refocusing methods to adjust our state either upward or downward. We also have higher-level adaptive strategies at our disposal, such as meditation, exercise, going to a movie, reading a book, or calling a friend; we can talk to someone when we are hurt, angry, sad, or fearful, aiming to down-regulate our arousal through self-expression. Alternatively, we can employ lower-level adaptive strategies, such as the use of alcohol, drugs, sex, violence, or any number of other behaviors, to adjust our state of arousal.

External regulatory functions are first performed by our earliest attachment figures, through skin-to-skin, face-to-face, vestibular, and prosodic interactions. Later on, friends, teachers, lovers, doctors, and others may fulfill external regulatory functions. Pharmaceuticals and street drugs provide external regulation, too, in the sense that they at least begin as external agents of state change. The psychobiological approach to couple therapy is particularly concerned with the external regulatory role of the adult primary attachment partner.

From a self-management perspective, we move from an automatic, inflexible, nonconscious level to a purposeful, flexible, conscious system of *self-regulation*, the latter being better suited to creating and maintaining social contracts based on fairness and mutuality. We begin to incorporate rudimentary self-regulatory functions at around 10–12 months of age, when our orbitofrontal cortex comes online (Schore, 1994, 2002c); the process continues throughout childhood. Impulse control and frustration tolerance are orbitofrontal, self-regulatory functions that are not fully completed until frontal lobe development reaches its pinnacle in early adulthood. As noted, we learn to self-regulate with the help of our first external regulators, our primary caregivers. Our young self-regulatory system is a fractal representation, or duplicate, of theirs. So, constitution and genetics aside, we are only as good at arousal regulation as were our earliest external regulators. Thus, if our primary caregiver was an effective modulator of his or her own feelings of anxiety, fear, anger, and excitement, we tend to become effective in turn.

An infant or child may be either wholly or partially neglected or otherwise deprived of good external regulation by a caregiver. In many such cases, certain mental, emotional, or bodily states are dismissed, discouraged, or devalued. When both parents consistently avoid a particular arousal or affective state, children must avoid or regulate these states on their own. The result is a poorly managed internal experience that can later produce negative social consequences.

For example, a young man comes from a family that has always favored the lower ranges of arousal, preferring quiet, low expectations and no drama from its members. Excitement of any kind was discouraged by both parents. Sympathetic arousal or intensity, positive or negative, was not a part of the family culture. Growing up, the young man stayed away from high-intensity friends but briefly dated a rather animated girl during senior year of high school. He found her liveliness attractive but intimidating; much to his dismay he could not tolerate her passion, especially when directed at him. He withdrew from any interactions that could have resulted in elation, joy, or desire, and instead swiftly shut down. For this young man, excitement or anything nearing excitement represented an *unregulated*, and therefore unmanageable, state. In adulthood his bride-to-be is similar to his high school girlfriend, and in fact struggles with the same problem but on the opposite end of the arousal spectrum. She's a master of high vitality states but avoids the lower range: repose, satiation, sadness, and depression. Together they form a *biphasic* couple—that is, one partner prefers higher sympathetic states and the other prefers lower parasympathetic states. In couple therapy, the task is to help him regulate (or tolerate) higher states and her the lower ones. As primary partners, each is in the best possible position to help the other, at least potentially. Each is also in the best possible position to hinder the other, and that is often the outcome. A psychobiologically oriented couple therapist may help such partners.

From a developmental perspective, each individual should be moving toward complexity—from self play to interactive play, from *autoregulation* toward *interactive/mutual regulation*. In couple therapy, we are concerned with the developmental state of each partner's prosocial capacities, which affect his or her ability to function at the highest levels of self-management within a relationship.

AUTOREGULATION

Autoregulation is the earliest and simplest level of arousal regulation. It is an insular, automatic process that requires little internal resource because it is noninteractive on an interpersonal level. For example, gaze-aversion is an infant's autoregulatory strategy for preventing over-stimulation and calming down. The infant will make eye contact with its caregiver but will eventually avert its gaze because eye contact is highly stimulating. If the caregiver becomes intrusive after the baby averts his or her eyes and tries to "chase" the gaze, the baby will feel defenseless against the overstimulation and turn to other, more drastic autoregulatory strategies (ducking away, arching its back) or resort to dissociation.

Autoregulation, in terms of a psychobiological approach to couple therapy, is a do-it-yourself management strategy for calming and stimulating oneself. Initially, it is internal, primitive, and nonrelational: The infant sucks its thumb to pacify itself, the toddler carries a "blankie" or other transitional object for self-comfort, the young child self-entertains with toys, the teenager gets excited by romantic fantasies. But autoregulation also entails more conscious, nonreflexive activities—watching TV, reading, eating, drinking or drugging, spacing out, obsessing, meditating, surfing the Internet, playing video games, and so on. On the creative side, autoregulatory behaviors can include dancing, singing, playing an instrument, writing, and painting, as long as they are nonrelational in the sense that another person is not required. They allow us to regulate our degree of stimulation without the element of interpersonal stress.

How we experience autoregulation is influenced by our attachment orientation. Interaction with another person generally requires more internal neurobiological resources, so for avoidant individuals, autoregulation is predominantly energy-conserving; reliance upon it over time consolidates a one-person psychological system of nonmutuality. The pleasantly dissociative state it confers allows for a blissful, focused unawareness of space and time, reminiscent of infant play states in which self-stimulation and self-soothing are unencumbered or interrupted by anxiety or insecurity. In the case of angry-resistant persons, however, the opposite prevails: For them, extended periods of noninteraction with primary figures lead to intensely dysregulated states; autoregulation for them demands high energy-expenditure, particularly when making the shift away from interaction.

It should also be noted that autoregulation can be employed in pseudo-relational interactions with other individuals, as occurs in some psychiatric and personality disorders. For instance, relationships of narcissistic personalities involve using others as mere extensions of the self, not as separate real persons (Kohut, 1977; Lichtenberg, 1991; Winnicott, 1969). In this sense, narcissistic-disordered individuals appear to be regulating interactively with others, but are in fact autoregulating—using others as objects of self-stimulating and self-soothing.

INTERACTIVE REGULATION

Interactive regulation is the process whereby at least two individuals comanage and dynamically balance ANS arousal in real time. Developmentally, interactive play by infants with their primary caregivers forms the foundation for mutuality and reciprocity. When interactive play does not take place, infants turn instead toward autoregulation as an adaptation to interpersonal neglect. They do so at great cost, remaining in exile from the interactive world as they grow older.

Whereas autoregulation is fundamentally self-absorbed, internally focused, and pro-self, interactive regulation is fundamentally interpersonal, externally focused, and pro-relational. An individual's reliance on autoregulation (one way, do it myself) or external regulation (one way, do it for me) is a sign of a one-person psychological orientation that is rooted in nonmutuality. Reliance on interactive regulation (two way, we do it for each other), on the other hand, points to a two-person psychological orientation that is rooted in true mutuality.

Attunement is the feeling of being on the same page, in alignment, or in synchrony—the feeling that launches primary attachment relationships. Attunement produces a sense of safety and security as well as attraction and is sustained by a couple's capacity to remain predictable and friendly on a micromoment basis. (*Micromoment* refers to the subcortical speed at which people appraise and respond to social situations; that speed is roughly between 30 and 300 milliseconds [Khan & Sobel, 2004; Krolak-Salmon et al., 2003; Morris et al., 1998; Shibata et al., 2008], which is very fast.)

Moments of misattunement between otherwise attuned partners are quite unpleasant. Reactions are reflexive and instantaneous and therefore cannot be fully controlled; once expressed, they cannot be taken back but should be repaired posthaste. Although skillful couples will quickly reattune without much awareness of what they are doing (awareness of misattunement lags behind the primitive operations already in motion to protect the couple from danger), discomfort will increase if partners take longer than usual to error-correct. Misattuned moments can spike partners' arousal in either the *hypo* or *hyper* direction, and too many such moments, without repair or error-correction, lead to an amplification of negative experience and a sense of threat. So in the region between misattunement and reattunement, time is not on the couple's side. In fact, when it comes to regulating rapidly increasing or decreasing arousal, time is of the essence.

Chapter 9

DYSREGULATION

Extended periods of misattunement between two people increase the likelihood of extreme arousal states, which in turn increase the likelihood of the internal and mutual mismanagement of those states. In other words, as arousal gets out of hand, couples move from love to war. The term *dysregulation* describes the somatoaffective, neurobiological condition that involves extreme negative alterations of the brain, the mind, and the body. In layperson's terms, dysregulation is equivalent to "freaking out."

CAUSES OF DYSREGULATION

Infants depend on their caregivers for help in regulating their internal states. The process is an exquisitely delicate and finely tuned collaborative dance. When the caregiver is too intrusive, too unresponsive, too reactive, or too preoccupied to maintain relational equilibrium with an over- or understimulated infant, however, errors or missteps occur. Normally, they are met with the caregiver's corrections and adjustments. However, when a caregiver cannot or does not correct or adjust, producing extended misattunement that goes unrepaired, the result is dysregulation of the infant's internal state.

This isn't to say that dysregulation is always caused by a caregiver. On the contrary, similar problems can occur when the internal world of an infant or young child is one of constant physical agony (e.g., in the case of colic, acid reflux, or other constitutional issues). The child's intense and continuous distress signals pave the way for mutual dysregulation due to the caregiver's inability to adequately soothe or comfort the distressed child. A child who is experiencing acute or chronic pain could present a regulatory challenge for any caregiver.

On an affective level, a parent's anger can become dysregulating when it becomes too intense and lasts too long. Frequent, extended outbursts of rage on the part of the father, for example, can negatively affect every nervous system in the family such that everyone becomes dysregulated along with him: A son rages in response, a daughter leaves the house, the mother cries and begs the others to stop; the younger girl keeps to her room and destroys her dolls and grows up to be fearful, disorganized, disoriented, and hyperaroused whenever she feels or encounters anger. Indeed, repeated frightening parental behavior is known to cause disorganization and disorientation in children (Cassidy & Mohr, 2006; Holmes, 2004; Lyons-Ruth & Spielman, 2004; Main & Hesse, 1990; Main & Solomon, 1990).

Attachment insecurity and dysregulation go together. The more insecure a partner, the more likely psychobiological dysregulation will appear as a regular feature in the couple system. This is ever so much more the case when both partners are further along the insecure attachment spectrum. Many insecure partners come with a history of unresolved trauma or loss: Their pockets of unmetabolized, painful experience can emerge under stress and increase instances of dysregulation. Because relational experience is interwoven with anticipatory systems such as the ANS and HPA, it not only profoundly affects one's attitude but also configures one's biology on a structural and functional level. Primary attachment relationships, whether characterized by sensitivity, insensitivity, or frightening unpredictability, powerfully alter the brain, mind, and body on the cellular level, even affecting DNA and gene expression (Schore, 2002a, 2002b; Cappas et al., 2005).

Individuals with unresolved early relational trauma, PTSD, or a chronic neuroendocrine response to threat are vulnerable to amygdalar hypertrophication and hippocampal atrophy (McEwan, 2003; Vyas et al., 2002, 2003, 2006; Tebarz et al., 2000). Individuals such as these become organized around trauma, fear, and aggression. There is some evidence to suggest that mothers being under high stress affects the prenatal neurobiological development of their infants (Davidson, 2008; Cottrell, 2009; Pardon, 2008; Oitzl, 2009).

Individuals with overgrown amygdalae and shrinking hippocampi may be prone to paranoia or an overly pronounced perception of threat and seem somewhat disoriented and unable to properly sequence events in time and space (a function requiring the hippocampus). High chronic stress, also a result of insecure attachment, leads to an overproduction of adrenal products, causing overpruning of cells during childhood and adolescence and neurotoxicity in adulthood (Schore, 2005; Teicher et al., 2002; McEwen, 2003, 2001, 2000).

In early development, attachment security also affects *parasympathetic tone*, which reflects the body's ability to relax and recover. Directed by the vagus nerve, parasympathetic tone is responsible for cardiovascular down-regulation and modulation of sympathetic arousal states. Insecurely attached children and adults may experience lifelong problems with impulse control and sympathetic acceleration (disinhibition) tendencies and poor vagal brake (inhibition) function.

Dysregulation between partners occurs in response to an intense and/or lengthy breakdown of interactive regulation. *Intensity* and *duration* are two dimensions of arousal involving negative emotion, and they correlate with dysregulation. Intense negative experiences of short duration are of little consequence, as are mildly or moderately negative experiences of longer duration. However, intensely negative interpersonal experiences of long duration lead to overwhelming interpersonal stress, resulting in relational trauma and a breach of the safety and security system. This breach leads to a threat response, a drive to get away from the object "causing" the stress.

Dysregulated couples' reactions can occur anywhere along the insecure spectrum and may include features of uncontainable arousal, intense affect, poor recovery, dissociation, and significantly compromised information processing. Partners lack either skill or capacity to self- or mutually regulate along the middle ranges of the arousal spectrum. Collectively, they are unable to maintain prosocial levels of arousal (i.e., those in which higher cortical areas are oxygenated and available for contingent responsiveness) and avoid reactive extremes—either fight/flight/freeze (sympathetic, associated with hyperarousal) or energy conservation/withdrawal (parasympathetic, associated with hypoarousal). In extreme states of arousal, the brain and neuroendocrine system undergo changes that support self-survival away from prosocial values and behaviors. In other words, during hyperarousal or hypoarousal, brain activity is limited to more primitive, subcortical processes dedicated to survival of the organism, first and foremost.

A couple becomes dysregulated when either or both partners fall outside of the social range of arousal (Porges, 2001) and are unable to reregulate downward or upward. Negative emotions become amplified. Behaviors related to hyperarousal tend to be overly expansive (e.g., mania, rage, terror, aggressiveness, grandiosity), and behaviors related to hypoarousal tend to be overly constrictive (e.g., dissociation, anaclitic depression, incapacitating shame, deadness).

HIGH-AROUSAL COUPLES

In high-arousal couples, both partners have biases in the high sympathetic range of the autonomic nervous system. Their arousal profile, which is remarkably stable and predictable, shows an excess of shared *high positives* and *high negatives*. The high positives can be attributed to their mutual preference for sympathetic states that include vitality affects such as excitement and mania, but also rage and terror. Their high negatives can be attributed to their shared avoidance or intolerance of low parasympathetic states that include affects such as sadness, grief, depression, and shame. Neither partner is equipped to interactively regulate painful affects; thus the calming and soothing function is missing in the couple. Commonly, both partners in such couples are angry-resistant—so, despite their fiery relationship style, they tend to stick together because of a strong clinging defense.

High-arousal partners have an extraordinarily rapid rate of kindling for anger and rage and typically accelerate into hyperarousal at the drop of a hat. Like the starting of a fire, the *kindling effect* refers to activation of a system or sequence that leads to a biological, emotional, or psychological condition such as a seizure, depression, anxiety, panic, or a bipolar episode, especially upon recurrence of that condition. For instance, untreated depression may lead to future kindling of depression (Ferrando & Okuli, 2009; Fries & Pollack, 2007; Scaer, 2001). When together, high-arousal partners are quite possibly on the upper boundaries of social arousal much of the time. The rapid kindling effect cuts both ways: They seem equally prepared for war as for passionate sex and can sometimes quickly shift between the two. Interestingly, many high-arousal partners have backgrounds of substance abuse, with a higher-than-average preference for stimulants, alcohol, and marijuana. (Nevertheless they are often resistant to controlled psychopharmacological intervention.) The couple therapist should always check for a history of legal and illegal drug use and a history of head trauma, and should also be alert to the possibility of frontal lobe impairment. (The almost complete disinhibition of the holding and waiting function may, among other things, be attributable to ventromedial prefrontal dysfunction.)

Because high-arousal partners lack impulse control, they continually "forget" about holding and waiting (impulse control), and their acceleration (disinhibition) tendencies and poor vagal brake (inhibition) function challenge the therapist, who would prefer to limit or interrupt in-session fighting. Once started, these embattled couples will not be stopped until they are good and ready; the therapist must wait to resume interaction with the couple until their arousal wanes.

Clinicians who are uncomfortable with high-intensity anger will find themselves holding onto their seats with high-arousal couples. Others will feel variously helpless, frustrated, impatient, and even bored: The repetitive rants can be exceedingly dull as well as discouraging. High-arousal couples *do* improve, but progress is slow: Although the capacity for self- and coregulation should improve with age and the developing complexity of the brain, mind, and body, arousal biases are not easily amenable to change (pharmaceuticals aside). As is the case with attachment structures, however, the goal is not to change partners' arousal biases but to make their primary attachment relationship secure.

LOW-AROUSAL COUPLES

Low-arousal partners are biased at the low parasympathetic range of the ANS. Most often, both are avoidant. Their arousal profile shows a predominance of low mutual positives and low mutual negatives. The low positives are mostly due to their lifelong avoidance or intolerance of high sympathetic states (including vitality affects such as joy, ecstasy, or passion); because of this pattern, neither partner comes to the relationship equipped to interactively regulate high positive affects. The low negatives can be attributed not to skillful interactive regulation of painful affects but to limited interactive demands and a mutual preference for autoregulation. Low-arousal couples tend to keep the volume low on arguments . . . and everything else. Nevertheless, these couples are chronically anxious. Their anxiety seems to be a function of insecure avoidant attachment during infancy. They are unheld babies who literally have no internal method for calming themselves down, particularly during periods of inactivity and quiet, at nighttime and in the morning. Sleep disturbances are common among these individuals, as are symptoms of obsessions, compulsions, and hoarding.

Low-arousal couples appear rudderless at times as if waiting for instructions from a parent. For this reason, these couples often overfocus on daily tasks and organizational difficulties, the content of which can become compelling and distracting for the couple therapist. Their avoidance of interactive regulation, mutual dependency, and physical and emotional intimacy may convince the therapist that their management concerns are most important. As partners they appear stalled and clueless, often fluctuating between needing help and refusing it. Since they are avoidant, they are single-thinking in their orientation, often expecting themselves and the other to do things alone and without assistance. Yet neither does anything very well alone, so they make promises they cannot keep.

One can imagine two avoidant, low-arousal partners stuck outside in a snow storm, sitting apart and freezing to death, neither realizing that together they could generate enough heat to keep warm. Because of that inability to recognize valuable resources "right under their noses," they perish. No matter how intelligent these folks are, their one-person psychological system of nonmutuality keeps them in an eternal state of neglect and aloneness. But because they are low-arousal, they operate under conditions of low interpersonal stress and so remain separate, together.

BIPHASIC COUPLES

Some dysregulated couples display biphasic features, whereby one partner exhibits a preference for higher sympathetic states and the other partner exhibits a preference for lower parasympathetic states. Collectively, they appear bipolar. Because biphasic couples argue primarily over misattuned interactions, particularly at reunions—which can occur many times during a day, even as partners go their separate recreational ways (one to the television, one to the computer)—therapists may come to feel frustrated and hopeless about helping them.

Therapists may also begin to harbor split feelings, negative or positive, toward one or the other partner, and might experience a strong countertransference in line with the couple's own suspicions that they are mismatched and wrong for one another. Of course, these couples, like all others, are not so much mismatched as unprepared to manage their opposing arousal biases, which amounted to a lesser problem during courtship when extended undistracted time together probably facilitated an averaging out of their extremes.

WHAT TO WATCH FOR

Therapists can identify dysregulated states in couples by observing changes in partners' voices, gazes, movements, facial expressions, breathing patterns, skin color, and so on. In a case of hyperarousal, the voice may change in pitch (up), volume (up or down), and tone (sharper); skin may become reddened and tauter; movements may appear faster, jumpier, arrhythmic, and menacing; the body may appear more rigid and constrictive. In hypoarousal, the voice may change in pitch (down), volume (down), and tone (dead); skin may become blanched and flaccid; movements decrease and slow; the body may appear collapsed or crumpled; the posture may suggest surrender and hopelessness or even nausea.

Therapists can also watch for signs of dysregulation in the couple's interactions. What distinguishes dysregulated couples from those merely in conflict is that they do not have the ability to coregulate during times of strife. If they were standing in a boat together, they would not be capable of balancing it, and as a result both would land in the water.

Regulated couples are able to go in and out of conflict, to tense and relax, without ever pushing either partner into hyperarousal or hypoarousal. These couples maintain a sense of play, whereas dysregulated couples do not. Well-regulated couples know how to hold on and let go; dysregulated couples do not. Well-regulated couples recover quickly from occasional spikes in their arousal system; dysregulated couples do not.

When dysregulated partners begin talking about an area of importance (something around which they argue), their interaction devolves into warring behavior: They interrupt each other, use dangerous words and phrases, and repeat the same arguments. One of the surest signs of incipient dysregulation is *content-spreading*, which is a branching out of complaints against another person. The growing litany of complaints is a symptom of interpersonal distress or injury, and occurs when distress goes on too long without repair. Therapists can be sure arousal is increasing and dysregulation is imminent when partners start adding to their complaint list or bringing up the past or bringing up other people (kids, parents, friends) to bolster their arguments.

Dysregulated couples typically do not hold, wait, or balance expansion and contraction, at least not very well. Holding, waiting, and limiting expansiveness are vital self-regulatory, executive functions of the right orbitofrontal cortex, an area of the brain that shuts down in situations of hyper- and hypoarousal. (In some cases the inability to hold and wait may point to a real neurobiological deficit.) The therapist must help the dysregulated couple regain and increase their capacity for holding and waiting if the therapy is to move forward. Effective interventions include those that have a regulatory impact on the couple system. One such intervention is the therapist's expectation that partners exercise their capacity to *hold* impulses and *wait* their turn, as well as limit the duration of the turns they take, because long narratives create flooding in the waiting partner.

While couples are in the throes of a threat response, hierarchical processes involving the prefrontal cortex give way to subcortical processes to ensure survival. During these periods of dysregulation, the ability to accurately represent and sequence events is highly compromised; so too is the ability to appraise intention. Yet insecure couples often become entangled in arguments involving the reconstruction of past events. In the clinician's office they will present wildly differing recollections as to content, sequence, and intent, and will remain locked into a painful, isolated reality of violent misattunement and persecution.

It is neurologically impossible for partners to set the record straight. The unrelenting attempt at reconstruction of a traumatizing event is itself retraumatizing. In addition, intense and repeated dyadic dysregulation is traumatizing and leads to threat-related psychobiological reorganization within and between partners (Charney, 2004). Memory undergoes a reconsolidation process, whereby visual and auditory reactivating cues associated with earlier dysregulated events become reintegrated "into an ongoing perceptual and emotional experience and become part of a new memory" that is contextualized around fear and connected with inhibitory avoidance mechanisms (Charney, 2004, p. 207). Thus couples cannot adequately regulate by trying to reconstruct past events. Attempts at repair must also fail as long as both partners believe that recall of such events is possible. The therapist should instead attend to the dysregulation occurring in the here and now.

The therapist should also assess highly dysregulated couples for prior histories of relational trauma, paying special attention to histories of neglect, because more often than not it results in alexithymia, focal affective blindness, and other sociocognitive and socioaffective disabilities, as well as in a psychobiological intolerance of close physical contact of even brief duration. (Traumatized individuals can appear physically and sexually compliant with their partners but dissociate in order to do so.) The therapist should gear the pace of treatment to the person less able to tolerate closeness, both in terms of physical proximity and duration.

The psychobiologically attuned couple therapist is always concerned with deficits relevant to social–emotional functioning, since they result in acute or chronic misattunement and poor error correction and thus interfere with skillful interactive regulation. Some deficits point to early insecure attachment, whereas others may be organic, drug-related, or due to other developmental or constitutional issues. Someone may appear affectively blind to particular emotions, for instance, or may have a difficult time finding detail in a partner's face or eyes or in intuiting a partner's thoughts, intentions, or emotions.

Neurological deficits resulting from brain injury, learning disabilities, and organic problems may present as problems with empathy, reading faces, interoceptive cues, theory of mind, and mutuality; these deficits may be constitutional or developmental in origin. Problems and limitations involving Axis I psychiatric disorders, such as mood and anxiety disorders, somatoform disorders, and relational trauma, including PTSD, can be viewed from the psychobiological plane. Problems having to do with cultural norms—when partners are from different cultural backgrounds—may be seen as deficits on the cultural–philosophical level. Attitudinal limitations about how partnerships are supposed to work can be understood as deficits stemming from a vision or belief system that guides them toward conflict rather than harmony.

We all have deficits in some area of performance—no one's brain is good at doing everything—but in most cases we are able to circumvent those deficits by utilizing clever workarounds, such as getting other people to do things that we are not particularly skilled at doing. So most deficits are not discovered unless we are faced with a particular task that tests our ability to do this or that. A couple may go for 20 or 30 years and never know that at least one partner has a deficit in a significant area that affects skillful coregulation. Partners may even come to believe that certain failures in attunement are purposeful and deliberate. Awareness of deficits can profoundly shift a couple's sense of what is wrong and what to do about it.

Secure couples rely upon interactive regulation—a prosocial, symmetrical, reciprocal strategy—whether or not they are under stress. They realize that they cannot thrive in the couple system by ignoring the affective arousal state of the other. In therapy they approach conflict-charged areas with some measure of care and mindfulness, and they mutually titrate levels of tension and relaxation. They can move in and out of conflict without resorting extensively to avoidance and withdrawal, and they are able to revisit areas of importance without fear of becoming overwhelmed.

Their two nervous systems continually attune, misattune, and re-attune through sensorimotor pathways and coregulators that include vision and sound (which play major roles in conflict management) as well as smell, touch, and taste. Secure couples are good at generating mutually experienced positive feeling, on the one hand, and at repairing and shortening periods of mutually experienced negative feeling, on the other. Theirs is a process of frequent proximity seeking and contact maintenance.

Insecure couples reverse this formula by withholding efforts to generate shared positive feelings while producing frequent and extended periods of mutually amplified negative states. Their default strategies for managing conflict—avoidant disengagement and intrusive overengagement—produce frequent and increasing bouts of mutual dysregulation and constitute, at once, cause and effect of their interactive patterns. Those regulatory strategies are distinctly asymmetric, nonreciprocal, and decidedly not prosocial. Distancing defenses, including dissociation, fall under the heading of pathological autoregulation, which, as a primitive homeostatic mechanism for self-stimulation and self-soothing, by definition involves massive withdrawal from a two-person system. Clinging defenses, including retaliatory rage, demand interaction, but in the context of a one-way strategy for internal state regulation that often is not accompanied by simultaneous ability to provide a reciprocal function.

Partners who attend to one another's eyes and faces are literally in an exquisite position to "read" each other's nervous systems. Doing this without dissociating enables a true interactive regulatory process that is inherently empathic because it picks up the somatoaffective resonance in the face and eyes of the partner. Full moment-to-moment engagement in this fast-acting process limits the influence of negative internal representations and helps reduce misappraisals of intent.

If, however, either partner moves into hyper- or hypoarousal (fight, flight, freeze, or conservation withdrawal), both will likely disengage from the interactive process and drop face-to-face contact, which may lead to dysregulation of the couple system itself. The insecure couple may develop an avoidance of face-to-face conflict management and disengage from real interactive regulation in response to threat. Since together they manage intensity and duration of negative arousal poorly, their dysregulatory process snowballs psychobiologically into a learned response whereby partners eventually view one another as predators.

In or out of conflict, engagement and disengagement within an insecure dyadic system involve issues of psychobiological dysregulation that the therapist must track and address. Chronic dyadic dysregulation as a product of an insecure couple system radically increases over time and becomes the central challenge to delayed therapy, and as such, degrades prognosis.

But failure to regulate should be viewed as a no-fault biological matter. There is no natural law that says that two nervous systems should get along—although our job as psychobiologically oriented couple therapists is to help partners do just that. While observing and tracking the wavelike arousal patterns of couples in treatment, therapists need to be mindful of the fact that, as each primary attachment dyad is intersubjectively unique, each forms a correspondingly unique *regulatory team*. It is entirely feasible, even likely, that couple therapy can succeed by helping partners view themselves as such while moving them toward improved regulatory competence. Safety and security within the couple system will improve as well.

The ANS is of particular significance to couple therapy because of its widespread effect on arousal, affect, behavior, stress, and recovery. In fact, ANS arousal is one of the fulcrums of the psychobiological approach because the arousal system is principally responsible for moving romantic partners toward and away from one another (in keeping with their respective attachment blueprints) from love to war. ANS regulation is foundational to attachment, and reparation of attachment injuries is foundational to successful intimate relationships. Neural development, attachment organization, and arousal regulation are intertwined, inseparable, interoperable, and circular, each affecting and determining the other.

PART IV

The Theory In Practice

Chapter 10

MARK AND MELODY

Secrets and Shame

The psychobiologically oriented couple therapist aims to reshape the arousal dynamics of a couple system so that it more closely resembles a secure attachment partnership with high positives and low negatives. The approach is developed around a deficit model rather than a conflict model. It recognizes that people come to the table with certain abilities and limitations that determine how well they get along with other people in general and with primary attachment figures in particular. Viewing attachment relationship problems and struggles as a matter of skills and deficits can greatly aid the couple therapist in formulating treatment plans and interventions that address what couples actually do and not what they say. The three cases in this and the following chapters illustrate the psychobiological approach to couple therapy in action.

INITIAL CONTACT

I (S.T.) have an idea of what I might be dealing with when I first hear from Melody. On the phone she describes her relationship problems with Mark. She has a lot to say and her thinking is inductive, meaning it takes her some time to get to the point. It's not that she isn't intelligent or even articulate. It's just that she seems oblivious to the limitations of my time and unaware of the purpose of the phone call, which is simply to make introductions, answer questions about the treatment approach, and set up an appointment.

I begin to think about how an angry-resistant individual tends to lose his or her listener, that is, fail to give his or her listener the main idea before starting in with an explanation. I hold the thought in the back of my mind as a marker. Melody's main complaint is Mark's secrecy, with which she is unrelentingly preoccupied. She has become increasingly certain that it meant he is cheating on her.

I hear from Melody four more times before our first session with Mark. She schedules 3 hours. With each contact she expresses worry that he is cheating and also that he will not end up coming to therapy.

Preoccupation and frequent contact with the therapist are two other markers of angry-resistant individuals, who typically require external regulation and verbal contact to calm themselves down. Avoidant individuals, in contrast, use autoregulation and err in the opposite direction by not reaching out to anyone.

Given Melody's description of Mark as secretive, unexpressive, and distant, I begin to make some preliminary assumptions about him as someone with avoidant tendencies.

A therapist must make early hypotheses about a couple but also must remain constantly open to contrary evidence, since things are never what they seem. The couple therapist should embrace this maxim and always keep it in mind: The human motivational system is too complex and contradictory to capture with words or ideas. A single mind is fluid, complicated, and continually self-modifying; two interacting minds are crazy-complex. Problems arise when assumptions are maintained even after they are proven untrue. (This is particularly the case when the therapist experiences, but does not understand, countertransference reactions.)

The partners are arriving in separate cars—something I discover when I find Melody alone in the waiting room. "He's on his way; he just texted me." I don't like to see individual partners prior to the first session, so I excuse myself and ask Melody to flip the call light switch as soon as Mark arrives.

Although there are exceptions to this and any rule, the couple therapist should view the couple as a single organism rather than as separate parts. On a psychobiological level, we are interested only in the attachment strategies active within the couple system and the moment-by-moment, nervous-system to nervous-system interaction between partners. We are not interested in partner narratives about the other partner in absentia, nor can we make much use of information garnered during separate meetings. In our model, partners are in each other's care and so must bear witness to one another's narratives anyway.

My first visual of Mark and Melody is of her trying to engage him while he's texting on his Blackberry. I greet and walk them back to my office. I initially allow the couple to sit undirected. At present only fixed seating is made available to them—a love seat and a sofa. Later I will move them to chairs that are highly adjustable and on wheels.

Melody sits on the love seat and Mark sits catty-corner on the sofa. I ask what brings them into therapy and Melody begins speaking. As she presents the problem, my eyes shift back and forth from her to Mark.

The psychobiologically oriented therapist scans each partner's face and body for shifts and changes in arousal by observing movement, posture, breathing, skin color, speech patterns, prosody, and the like. Shifting his or her own gaze back and forth helps the therapist acquire nonverbal corroborative information, or "tells." (That's con-artist speak for giveaways, and they are a valuable part of the professional gambler's toolkit—since gamblers, like therapists, are always on the lookout for nonconscious bodily cues to other people's emotions or intentions.)

The therapist should pay special attention to the listening partner because that person's face and body can be more expressive while unencumbered by the resource-hungry speaking function. (When a speaking partner stops talking, emotion will often wash over the speaking partner's face and sometimes provide a clue to what might be going on inside.) The therapist will be focusing overall on arousal, especially at the beginning of treatment when assessing nervous-system to nervous-system capacities for self- and mutual regulation, the two prosocial modes of arousal management.

When observing Melody and Mark, I watch to see how well they notice slight shifts and changes in each other, how they interpret those changes, and what they do or don't do about them.

"He has been very secretive with me for the last year, and I know something's going on," says Melody. "He denies it all right, but he comes home late and he won't let me see certain things like his cell phone call list and . . . I don't know . . . I don't think he's telling the truth." Melody's arousal is going up. Her movements are sharp and jerky and her breathing has increased. I turn to Mark and ask, "What is she talking about?"

The therapist cross-checks partner information both to monitor perception and as a reason to move back and forth fluidly between the members of the couple, an activity that doubles as a partner regulatory function. Moving back and forth is also a mechanism for titrating arousal within and between partners.

Asking partners what they notice and how they interpret what they notice implies something important about the therapeutic stance. The job is, in part, to show both partners how the other works—not how they would like the other to work but how each actually works. It's a little like helping them develop owner's manuals for one another, which they must do because they are in the care of one another; they go home with one another, not with the therapist.

"I'm not having an affair," Mark says. "I'm not seeing anybody." His lips are smacking, indicating a dry mouth, a possible indication of increasing arousal. It isn't yet clear if he feels attacked or is hiding something.

When our arousal goes toward fight–flight–freeze, fluids leave our gastrointestinal system; blood moves into the striated muscles to ready us for action.

"I don't know where she gets these ideas," Mark continues, "I have not been unfaithful to her at all." Melody's eyes roll as he turns his head away and makes a grunting sound.

"I don't think she believes you," I say to Mark.

"I know!" he says, "And I don't know why!"

During the first session, the therapist should allow for some therapeutic triangulation—that is, for partners to address the therapist and not each other as they describe the relationship or answer questions. But soon triangulation should be discouraged and partners redirected to one another. The therapist helps partners understand that forming any dyadic alliance with the therapist (who is, and should remain, an outsider) creates an immediate breach within the attachment system and negatively affects the outside ("abandoned") partner's arousal. These breaches never come cheap, and the abandoning partner will pay in some manner.

"Ask her."

Mark turns to Melody and asks, "Have I given you any reason, any reason at all, to suspect me?"

"Oh, let's see," Melody replies, touching each finger as she counts, "there's the not answering the phone; there's your always texting on your Blackberry instead of being with me; there's that time I came to your office and surprised you, and you took forever to come out to greet me and looked all weird like I'd just interrupted something. . . . Shall I go on?"

Melody crosses her left leg over her right, leaving her left foot free to dangle and shake wildly. Her breathing quickens and her nostrils flare. I look back at Mark. He seems very still, his breathing shallow. I remind him to breathe by taking a deep breath myself.

The therapist remains alert to stillness, especially to shallow breathing or lack of breath in him- or herself and in partners, as this is often a sign of increasing arousal. Stillness and shallow breathing can be a sign of freezing, dissociation, or lack of body awareness that can quickly lead to runaway hyperarousal and dysregulation.

A few more moments pass in silence and Melody speaks up. "Why don't you tell him about what happened when I went away to Cabo?" she challenges, with a mocking tone and glaring eyes. Mark, who had been leaning forward, sits back and sighs deeply. "I didn't answer my phone, excuse me, our phone. Is that what we are talking about?" She does not respond but continues to glare at him. Mark continues, his voice controlled, "You left, you went away and I was there, with Brian . . . and Brian's friend. I was at our house entertaining my friends. I had a few drinks and that's all. You called me from the airport and—I—DID—NOT—HEAR the phone ring," he says, suddenly becoming loud and emphatic, his temper clearly rising. "Okay? We were outside in the patio having drinks and talking."

Melody responds quickly and sharply, "Why don't you tell him who your friend was . . . who . . . who Brian's friend was? Why don't you tell him that? What was her name? Frieda?"

"Actually," I say, "I don't really need to know anything about this directly. How about the two of you continue with each other and if I have any questions, I'll ask."

Each partner's behavior has quickly become rife with predatory signals. Mark's initial underresponsiveness and dismissiveness are threatening to Melody. Her vocal tone becomes sharp, her physical movements become abrupt and quick, and her questioning takes on the style of an interrogation. Mark's sudden shift from quiet stillness to belligerence, in combination with Melody's confrontational-seeming behavior, move the two of them toward a heightened threat condition. In this particular instance, they are not able to continue without my help.

I roll two chairs into the room's center and tell them, "Move to these chairs and continue."

They both get up and move without hesitation.

When a couple gets going into arousing material, they should not be in fixed seating where they cannot move freely or face one another without twisting their bodies. The therapist, too, should be seated in a fully adjustable, swiveling chair on wheels so that he or she can move freely about at will and observe subtle movements and adjustments. Rolling chairs allow the therapist who is working psychobiologically (i.e., with fast bottom-up interventions) to get in and get out as quickly as he or she can with minimal intrusiveness. Props and other items are kept close by so that their use isn't overly telegraphed, and they can disap-

pear as inconspicuously as they arrive on the scene, making way for on-the-spot implementation of interventions that promote experience and avoid too much thinking (e.g., swift movements, short verbal commands, and other surprise triggers of somatoaffective reactions).

Mark and Melody make eye contact for a few moments, then Mark breaks the contact and looks at me with an uncertain expression. I ask, "Why did you break eye contact with her?"

Mark shrugs and asks, "What are we supposed to do here?"

"Frieda," I respond, gesturing to Melody. She folds her arms, looks at me, and says, "Yeah, Frieda! What about Frieda?"

"Don't look at me. Look at him," I say pointing to Mark.

Melody turns back and says, "Okay, you heard him." With that they both break into a snorting laugh.

I have been noticing that both partners are sitting with legs crossed and feet dangling and wagging back and forth at a similar pace.

Partners tend to match one another in a variety of ways, for example, in their choice of clothing, gestures, expressions, vocal utterances, postures, and movements. Choice of clothing aside, matching behaviors occur very quickly, often simultaneously, sometimes with just a brief time-lag.

Matching is a positive marker that suggests a measure of connection and attunement, regardless of mood or affect. Extended periods during which partners do not match is cause for concern, as one or both partners may not be fully present in some way. The clinician should remain alert to matching, and comment when he or she observes it. Commenting to partners reinforces the idea that they are a couple and affirms that, regardless of what they may currently feel, they are wired together.

Melody and Mark are "tail wagging": Their feet are wagging rhythmically in unison. Some tail wagging is slow and relaxed, as when partners are not in distress. Tail wagging looks different when partners are in distress, and Melody's and Mark's feet are definitely wagging wildly at this moment.

"That's nice," I say.

"What's nice?" demands Melody. "What about this is nice?"

"What's nice is that the two of you could make each other laugh, as you just did, even during moments of distress. That's important. Also, I notice the two of you wagging your tails. You're matching right now: Both of you have your legs crossed with your feet moving at around the same pace."

"So what?" Mark asks with a dismissive tone.

"That means that despite everything else, the two of you are connected—even if you are unaware of it, you are both connected—unconsciously perhaps but connected just the same."

"Oh," utters Melody as she turns back toward Mark, and they share a smile.

"Imagine that, we're connected," says Mark, gestating a rare smile. As my eyes move back and forth between the two of them I notice Melody's eyes begin to well up.

Wheeling my chair closer I look at Mark and say, "Do you see that? Do you see what's happening in her eyes?" Mark's face scrunches up as his eyes begin tearing up as well.

"Hmm, interesting," I say. Turning to Melody, I ask, "And do you see that?"

"Um-hmm," she says softly while trying to hold back more tears. I use this opportunity to once again establish them as a couple.

Any shift or change in arousal or affect presents an opportunity for amplification as long as the therapist comments as soon as possible. Calling attention to affective shifts tends to amplify affect and raise awareness. Delays of several seconds or more will not have this effect.

I continue in a serious tone to offset Melody's lingering cynicism, "You see, here's another way you're both connected. You two are wired together, like it or not; you both are connected. Where one goes, so goes the other. That's the way it's supposed to be."

This comment is an introduction to the principle of affect contagion between primary partners. They are affectively connected and, as such, cannot be immune to one another's emotional or arousal state. This is normal and considered a psychobiological given.

I turn to Melody and say, "I know there's a lot going on here, and we haven't really even gotten to any of it. But I want you to understand that despite what you think about Mark and what he may or may not be up to, when you're moved, he's moved too, and vice versa. This is extremely important to hold onto because many couples do not have this and the two of you do."

Mark, while watching Melody dissolve into more tears, says, "This is nice and everything but what do we do, Dr. Tatkin, about this thing with Melody, this thing she has about me . . . that I'm cheating."

Melody quickly responds, "You were going to say something about Frieda."

Mark lets out a sigh of frustration, turns to me and says, "Look, Frieda is a friend of my friend, Brian."

Wheeling my chair back and away from them, I gesture him back to Melody and he continues, "She's not my friend. In fact, I don't really even know her, so lay off this Frieda thing."

"Well, that's certainly not going to work," I chime in from across the room.

"What do you mean?" asks Mark.

"You were good up until 'so lay off this thing Frieda thing.' You really believe that's going to make Melody feel better?"

"No, I guess not" he replies.

"So try again," I say.

"You and I both know you freaked out because . . ." Mark says before I interrupt again.

"What?!" Mark responds with hands open and exasperation in his voice.

"You're not so good at this, are you?" I say. Melody suddenly laughs and then quickly covers her mouth.

"Hey!" I say to her, smiling, "You're not much better, so watch out."

Melody puts her head down, still laughing, and says, "I know, I know."

I turn to Mark and ask, "Do you know what I meant when I said you're not very good at this?"

"I think" he replies. "You're saying that . . . um . . . no, I guess I don't understand. Tell me."

I roll my chair forward toward Mark.

"When your partner is in distress," I tell him, "you don't want to lead with anything other than what would relieve her. You have to give her some relief here and fairly soon; if you don't, you're the one who will pay for it. She feels threatened by this character, Frieda. You started off, it seemed, by trying to offer her some relief but then told her to stop bugging you about it. There's no way in hell that will ever work, not just with Melody, mind you, but with anyone on the planet, including you! That's incredibly dismissive."

Out of the corner of my eye I can see Melody becoming activated by what I'm saying. I anticipate her interruption.

"Hold on," I say to Melody with my hand out to her in a stop gesture.

"I see," says Mark.

"And on your next try you led with something like, 'You and I both know that you freaked out' and . . ."

"I got it. I got it," says Mark, interrupting me. "That sounded attacking. I got it. Let me try that again."

"Go!" I say and quickly roll my chair backward, giving them the floor.

"Frieda is . . ."

"You're going to do it from that far away?" I interrupt again.

"Ahhh!" Mark yells softly with his hands now up.

"I'm just sayin' . . ." I respond with an impish smile and my hands up, matching his. Everyone laughs.

Looking at Melody, he says, "Where did you get this guy anyway?"

"Yellow pages," I say, responding for her. Again, laughter.

I use humor as a means to regulate the couple, shifting back and forth between tension and relaxation, seriousness and play. I can usually sense how far I can go, not just with humor but with bluntness and confrontation. Of course, if I err and make a mess, I have to model cleaning up after myself, making sure I adequately repair.

Humor is idiosyncratic and, as such, not every clinician's style. Each therapist must find a personal style that is true to his or her nature. Ideally that style will represent the broadest dynamic range he or she has to offer. The experienced psychobiologically minded couple therapist should find a way to remain relaxed and available to rapid expansion or contraction, in the arousal sense, in keeping with the current state of the couple in the room. An overly expansive or constricted therapist runs the risk of misattunement with either or both partners.

Mark rolls his chair closer to Melody. "I'm sorry if I gave you any impression that Frieda or anyone else is more important than you. Frieda is no one to me. No one. Okay? I wouldn't do that to you." Melody's face immediately softens and her body relaxes. Mark is finally providing some relief. Unfortunately, he then adds, "I wouldn't do that to you, and you know that." Melody's face and eyes react instantaneously.

"No, she doesn't," I say. "If she knew that, you wouldn't have a problem."

"Right," Mark responds. "Sorry. I guess you don't know that. I wouldn't cheat on you."

"I won't cheat on you," I say, correcting him.

"I will not cheat on you," Mark restates, taking Melody's hands into his. "I don't want to be with anyone other than you."

By now, both partners have slowed considerably. Melody listens carefully as Mark steps cautiously, watching her face.

"She still doesn't understand why you didn't answer the phone," I say, prompting him further.

"I didn't answer the phone, and . . . I'm sorry," he says, dropping his head down.

"Keep watching her face, Mark" I say. He rights himself and goes back into her eyes.

"And then when I did, you heard me sound kind of strange, and I told you that I was drinking a little and had friends over." He pauses for a moment as he checks Melody's face for a reaction, as if approaching land mines. Softening, he continues, "I knew you were pissed off at me. I heard it in your voice. Unless I respond to you right away, you get all angry with me . . . and . . . and . . . ." Mark's head drops downward again.

"What?" Melody interrupts. "And what?" Her arousal visibly increasing, she starts to take her hands back. "What? Are you blaming ME for your not answering the phone? Like I'm some sort of bitch or something?"

"That's not what I'm saying," Mark barely utters with his head still hanging low.

"Because let me tell you," Melody blares, "I am not the problem here! I have not been distancing from you, or keeping secrets, or making you feel insecure."

Mark turns to me and says, "I feel like I'm a little kid. I hate that, and I don't know what to do about it."

"Melody," I say to her, rolling my chair toward both of them. "When you look at Mark right now, what are you seeing?"

Melody looks at Mark and pauses for a moment.

"He looks ashamed," she says. "He looks ashamed like he's done something wrong."

"Really?" I ask. "Like he's done something wrong?"

"Yes," she replies.

"I want to do something," I say, as I tell them how to adjust their chairs so that Melody's seat is at its highest position from the floor and Mark's seat is at its lowest.

"Oh, God," says Mark, dropping his head again. "I think I'm going to be sick. This is how it feels to me, just like this."

Melody initially laughs and then shifts to a plaintive tone. "What? What's the matter?" she says to Mark.

Mark turns his head away from Melody, who appears to tower over him and says, "I don't like this."

"What?" Melody asks again, only now more concerned. "I don't understand." Melody's distress is increasing rapidly as she is unable to understand Mark's reaction. His turn away from her seems to spike her arousal.

"Melody," I say in a soft tone, "what if Mark's reaction isn't a sign that he's actually done something wrong? What if he's reacting to you? Pay attention to your physical position right now in relation to his. What do you notice?"

"I'm big and he's small," she replies.

"Exactly," I say back.

"Oh," Melody says with surprise, as if she's just understood something. "Oh, God."

Mark, head already down and resting on one of his hands, starts to sob uncontrollably. Melody immediately attempts to go to him but he puts out his other hand, motioning her to stop.

"Wait . . . wait," he says, in between waves of grief. "Just . . . wait."

Melody's face appears racked with pain, and she looks like she can barely hold back from going to him.

"You see," I say softly to Melody, moving my chair toward her, "I think you have misunderstood Mark—not that he doesn't play a role in this, because he does. I don't think he's understood you either. His dismissals, his lack of responsiveness, and his distancing create tremendous anxiety and insecurity for you. He responds to your fears improperly; at least for you his responses are improper. They're threatening for you." Although I direct this toward Melody, who continues to focus on Mark's collapse, I know I am addressing Mark at the same time.

"I think you may at times misinterpret his silence as hostility when it's actually fear. He seems to freeze at certain points with you, and because he does not respond in any way, I think that is felt by you as an attack."

I turn to Mark and say, "Melody relies more on interaction than you. What I mean is, she is highly verbal and relies on verbal communication quite a bit, but she's also looking at your face and your body, and there are times when you don't move, your face doesn't express, you don't make any sounds, and while this may seem to you as polite listening, your nonresponse is felt as negative to her. You have to understand that a 'nonresponse' isn't neutral; at least, it's not perceived as neutral by most people. In the absence of a response people are more inclined to take the nonresponse as negative. This is especially so when people are in distress. When you don't nod, grunt, or otherwise acknowledge her in a timely manner, she begins to become more distressed because she's depending on fast interaction with you."

I turn back to Melody and continue by saying, "but I think you might be faster at this than he is." She nods her head in acknowledgment and says, "I think you're right—I can see that many times." I turn back to Mark and ask, "Does that seem true for you?" He's still moving as if going through molasses but seems to be more responsive at this moment and nods in acknowledgment, uttering a small "yes."

Going back to Melody now, "I think what happens when you get distressed is that Mark responds as if he's being attacked and either attacks back or withdraws or freezes. This is a reflex of his, but you experience it as an attack."

I stop for a moment to view their faces and to read my own body. (Talking tends to interfere with somatosensory awareness, making it very easy to become misattuned.) "For both of you, arousal begins to climb fast; you react quickly to one another, misappraise one another, and increase your mutual threat level to a point where things fall apart."

As I talk I'm looking at both of them, and I can see them both nodding in agreement. I take this as permission to continue, so I do.

"I think then what happens is that the two of you become dysregulated and unable to calm one another, and this results in repeated events that become traumatizing for both of you. Then you just avoid one another. Neither of you is doing this purposely. I don't think either of you wants to be threatening. You didn't get together to do that. But I think there are important things about each other that neither of you has understood, ever. I'd like to find out some of those things. Okay?"

Both slowly nod.

SESSION THREE

We jump to the third session because session two represented a honeymoon in reaction to session one. It is often the case that the epiphanies of the first session result in a love fest during the second; in the third session we see the return of warlike behavior but with more intensity. Therapy can have unintended iatrogenic effects: Some couples will look worse just following initial treatment; for others a good session instills hope that things will get better until the partners discover that nothing has really changed. Neither Mark nor Melody was subtle at telegraphing their displeasure when I greeted them in the waiting room. As soon as we got seated, I brought up the obvious.

"Okay. What happened?" I ask while scanning both partners.

Melody sits back in her chair with arms folded, legs crossed yet in motion, and lips pursed. She just glares at Mark.

"She's mad at me again," Mark says cautiously while keeping his eyes on Melody. "It's the same thing again. She thinks I'm cheating on her."

"I don't understand, what happened?" I say, though I can guess what happened.

"After the last session we went home, got into bed, made love for the first time in weeks, and then just as I was about to fall asleep, she asks, 'What really happened between you and Frieda?' and I

132

was flabbergasted. She broadsided me with this question just after we had this really nice evening together . . ."

"That's not the whole story!" Melody interrupts.

". . . and I was very tired and trying to sleep. I had to get up early the next morning for work and . . ."

"That's not the whole story!" she interrupts again. "Tell him! Tell him the truth because if you don't, I'm not doing this anymore! I'm telling you right now I'm not doing this anymore!"

I redirect Melody. "Why don't you tell HIM what the truth is. Apparently he's the one who needs to know, not me."

Melody refocuses on Mark. "You're bringing up one part of what I said and that's unfair. I only asked you about Frieda after you wouldn't talk to me about that time I surprised you at your office. I still can't understand why you would just brush me off like that, even now, after Dr. Tatkin told you how your withholding things from me is wrong."

"Hey!" I say to both of them. "Don't bring me into this. This is between the two of you."

I roll my chair farther back to remove myself from their immediate field.

Mark leans forward toward Melody and yells, "I did not withhold anything from you. I just wanted to go to sleep, and you wouldn't respect that. It's always on your timetable! You don't work, I do! You don't seem to realize that." Melody fires back. "Wait a second! Don't turn this into a 'you work' and 'I don't' kind of thing. I do plenty for you. I do housework, and . . ."

Mark interrupts her and says, "And I bring home the money that allows you to do what you want and you don't appreciate that!"

This is the point at which the content turns to "blah, blah, blah" because the partners have moved one another into hyperarousal (fight–flight–freeze). They are, at this point, psychobiologically "altered." I push my chair back and let this play out for a while.

In some ways, listening and watching couples in conflict is like attending to sound and light waves. Their collective arousal moves up and down, much like various movements of a symphony. How much variation is there between highs and lows? We know that heart rate variability is a sign of health. If arousal variability within the couple system is also a sign of health, then stable couples should demonstrate more variability than unstable couples. How long do they stay at any given peak or valley? The clinician should become concerned when intense arousal or affective states, either high or low, stay online too long. Strong intensity *at* long durations *is a recipe for relational trauma.*

Are the ups and downs rounded, as in sine waves, or jagged, as in sawtooth waves? Get a sense of how partners transition each other between emotional states. Are there moments of play, or is it all serious business? Successful couples can play in the midst of conflict. Interactive play is an enormously effective coregulatory stratagem. Do they alternate between tension and relaxation, or do they remain in tension for too long? Do they provide quick relief for one another, or do they delay relief, unaware of the immediate toll such delay takes on each partner?

After several minutes Mark turns to me.

"Why did you stop just now?" I ask.

"I don't know," he says, "I suppose we're done."

I turn to Melody and ask, "Are you guys done?" She shrugs and while rubbing her face says, "I don't know."

I turn back to Mark and say, "It sure doesn't seem like you're done to me. Neither of you looks too happy."

"We're not," says Mark.

"Then you're clearly not done," I respond.

"What do you want me to do?" Mark asks.

"I don't know," I reply, "but the two of you made a mess and you both have to clean it up, at least for now. Otherwise, at what point in the day do you plan to feel better? Tonight? Tomorrow? Next week?"

Mark and Melody sit quietly, looking at one another like siblings expected to make nice and get along.

Tensing and relaxing: *One of the goals of our psychobiological approach is for the couple to be able to talk about anything without becoming dysregulated. Neither partner should be afraid of becoming overwhelmed, trapped, or held too long without some relief, which can come in the form of playfulness, humor, distraction, affection, repair, or agreement, even agreement to table an issue until later. We look for* alternating tension and relaxation *during any one sitting, discus-*

sion cycle, or interactive block of time—a kind of peristalsis that is part of effective partner coregulation. Partners' ability to read one another's arousal is fundamental to the more complex skill of titrating tension at will. Partners must learn how to move in and out of tension, holding and letting each other go as necessary. The therapist models this regulatory function at all times when working with the couple.

Taking things out and putting them back: *Just as parents expect children to put things away after taking them out, the couple therapist expects partners to put certain business behind them before moving on. In other words, partners must make creative efforts to ensure that each is okay at the completion of any difficult interactive episode. This isn't to say that the matter is resolved, just that by the end of that particular round, both partners are okay enough to go on to something else together. In session, partners are directed back to one another to find an effective way to tie off the episode before going forward. If, at the end of any back-and-forth interaction, either or both of them look defeated, helpless, or otherwise distressed, they must be redirected and further guided.*

"Okay. What should we be doing?" Mark asks.

"Well," I say, "do you folks always end up in this spot where you both kind of give up?"

"Yes!" blares Melody with her head down and hands still on her face.

"I don't understand. Why do you to have to end up here? Why can't you talk about difficult things like this and land on your feet, at least for the time being?"

"How are we supposed to do that?" says Mark.

"Distress between the two of you should never go longer than an hour," I tell them both. "That doesn't mean that you can or should fix things completely. Regardless, there is no reason for either of you to ruin your day together. A day is way too long."

Between any points of injury/distress and repair/relief, the clock is ticking and time is not on either partner's side, so when hurt arises we take a "stop-the-presses" approach and deal with it. Nothing good can follow when one partner is hurting. As in a three-legged race, both partners will only get to the finish line if both are still standing; if one goes down, both go down.

"But she won't let go, and I can't make her. Nothing I do or say seems to work. She'll be angry with me for days. You see what she does."

"Do you think she's crazy?" I ask Mark.

"What?" Mark replies with a surprised look of embarrassment.

"Do you believe she's crazy?" I say again. "She doesn't seem to let go of this, and you've done everything you can to convince her. I wonder if you believe she's crazy."

"Maybe . . . yeah," Mark cautiously replies.

"I can't believe this!" Melody says, as she springs up, her face red and her eyes widened. "Maybe I'm crazy because you don't really do or say anything except make excuses and expect me to just shut up and get over it!" Melody's breathing has now quickened, her face tense, her eyes oscillating between rage and hurt, her hands curled in a fist, her legs straight on the floor with muscles tensing. She holds this position waiting for Mark's reply.

Mark seems to have stilled, appearing frozen with his eyes locked onto Melody's. I wait to see what comes next. A minute or longer goes by and now Melody drops her tension and goes into a collapse, shoulders slumped, her head rested into her right hand; she sighs deeply as if hopeless. Mark still looks frozen and says nothing.

In couple therapy nothing is what it seems, but countertransference may cause us to jump to certain conclusions. For instance, if a partner appears to hold on to something, relentlessly batting away the other's repeated efforts to explain or repair, the couple therapist may become frustrated with the complaining partner and assume that he or she is causing or maintaining the problem. That partner can appear unrea-sonable, even crazy. However, the therapist would be advised, in this case, to look in the direction of the "unfairly" accused partner. He may only appear to be doing everything he can. We can't see wind but we can see its effect on trees, so we know it exists. We may not be able to see what Mark is doing to torment Melody, but we can see its effect on Melody and that is what counts. If she's not finding relief, it's because he's not providing it.

Another few minutes go by when Melody quickly lifts her head up and says in a much softer tone, "It's always the same fucking thing. You just sit there and leave me hanging."

I turn to Mark and ask, "What is she talking about?"

Mark says, "I don't know. I don't know what to say. I feel like whatever I say she's going to jump on me."

"Why did you refuse to answer her questions that night about the office visit?" I ask Mark.

He looks up. "What?" he says, sounding surprised.

I repeat what I said.

"It was late!" he says loudly as if suggest my question was ridiculous.

"So?" I say, shrugging my shoulders.

"So?!" he says with a look of astonishment. "So? Let's see how you function after only 5 hours of sleep."

"She's your wife, your primary partner, your one and only. She's in distress. That comes first, doesn't it?" I turn my gaze to include Melody. "That's the deal, right? If either of you is in distress, that comes first? Is that part of your job description? You tend to each other first, before all other matters? Yes? If not, I can understand why you're having problems here."

I turn again to Mark, rolling closer to him. "Do you really think you can disregard her distress and have a good sleep or good next day?" I ask rhetorically in a much stronger tone. Shifting my position away from Mark, I redirect to Melody.

"Does either of you really believe you're that separate from one another that either of you can simply ignore the emotional state of the other without going there too? Because that is a big mistake. It isn't possible; it never was. You two are connected to each other; where one of you goes the other goes too."

I return my focus toward Mark. "If you felt physically ill that night," I ask him, "would you expect Melody to get angry with you because she needed to sleep?"

"No," he responds sheepishly.

"Then why would you do that to her?"

Whenever the couple therapist becomes active, that is, when intervening in any way, he or she is responsible for tracking and titrating each partner's arousal. As I confront both Mark and Melody, I make use of my proximity, voice, and focus as a way to tense and relax, move in and move out, hold on and let go of each partner as I notice their arousal moving up or down. I am careful to shift my position and focus away from Mark as soon I sense he's becoming activated by my attention on him and use Melody as a way to let him relax. Of the two, she tolerates more focus than he, and so I often stay with her longer. I will also shift my focus to the space between them in order to implicitly confront the couple itself. Using this method, I can often get away with confronting them with great intensity and not drive either into hyperarousal.

Realizing that Mark has taken this in, Melody immediately softens and moves her chair closer to Mark.

"I'm sorry I made you talk that night," Melody says softly to Mark, whose head is still down. "I started that fight and I shouldn't have."

Mark weakly lifts his head as if drained of energy and says, "No, you just wanted reassurance, and I did the opposite. I made you worry more."

Mark's apparent energy drain represents a mild parasympathetic drop, a depressive reaction, something Mark is more inclined toward when feeling alarmed. The therapist must track drops such as these because they are hard to recover from and, if severe, can signify more serious dissociative issues and unresolved trauma.

After brief pause Melody says, "I didn't realize until right now that I was angry with you for wanting to go to sleep. I was feeling so good that night, really that whole day. . . . After we made love and you wanted to go to sleep, and you were leaving me, that's when I brought this up."

The angry-resistant person experiences a counterreflex to positive approach and reunion by pushing away or behaving negatively.

"I was masturbating," Mark says, in a barely audible voice.

"What?" Melody replies.

"That day when you came to see me at the office . . . I was masturbating. That's why it took so long for me to come out and why I seemed so weird."

"Oh, babe," Melody responds lovingly.

"I was surprised and embarrassed," Mark says as he looks up. "I didn't want to tell you that. I tried to act normal. I saw that you reacted, but I didn't say anything. I just hoped you would let it drop."

She moves closer and pulls him into an embrace. "I thought . . . I don't know what I thought," she says cuddling him. "You can tell me things like that, you know that, don't you?"

"No," Mark softly replies.

"I'm sorry if I made you feel like you can't," she says to him in a contrite tone of voice. "I really am. We should be able to say things like that to each other, don't you think?"

Mark quickly replies, "I do. I'd like to be able to tell you and not worry. Thank you . . . and I'm sorry for not telling you sooner."

They continue their embrace for several moments, each appearing soothed by the other, each with a smile.

"Were you thinking of me when you masturbated?" Melody asks Mark.

CONCLUSION

Mark and Melody's treatment, though intense in the beginning with sessions running 2–3 hours, soon tapered off in both frequency and session length into the occasional 1-hour follow-up. Psychobiological methodologies, though not conceived as brief therapy approaches, tend to be very effective right from the start.

Mark and Melody initially presented as an insecure couple with moderate dysregulation. By the fourth session, dysregulated episodes had all but disappeared from the relational landscape. By the fifth session, both partners ceased all threats against the relationship, and breaches in the attachment system were repaired within hours instead of days. Soon, their mutual commitment to fix errors, repair injuries, and minister to one another's distress greatly limited and reduced shared negative moments. Their newfound ability to attend to each other's distress made the value of their relationship exceed all expectations, leading to a higher frequency of amplified shared moments. In other words, the once insecure relationship was now functionally secure.

Chapter 11

DAVID AND MARGARET

A Sexless Marriage

David and Margaret, a couple in their late 40s, come in at the behest of Margaret's individual therapist, who believes that Margaret is not making headway in her individual therapy.

SESSION THREE

In our two earlier sessions I (S.T.) learned that David and Margaret both suffered from multiple ailments, some apparently undiagnosed. Margaret complains of fibromyalgia and rheumatoid arthritis. David insists he is environmentally sensitive and given to severe bouts of sinus inflammation that keep him awake at night; he makes frequent sinus-clearing sounds that suggest problems with breathing. His night-time breathing problems are the stated reason for their sleeping in separate beds.

The marriage has remained essentially sexless from the time of dating, and neither particularly seems much bothered by this. Romance, excitement, or playfulness rarely visits their relationship. Previous relationships for both were no different. They are very hard workers but are poor home and finance managers. Despite their excellent work ethic, neither seems particularly good at making money. As a result, they are always trying to make ends meet and just barely get by. Though seemingly calm, they both report chronic anxiety symptoms and describe themselves as good friends but "lost at sea."

The AAI reveals that both were avoidantly attached when they entered the relationship; they shared significant early neglect, and both reported having spent a great deal of time alone. History and presentation throughout the sessions show a common preference for lower parasympathetic states, supporting the view of the couple system as low arousal.

They are not unattractive people, yet they look a little unhealthy and a bit unkempt. Margaret appears fatigued, her skin blanched, eyes unclear. She moves like someone physically pained and looks older than her 46 years. David looks gaunt and fatigued with dark circles beneath his eyes. Both are dressed comfortably in sweats with hair that looks as if they just woke up.

I open the door to the waiting room and see them quietly sitting next to each other reading magazines. I greet them and as we proceed toward my office, which is situated in a large suite at the end of two long angling hallways, I am struck by their posture and way of walking. Both move awkwardly. Margaret, a little plump, walks with difficulty as if she is experiencing pain in her legs. Her shoulders are slumped forward as she walks with an uneasy gait, wobbling a bit. David, of thin build, walks with his hands in his pockets, his shoulders also slumped forward.

After initial sessions where I lead couples to my office, I tend to hang back to see if they can find their way back there. This sometimes serves as a directional memory litmus test. David, for the second time, loses his way, and Margaret follows. I redirect them both.

Directional confusion can derive from psychological, neurological, or substance-related problems, but patients who consistently forget how to get someplace may simply be suffering from acute or chronic stress. Stress can compromise the hippocampus, which is associated with memory, specifically short-term and episodic memory. Episodic memory allows us to recall events, times, places, and attendant emotions in connection with our experience; episodic memory combined with semantic memory (words, language) we call declarative. Partners under chronic stress will demonstrate continuous problems with short-term memory and declarative recollections of events. Chronic activation of threat systems (a brain continually at war) negatively affects hippocampal memory.

I sit in my wheeled office chair and notice that each chooses the same seat as before: Margaret sits in the love seat at the far end of the room, while David takes the far end of the couch catty-corner to it. In terms of the available seating options, neither could pick a further location. Margaret leans over and grabs the ottoman, pulling it toward her so that she can lift her legs up and lounge comfortably on the love seat. David sits with his hands folded between his legs, making as little use of available sofa real estate as possible.

What is the meaning of their physical distance? Is this positioning a specific symptom of their current marital condition, or is it a general indication of their attachment orientation? If the latter, it may signal avoidant attachment, of which supportive evidence would be low proximity seeking and low contact maintenance. If avoidant attachment is confirmed, their chronic, low-contact orientation likely preceded the relationship and may be a contributing factor to their physical ailments.

Many avoidant adults were physically deprived of hugging, cuddling, and stroking during all or most of their infancy and childhood, making physical affection awkward throughout their lifespan. During the developmental phase of infancy that Margaret Mahler (1974) termed symbiosis, *infants and caregivers use a great deal of ventral-to-ventral contact, a folding into one another in a kind of merger. Mahler found that some mothers were uncomfortable with this phase, however, and would avoid sustained ventral-to-ventral contact with their infants.*

The human neuroendocrine stress system (the HPA) prepares us for action, usually in response to a threat. The HPA is supposed to turn off when threat abates, but with people who are insecurely attached and/ or suffer unresolved loss and/or trauma, the HPA is like a spigot stuck on, continually spending resources, straining major systems, prematurely wearing them out. Physical contact, such as cuddling, hugging, kissing, and stroking, effectively shuts down the HPA, which is why most parents, regardless of culture, reflexively comfort their distressed babies and children with physical contact. Indeed, trauma specialists increasingly believe that the old cognitive–behavioral notions of talk therapy may not only be ineffective but may also be harmful for treating trauma. Victims of 9/11 who did not develop PTSD often turned to physical comforts such as massage, acupuncture, and increased physical affection from others (Maville et al., 2008).

Both David and Margaret are quiet, and neither seems willing to start the session. I move the two wheeled office chairs to the center of the room.

"Let's have both of you move to the chairs," I suggest, but neither moves.

"Uh," says David while looking at Margaret, "I don't think she wants to do that."

I look over at Margaret, who is looking now at me.

"Is that right?" I ask her.

Moving a finger to her mouth she says, "Well . . . yeah, but I don't think he wants to either."

"Really?" I say. "And why is that?"

Both remain silent for a moment and then Margaret says, "I think, for me at least, it feels a bit too confrontational."

"Is it the same for you?" I ask David.

"Yeah . . ." he says, "I guess it does a little. We don't really do that in real life."

"Really?" I say in a surprised tone. "You guys don't sit across from one another? Ever?"

"No, not really," says Margaret, slightly chortling with finger still in mouth.

"Well," I say, "let's see what happens if you both get in the chairs for a moment. I want to try something."

I turn both chairs toward me and move them together so that David and Margaret will be side by side. They each move into place and I ask, "So how's that? Is that more comfortable?"

"Yeah . . ." they seem to say simultaneously.

"Really?" I say, again sounding surprised. I turn them around, facing one another. "Better than this?"

Within moments, Margaret adjusts her chair back to face me; David follows.

"Huh," I say, "what did you guys do when you were dating? How did you manage not facing each other?"

David swivels his chair around to look at Margaret, who is still facing me.

"I don't know," he says while looking at her. "Did we not sit across from each other? I think we did, like when we'd go out to dinner."

Margaret swivels around toward David. "I don't know," she says.

David swivels his chair back toward me. "I'm sure we did," she continues, "but I remember sitting next to you a lot."

She turns to me. "I know that sounds really weird," she says with a laugh, "but even when we sit across from each other, I don't get the sense that we look at each other much. Do you?" she asks David, who continues to look forward shaking his head in agreement.

"Hold on a second," I say while fetching a softball-sized Nerf™ ball. Would you be willing to try something new—playing with a ball and seeing what happens? With some skepticism and a bit of laughter, they agree. "David, I want you over here," I say, pointing to one side of the room. "Margaret, I want you here," pointing to the other side of the room. "Sit so you are both facing one another." I throw the Nerf ball to Margaret, who catches it.

"I want you both to keep the ball in play. Don't stop. You can talk about anything you'd like. Just don't stop playing catch. Go."

I roll my chair back and away, as if removing myself from the scene. David and Margaret look at one another in astonishment and start to laugh.

"Come on," I say to Margaret playfully, "try it. Start throwing the ball."

Margaret begins to lob the ball to David. He catches it and lobs it back. Minutes pass as they continue to play catch, when Margaret says, "So, what do you want to talk about?"

David catches the ball and holds onto it while he thinks.

"Keep the ball in play," I tell him.

They both laugh, and he throws the ball.

"Maybe we should talk about last night," he says to her.

"Okay," she replies.

Several moments go by as they play catch in silence. Margaret suddenly holds onto the ball, thinking, and before I can say anything, throws the ball to David.

"I really didn't mean to make you feel bad," she says to him.

"I know," he says, "but you didn't understand why I had to follow through on my promise. I told him . . ."—holding the ball, David turns to me—". . . my client, he expected me. . . ."

I interrupt him, "Keep the ball in play; I don't need to know anything about this. Just keep talking to her."

"Oh," he says, surprised, "okay, well," turning back to Margaret he throws the ball.

"I know you made a promise," Margaret says, picking up where he left off. "I respect that about you. I really do. I just think that you don't know when to quit sometimes and just get some rest. You were exhausted . . . we both were; it was a long day and then you were going to stay out even longer, late at night and in the cold."

"I know," says David, "and I didn't expect you to come with me. I knew you were tired. You worked really hard this week, and I felt bad about going out, but I couldn't let this guy down."

David, becoming more aroused, again holds onto the ball.

"Keep it going," I say.

He throws it over Margaret's head and she reaches up, misses, and stumbles back to retrieve it.

"I'm sorry," he says.

Margaret returns to her seat and throws the ball at David's stomach. It bounces off and back to Margaret. They both laugh.

"Did that hurt?" Margaret asks, with a mischievous smile while throwing back to him.

"No," David replies, smiling. "Of course not." He playfully tosses the Nerf ball at her stomach this time. They again share a laugh, bigger this time, and continue to talk about their overwork problems and lack of fun time together.

This exercise is strictly psychobiologically informed and requires no clinical intervention other than reminding both partners to keep the ball in play. David and Margaret share an intense discomfort with face-to-face interaction at near distances. Facing one another has been tantamount to confrontation for both of them, an interpersonal stress they experienced with their early attachment figures. Both have felt debilitating pressure to perform in some way and could not properly "think" or "speak" under conditions of threat. Neither behaves loudly, aggressively, unpredictably, or abusively under such conditions; both tend to freeze. Both evince seriousness, introversion, and a lack of playfulness of any kind.

Throwing and catching the Nerf ball accomplishes a number of things. It forces them to look at one another and maintain the eye contact necessary to track the ball. The task gives them a purpose that releases them from pressure to do or say anything other than simply pass the ball back and forth. It moves the focus from their smooth muscles (anxious tension in the stomach area) to their striated muscles (arms), allowing them to unfreeze. Finally, the development of a mutual rhythm leads to a relaxed, trancelike play state that engenders a natural conversation about the relationship and provides several moments of mutually amplified positive feelings (laughter).

SESSION FOUR

Both partners reveal that they had fun the last time and even went home and broke out their ping-pong table.

"I want to bring something up," says Margaret, directing a question to me. "Do you think it's possible for two people to be wrong for one another? I mean, I was a different person before David. I was more outgoing and attractive; I think people found me attractive. Anyway, maybe David and I just aren't right for one another."

Partners are on a trajectory long before they meet; the AAI provides some understanding of that route. However, their narratives would have us believe, as they do, that their experience begins with their partnership. That is because the human mind, particularly the left hemisphere, abhors a vacuum no less than nature, so in the absence of a coherent autobiographical narrative (both individual and couple), the left hemisphere confabulates or fills in blanks in order to provide coherency or a reason for why things are the way they are. (Ask a child why he or she broke the vase and, lacking a real understanding, the child will answer with an implausible explanation. This is not lying; rather, it is the left hemisphere's attempt to bridge the implicit realm with explicit reality in the service of interpersonal repair and pain relief.)

When partners ask, "Are we right for one another?" or say, "Maybe we just aren't compatible," the psychobiologically oriented therapist, armed with an understanding of compatibility, knows that the question to be answered is, given their individual attachment histories, how far can these partners advance together before their capacities to coregulate and maintain safety and security reach their limit? And when they reach that limit, what might we expect to occur between them? Would we expect an affair? Would we expect secrets? Would we expect dysregulation?

"In what way are you wrong for each other?" I ask.

Margaret hesitates, looks over at David, and then says, "Well, sex, I guess."

"Do you guys have sex?" I ask.

"No, not really" says Margaret, smiling with embarrassment. "I mean, we . . . we have, but it's a problem with me."

"And that's another big thing, another big problem we have," says David. "We don't really make love, and I don't really feel that she wants to make love to me."

Margaret, looking at David, smiles a little and says, "Well, I don't want to embarrass you but . . . should I say it?"

"Sure," says David, "say whatever you want—it's okay."

"Well, sometimes I don't . . . well I did . . . I have a problem with David's hygiene." She continues to smile as she studies David carefully, and he now matches her expression of embarrassment. Neither appears particularly ashamed of the topic.

At least in terms of arousal, embarrassment and shame are different. David and Margaret appear embarrassed. They laugh, turn red, and generally seem to move up in arousal, stimulating one another. Neither appears to drop down in arousal, which is typical in shame. Their faces are not strained; there is no awkward swallowing, facial or postural resetting, or tightening around the jaw. They check with each other, and David gives his sincere approval for Margaret to continue. Shame is a deeply painful parasympathetic affect. Some shame-averse individuals can suddenly pop up into rage; others will drop, collapse, and withdraw. I watch David's face closely for signs of shame as Margaret talks. He clears his throat once, which could be a sign of a sympathetic spike.

"Should I continue?" Margaret asks David.

"It's all right," he says, smiling. "I've heard it before."

"Sometimes I just really don't like his hygiene." She continues, saying some very personal and private things about his breath, his smell, and other matters involving the near senses. "It's like he doesn't really care that it would bother me. He doesn't think about things like this. It really grosses me out."

David now laughs. He looks at me and says, "Of course I wash and clean myself, and I brush my teeth every day. What you don't know is that she's just very particular." He continues to smile. "She's easily grossed out, but so am I. She and I have talked about this before, see, because I also have a problem with how she smells and how she tastes."

I look back and forth between them and I notice, to my amazement, that they appear comfortable talking about this. Neither seems to be getting angry with the other.

"Is that right?" I ask Margaret.

"Yeah, he feels the same way about me," she says unashamedly. "For one thing he doesn't like my breath," she says, still looking at him.

"Maybe it's the medications you're taking now," says David. There's a short pause and then he goes on. "I think we kind of get a disgusted feeling toward each other . . . like, neither of us is thrilled about being intimate with the other."

Margaret picks up where he leaves off. "I mean, I really love David, and I know he loves me but when it comes to being physical, we just never really liked it very much with each other."

I ask her, "Have you liked it with anyone before?"

"Yeah," she says.

David pipes in, "I don't think that's really true. I don't think you remember all the things you told me before about feeling unsexy and not really liking kissing and stuff like that."

Low libido and the "ick" factor: *Low-arousal avoidant couples typically describe low libido, not just with one another but throughout life. Some partners will not admit this initially because of shame and memory confabulation. With some careful examination, the therapist will likely find that both partners' libido was never very high, although their fantasy lives may have been quite elaborate. Low libido is not their only problem, however; they tend to possess an acute "ick" response to all near-sense experience—namely, touch, taste, smell, and near vision.*

Much of this near-sense problem can be attributed to very low contact throughout childhood. Several studies have shown that problems arise with low-contact caregivers, including those who favor cradling their infant on the right instead of the left (Bourne & Todd, 2004; Manning et al., 1997; Sieratzki & Woll, 1996). Some studies have noted cases of mothers having aversive reactions to the smell of their own babies, and vice versa. Many avoidant individuals who have lacked skin-to-skin contact in early childhood report discomfort with gustatory, olfactory, and tactile experiences with others throughout life. Some of these difficulties may point to a problem in early sensory integration development. Either way, the "ick factor" must be investigated in terms of the psychobiological attention to attachment and the somatosensory and nervous systems, and dealt with through psychobiological interventions to move the couple together.

"Yeah, you're right," she says, with eyes glazed over as if watching an internal movie about her romantic history. "I've never been with anyone long enough to know," she says, smiling now, almost laughing. "David's the longest relationship I've had. Right?"

She checks with David. "Right," says David, "as far as I know, you just dated briefly here and there. But I've got to say that it's been the same for me. Margaret is by far the longest relationship I've ever had. I never felt attractive enough. I was way too shy to meet girls." They look at one another as he talks, checking with one another while holding each other's gaze.

"I guess," David continues, "neither of us is very experienced in the love and romance arena."

"Do the two of you sleep together at night and get up together in the morning?" I ask. David and Margaret begin to laugh and almost in unison say, "No."

Sleeping and waking together: *Falling asleep is very difficult for many adults. It is a lonely transition; even if a partner is nearby, we enter the state by ourselves. Many people fill the hours before bedtime by working, listening to music, reading, or watching television, so that they can bypass the transition from wakefulness to sleep altogether and simply pass out when they are too exhausted to stay awake any longer.*

The opposite transition, from a sleep state into a wakeful state, can also be stressful. When we "wake up," we emerge from a fully internal, emotionally-laden dream world into a state of mild disorientation as our frontal lobes lag in sleep inertia and stolid reality gradually, sometimes ungraciously, comes back into focus. For the insecurely attached individual, waking up can be even more unpleasant than fall-

149

ing asleep. Both transitions can have a profound effect on both mood and energy during the daytime.

Many of us had the benefit of growing up with regular bedtimes and routines. We may have been tucked in, read a story, or sung a song. Ideally, as children we learn how to make the transition while in the hands of another who is unafraid and accustomed to the experience. Through this other person we gain a felt sense of safety. However, some of us were not so lucky and did not grow up with memorable bedtime rituals and routines. This lack of supportive routine to help us gradually down-regulate our internal state can affect our sleep hygiene later in life, and show up in the therapy session as various problems with co-sleeping.

Cosleeping helps regulate sympathetic nervous system activity throughout the nighttime (barring, of course, such disruptive factors as sleep apnea, snoring, restless leg syndrome, and more bizarre forms of sleep disorder; Troxel et al., 2007). But too many couples fail to recognize the psychobiological importance of sleeping and waking transitions.

The psychobiologically-oriented couple therapist pays special attention to sleep and wake rituals between partners and checks responses between partners when either finds him- or herself alone in bed during the transition time from wakefulness to sleep, in the middle of the night, and upon waking in the morning. Depending upon one's attachment organization and self-regulatory capacities, the unexpected site of an empty bed can cause considerable distress.

Even partners with biphasic issues or sleep disorders can ritualize a small portion of the ending and beginning of each day. For example, partners can read to one another, play a board game together, gaze at one another, talk quietly about their day with one another while gazing, pray together, wish people well together, express gratefulness for kind deeds together . . . the list is unlimited. Once one partner falls asleep, the other partner can get up and do whatever he or she wishes. Caveat here to the avoidant partner, who naturally gravitates toward autoregulation, predominately a dissociative state that replicates early neglect and abandonment: Because the avoidant person's adaptation to neglect through autoregulation is ego syntonic, he or she is unlikely to realize just how dysregulated he or she becomes when alone in the wee hours of the night.

"How come?" I ask.

David speaks, "Well at night . . . well, we get such little time to ourselves that at night we like to just watch TV. But Margaret likes her shows, and many of those I can't stand, so I'll go into the other room and watch mine."

"Do you ever watch anything together?" I ask.

"Sometimes we do," says Margaret. "There are some shows that we both like."

"When you watch the shows together, do you talk about them and share the experience while watching?" I ask.

"No," they both say, almost in unison.

"Why not?" I ask.

They both look at each other and shrug and David says, "I don't know, we just don't. Usually Margaret gets sleepy and falls asleep on the couch, and then I just go up to bed."

"You mean, you don't wake her up and bring her with you up to bed?" I ask.

"No," he responds.

In primary intersubjectivity *(face-to-face contact), partners use one another as objects of attention for stimulation and soothing; this is mother and baby looking at one another, as it is adult romantic partners gazing eye to eye.* In *secondary intersubjectivity,* in contrast, *partners utilize a third object of attention for stimulating and soothing as an alternative to direct use of one another. This is called joint attention. From a very young age children normatively engage in it with caregivers and others. Partners naturally do so when attending to third things, be it their child, a beautiful landscape, or an exciting performance—whatever, positive or negative, inspires them to look at one another for purposes of positive amplification.*

Parallel play (partners autoregulating together) differs from joint attention in that partners attend to a third thing without any intent to inspire mutually amplified positive moments. In other words, they are alone together on separate parallel tracks. Couples comprised of avoidant partners are much more likely to employ parallel play over joint attention and certainly over primary intersubjective contact. As a result, they enjoy far fewer mutually generated positive moments.

"The thing is," Margaret says, "I feel so incredibly lonely at night, but I don't like him bugging me." She laughs. "Is that bad?"

"Yes, that's bad!" David responds. "That's very bad. Of course that's bad. We're like roommates! I don't like it when we don't go to bed together."

"All right, so let me ask some questions," I say, "but first, let's move the chairs away and sit on the couch as they would while watching television.

"Now, how do you guys watch TV? Where do you sit in relation to each other?"

David positions himself on one side of the couch and Margaret on the other, with her legs up toward him. "Like this," says Margaret. "Sometimes like this too." She moves onto the floor, resting her back against the couch.

"David, when she's in that position do you move or stay in the same place?"

"I just sit here," he says, "no matter where she is."

"Okay," I say, "move yourself down to her, David, and sit beside her." He does. "Now, take her hand." He does and laughs a bit.

Margaret shakes his hand off. "Yuck. It's all sweaty," she says while sticking out her tongue.

"Margaret, rather than do that, get something to dry his hands so that it feels better to you." She gets up and finds a blanket and gently wipes his hand and puts it back in hers. "That's better," she says looking into his eyes.

"Thank you," David responds with a smile. "That feels much kinder. I miss holding your hand."

David turns to me and says, "Now this is where I begin to feel lonely sometimes. My fear is that we will both just sit here in silence while watching TV and then Margaret will just fall asleep."

"Which one of you holds the remote?" I ask.

"I do," David responds.

"Okay," I say. "David, this is what you do: At every commercial break, mute the sound on the TV set . . . go ahead, pick up the remote and mute the sound."

"Oh, you mean for real," David asks.

"Yes, I mean for real, do that now. You can use the one on the table."

"Okay," he says, "I'm putting it on mute."

"Okay," I say, "now turn and look into Margaret's eyes."

"What if her eyes are looking straight forward," David asks.

"Then gently pull her face toward you," I respond. He does this and both he and Margaret break out laughing. I tell them that this is a mutually amplified positive experience right now, and that this is what they miss too often, especially in the evening and probably in the morning time too.

"Do this at every commercial break: Make contact with one another, whether it's to talk about the show or just to check in with your eyes; laugh if that comes up or fight if that comes up. One of you may feel irritated by this and it might start a small fire. No problem. I just want you both to interact at night. In between commercial breaks I'd also like you to look at each other at different times, just checking in with each other. Nothing special, just look at each other so that you remind one another that you're sitting together watching this or that program."

"You know," David says, "Margaret has this thing where she spaces out; she'll just stare straight ahead, and I can't tell where she is or whether she's okay. What do I do about that?"

I have both of them stand up for moment facing one another, and then I ask David to move right into Margaret's face, with his forehead touching her forehead, and to hold that position for moment. This immediately causes laughter. David's and Margaret's faces light up, redden, and their eyes open wide and brighten.

Children and parents often go forehead to forehead as a playful, giddy bid for closeness. Kids do this naturally (Mahler, 1979), and parents may do it with them because it's fun and goofy, but people do not ordinarily think to do it when dealing with a partner who is lost in autoregulation, meaning somewhat dissociated and focused on something else. Just doing it makes people laugh. After all, with foreheads touching, near vision distorts like a funhouse mirror—two eyes become four.

If kids and parents can make good use of this technique, so too can adult couples; it's uplifting. Filling the other's visual field with one's face and maintaining skin-to-skin contact can really focus that person, especially if he or she is given a few moments for his or her eyes to soften—and four eyes are less threatening than two. Going head to head can be a particularly useful intervention with a partner who is down-regulated because it has such a stimulating effect. For depressed or low-arousal individuals, the position will likely cause a spike in arousal, popping the lowered partner upward, if only temporarily. As in the case of a mindfulness meditation technique, the entire visual field is taken up, here by the other partner's imposing face. The touch of skin and the goofiness of this perspective almost always give way to a giggle or two. Moreover, it's playful and sweet.

"This is so goofy," Margaret says while giggling.

"I know," I say, "this position is highly activating because your foreheads are touching and your faces are filling up the visual field, even though in a blurry and double-visioned way. This is something each of you can try when you want to up-regulate or stimulate the other. It is also something you can try when one or both of you become preoccupied or spaced out. This action, and others like it, can quickly shift your state of mind and body, and this is what we want: ways that we can quickly shift one another up or down, as necessary."

David and Margaret continue to hold the position, looking like two giggling children having fun. We continue this exercise trying different configurations on the couch and on the floor as though they were in bed. The movements and poses give us all a sense of what happens in micromoments, nonverbally, between partners, affording me a real-time opportunity to create interventions that might shift their experience in one direction or the other.

CONCLUSION

In these two sessions David and Margaret experienced measurable amounts of interactive play that became useful on several levels. They found that certain kinds of play, such as catch, ping-pong, and anything else involving face-to-face interaction, allowed both of them to relax, enjoy each other's company, and talk about difficult issues, when needed. The experience opened the relationship to moments of mindful reflection and loving experience of playfulness and novelty. The interactive play variously reduced or removed the interpersonal stress that overwhelmed them both when facing one another and talking about difficult matters; use of their striated muscles helped dissipate anxiety and convert the energy for movement. More important, interactive play provided many more opportunities for mutually amplified positive moments, which had been so sorely lacking due to both their common avoidance and their common low-arousal bias.

David and Margaret came to understand something about their relational trajectories—why they came together and how they have been, and continue to be, more alike than they ever thought. The narrative of their sexual problems, which reflected their mutual contact avoidance, was reframed as a natural outgrowth of their early attachment experiences as low-contact babies. Both partners came to understand that although they shared a physical aversion with regard to their near senses, they needed physical contact—not only for their physical health and well-being but also as an effective means of shutting down their stress systems.

We increased physical proximity and contact maintenance by shifting parallel play into joint attention activities and nighttime rituals. We also found effective ways to stimulate them in the session that they could take home and do on their own. By their next session, David and Margaret were getting to bed together, playing together more, and beginning a long journey toward welcoming and sustaining physical and emotional dependency. Their near-sense aversion to one another gradually shifted enough to allow for more physical closeness and affection, especially at nighttime. Despite this improvement, they would never be as comfortable with physical intimacy as higher contact, more secure partners.

It is extremely important that the therapist working with low-arousal couples like this one resist the temptation to focus on the litany of daily management complaints that often take center stage during sessions. Understand that these couples have a kind of phobic reaction to physical contact, comfort, playfulness, and dependency. The therapist's countertransference may dictate avoidance of these issues, in alignment with the couple's avoidance; following instead the many red herrings and distractions that appear will seem easier than moving the partners together. It is worth remembering here that low-contact, low-arousal, avoidant partners can become physically ill because their HPA systems cannot ever fully shut down without physical comfort or interactive regulation. Their "allostatic load" (i.e., the price in stress these partners pay for their coping imperatives throughout the lifespan) remains too high in the absence of satisfying their basic human needs for safety and security.

Chapter 12

PAUL AND JANE

Crossed Signals

Paul and Jane are a married couple in their mid-30s with two small children. They met at an Ivy League college, went to graduate school together, and then pursued separate careers in physics. Jane left her job in preparation for her first pregnancy and has not been back to work. It was she who contacted me (S.T.) for couple therapy, saying she feared that she was "messing up the marriage." The first session was scheduled for 3 hours.

Paul and Jane are attractive people with warm smiles, and although they are both articulate and well spoken, it becomes apparent that they frequently misunderstand each other on neurobiological levels. As we enter my office I show them to the two chairs facing each other. We all sit, and I notice they each swivel their chairs away from the other and gaze downward.

"So, what's going on between you two?" I ask, as my eyes scan back and forth between the partners. They look at one another, each seeming to politely ask who should go first.

"She gets upset with me when I discipline the kids," says Paul. "I can't seem to say or do anything to either kid without Jane disapproving."

"I think I get too fussy, too worried about them," says Jane. "I have a hard time when Paul tries to discipline either one of them, but especially our daughter, who's very sensitive. Paul's voice can get very boomy and intimidating—at least I think so."

Jane's focus on Paul's voice seems to point to a psychobiological issue, a sensory trigger perhaps embedded in her own attachment history.

"My voice does not get boomy," responds Paul.
"How do you know how your voice sounds to Jane?" I ask Paul.

The couple therapist commonly hears partners dispute each other's tone of voice, facial expression, or attitude implied by gestures or posture. In a psychobiological approach it is perception, not intent, that matters in primary attachment relationships. Whoever does the perceiving wins.

"I guess I don't," Paul replies with a smile. "But I don't think it's boomy. When I discipline the kids my tone of voice changes, that's true. It will probably sound commanding, but I'm not feeling out-of-control angry or anything like that."

Although we are primarily visual animals, sound, especially the human voice, represents a powerful regulatory mechanism that can both soothe and excite the nervous system. Both men and women utilize vocal prosody to soothe, lull to sleep, or to alert and alarm. Because the auditory cortex is proximal to the amygdala, a partner's vocal pitch and tone can trigger traumatic procedural memories. PTSD is often triggered by sounds. Partners typically complain about each other's vocal volume, tone, and pitch, particularly when in distress. As with all senses, stress alters both motor and sensory (output and input) activity. With couples, it is difficult but necessary to parse reactions in both directions and in both producer and receiver of stimuli.

On a very nonpersonal level, the couple therapist should be alert to the fact that many researchers believe that male and female vocal differences serve evolutionary purposes pertaining to love and war. The role of voice has historically played a large role in romantic seduction, childrearing, storytelling, alarm sounding, and domination–submission interactive patterns.

"Do the children ever seem afraid of you?" I ask Paul.
"No," replies Paul, "I don't scare them either. I would know it if I

did. And she doesn't think so either. But I *can* get them to do things sometimes that Jane can't. If I see that Jane is losing control with one of the kids, I'll step in and help her, but then she gets mad at me. I'm trying to help her, and it becomes about me suddenly."

I turn to Jane, who shrugs. "What was that?" I ask her with an interested smile. "You shrugged."

In a conciliatory tone, Jane replies. "He does try to help me. I get frustrated sometimes, and he'll come over and step in—but then I get angry with him because he seems so harsh. Like this morning," she says turning to Paul, "with Dina . . . getting her dressed."

Paul looks confused. He asks, "You got upset with me this morning?"

I'm always interested when one partner acts surprised when the other partner says he or she was upset. How is it that he did not know she was upset? Did he not notice? After 12 years?

"Yes," Jane replies, "you were getting Sam breakfast and I was trying to get Dina dressed and she was fussy as usual and I started to get angry. You came into the room and started yelling at her."

Paul, in disbelief, says, "I *yelled* at her? You think that was yelling?"

"Yes, absolutely it was," Jane replies.

Yet another difference in perception and recognition comes up, which should be more compelling to the couple therapist than the content. I want to learn why Paul and Jane experience such perceptual differences. One way to find out is to stage reenactments or mini-psychodramas that approximate the dysregulating scene. I decide to have Jane and Paul do exactly that instead of talking about it.

I ask both partners to stand and recreate the morning scenario with Dina for me. Jane acts out her interaction with Dina. Because Paul enters the room only when he hears Jane's distress, I must assist Jane in reproducing the vocal stress that cues him. Her first attempt seems to lack sufficient force.

"That's not how you sound when you're frustrated with her," Paul says to Jane. "Your voice is much more shrill."

When utilizing psychodramatic methods the couple therapist must be able to reach certain levels of arousal in order to model and guide partners. This is an external regulating function that holds out a metaphorical hand to another while moving up and down the arousal spectrum.

The clinician must get explicit permission from partners to do this. It is important that they understand the therapist's intentions in both the reenactment strategy and the "arousal coaching," so that the therapist is an ally and not simply a retraumatizing figure.

The psychodramatic reenactment, like all other interventions, has multiple purposes. The reenacting provides a field upon which to further assess difficulties and deficits, a regulatory opportunity to move partners up or down the arousal spectrum, and an intervention that switches the tone from serious to playful.

Working at the level of arousal at which the couple becomes dysregulated allows the therapist to work with the troublesome state in real time. Since procedural memories are experience-dependent, injury at this level can also become repair. Also, dysregulation means that higher cortical processing is compromised, making contingent and novel response to threat impossible. The therapist therefore functions as the couple's (or partner's) frontal lobes and intervenes quickly and unobtrusively while partners are in a dysregulated state. The therapist literally moves in, corrects, and moves out. The correction can be a word, simple phrase, a movement, touch, or any other act that rapidly shifts the state of both partners.

In this instance, I must help Jane accelerate toward the high sympathetic range of arousal, so I intentionally increase the speed of my movements, the speed of my speech, and the amplitude of my voice. My use of movement, speech, and vocal intensity seems to help move Jane upward toward where she was earlier in the morning with Dina.

"We're not going to do this again," Jane says to an imaginary Dina on the floor.

"Louder!" I say raising my voice more.

"We're not doing this again!" she shouts. "We're not making Daddy late! You can't put the sock on yourself."

"That's it," says Paul. "That's the sound. That's what gets me to come into the room."

I suspect that Paul is responding to Jane's voice as an alarm or distress call. I want to confirm this before going further, not just for myself, but also for both Jane and Paul. There's no hurry here, so we can afford to slow everything down to its smallest component.

"Before you do anything," I say to Paul, "what are you noticing in your body?"

He puts his hand over his chest. "My heart's racing," he says, "I can feel it. Her voice sounds like something I can't ignore."

"Like a siren?" I ask.

"Yeah, exactly like a siren."

Alarm cries, in humans and primates, serve pair-bonding and survival purposes. An infant's cry activates a mother's approach response. Sentinel warnings of approaching predators elicit a cry of urgency, the pitch and amplitude of which can signal to others the approaching predator. The predator–prey cries signal aggression (attack) and attempts at pushing away (distancing), respectively (Blanchard & Blanchard, 2008). Though alarm calls engage Broca's area, they do not involve language centers or the neocortex, and are not learned. Rather, alarm and signal vocalizations are mediated by the limbic system and are built in as nonvolitional responses to distress or threat (Wilkins & Wakefield, 1995). Empathic response to infant cries varies between fathers, mothers, and nonparents of both genders. Female vocal pitch, particularly during an alarm cry, is more piercing and carries further, which is perhaps why females tend to act as sentinels to bring others in toward them. The male vocal pitch, being lower, tends to express dominance, which is perhaps why the male alarm cry tends to stop others from approaching. The male commonly uses a deeper, more booming voice to invoke stopping or freezing reactions in misbehaving children, with the female often being less successful in this regard.

As mentioned earlier, the human vocal alarm, like a siren, pierces the senses with urgency, activates the amygdala and the HPA, and mobilizes striated muscles to act either to run *toward or* away *from the call.*

We want to know what is going on in Jane's body as well. Is it a match with what Paul experiences?

"And you?" I ask Jane.

She throws up her hands while moving around, agitated. "My

heart is pounding," she says. "I just want to leave her here and get away. I know that's a terrible thing to say."

Here's an instance where Jane seems to feel bad for feeling what she feels. It is perhaps another indication of insecure attachment with important figures. I expect this will be clarified further during other moments, including when performing an AAI.

"No, it's not a terrible thing to say. Not at all." I tell her. "Okay. So what happens next?"

Paul says, "I drop what I'm doing with Sam and I come into the Dina's room. I already know what she's doing to frustrate Jane."

"How do you know that?" I ask him.

"Dina has been wanting to put her own socks on and she takes forever, picking one sock and then the next. Jane tries to help her, but Dina gets upset and wants to do it herself. Jane feels the pressure of my having to leave for work. I take Dina to school."

"Okay," I say. "That makes sense. Is he accurate with that, Jane?"

"Yes," she quickly responds.

We always want to cross-check information with each partner, again for assessment and intervention purposes.

"And you can hear Paul coming toward you?" I ask Jane.

I ask this question to break down the event into very small pieces, as if going frame by frame when watching video interaction. We're checking perception, awareness, and appraisal of meaning and intention.

"I don't know," she replies.

"That's okay, that's okay," I reassure her.

"Yes," she says, "I can hear him coming."

"You dread hearing him come or you feel relieved hearing him come?" I ask her.

This question is intended to elicit information about her appraisal of Paul's move toward her. Is it loving or warlike?

"Dread," she says, "I dread him coming."

And the answer is, warlike.

"Paul, you go into the room and do what?" I ask.

Paul pretends to open a door; I stop him and ask about this.

"The door is closed?" I ask him.

"Yes," he replies.

"Is it always closed when you come into a room to find Jane and Dina?" I ask him.

Paul replies, "I think the door is always closed."

"Is that right?" I ask Jane.

"I think that's right," she responds. "My mother never liked to make a scene in public. I think that's it. I will also close the door when Paul and I have arguments."

This is another clue about early attachment that I hold in mind for later.

"Okay, we'll come back to that later. Paul, continue what you were doing before I interrupted," I say, moving away from the couple.

"Dina. Let Mommy put on your sock," he says in a stern but well-controlled voice to the imaginary Dina on the floor.

There's a long pause. "That's it?" I ask them. "Is that what he does?" I ask Jane. "In that tone of voice?"

Jane thinks for a moment. "Maybe a bit louder and boomier," she says.

"Paul, do it louder and lower."

He repeats what he said, this time more loudly and in a lower tone. Jane is quiet.

"What's going on?" I ask her.

"I don't know," she looks up sheepishly. "It seems worse at the time." She looks at Paul's face. "I don't think it's just his voice actually. I'm reacting to his face. It looks angry to me."

The psychobiologically oriented couple therapist will often be surprised to discover information that, upon closer inspection, leads in unexpected directions.

I look over at Paul, who's looking back at Jane. His eyebrows are furrowed, but I can't see anger on his face.

"Where do you see anger?" I ask Jane.

"I don't know," she replies, "his eyes."

"Point to where you see anger," I ask.

Jane points to Paul's left eye. "There," she says. "He looks angry there." I consider an exercise that might help them.

I ask them to sit close to each other, cross-legged on the floor facing one another.

"Let's try something new," I suggest, and see that they are curious and willing. "Will the two of you to just look into each other's eyes for a few moments. Don't talk. I'll tell you when to quit. Go."

This exercise allows me to see what happens to both partners when they sustain eye contact. I'm looking for clues in arousal, such as body movements, gaze aversion, laughing, or talking. I'm also going to check their moment-by-moment appraisals of one another.

I leave them in this position for several minutes. They both seem to maintain their gaze. Periodically, Jane's body seems to tense in the legs and in her jaw. "What's going on in your body?" I ask her. "You seem to be tensing your jaw."

"Whenever I see his face look angry, I tense up."

I pick up a stiff sheet of white paper. "Jane," I say, "keep your eyes on Paul. I want to try something." Standing over them, I go to her right side and position the white paper so that it covers Paul's left eye only. After holding it there for a moment or two, I move the paper so that it covers Paul's right eye.

"Oh," Jane utters immediately. "Oh, that's not good. That's not good at all."

"Why?" I ask.

"He looks angry when you do that," she replies.

I take the white paper and do the same thing, only this time covering Jane's left and then right eye.

"That eye," says Paul referring to Jane's left eye, "that eye looks kind of sad, maybe a little scared."

Although the eyes have both contralateral and ipsilateral connections to the brain hemispheres, the left eye and muscles surrounding the left eye are believed to be influenced mostly by the right hemisphere (Kawashima et al., 1999; Nicholls et al., 1999). The left side of the face, in fact, is largely controlled by the right hemisphere, which is dominant for social–emotional processing.

I sometimes find that trauma victims favor looking into the eye that is nondominant for emotional expressiveness, and this is usually the partner's right eye. Indeed, Jane finds Paul's left eye disturbingly angry and his right eye more neutral. A question remains as to whether she is misappraising the emotion she reads from this eye. She's reading anger when Paul denies feeling any anger.

I ask the partners once again to maintain eye contact and ask Jane to tell me when she sees Paul's eyes becoming angry.

"Paul, I want you to look into Jane's eyes and describe them to me."

"They're really beautiful, serene, and maybe a bit sad," he says.

"Just describe them as you would if you were a painter, an artist," I say.

"They're light brown with a dark brown circle. I can see three points of light bouncing from them, like stars. The whites of her eyes are really clear with just a bit of red in the corners," he says, while carefully studying her eyes.

"It's gone," says Jane. "I don't see the anger at all. His eyes look loving and soft. This I like."

Paul's face turns perplexed and worried.

"What's wrong?" I ask him.

"Well," he says, "that's weird because I don't know what I did that was different."

"I know," I say, trying to reassure him. "Don't worry about it for now, okay? Paul, I'd like you to keep your eyes on Jane, only this time think about what happened this morning with you, Jane, and Dina."

In only a couple of moments Jane reacts and says, "There it is."

I ask Paul, "Do you notice a change in your body as you think about this morning?"

"I can feel myself worry about it, about the future, when it happens again," he says while putting one hand on his chest and the other on his stomach.

"Do you feel any anger?" I ask.

"No," he answers quickly, "not in the least. I feel worried."

"Okay," I say. "Now, Paul, I'd like you to maintain eye contact with Jane and I want you to start to stare through her; just stare as if looking through her."

I suspect that Paul's eyes take on different appearances depending upon his focus—internal versus external. Jane reacts differently according to Paul's focus of attention. When Paul focuses externally on her face, she relaxes and doesn't experience Paul's face as threatening. When he's focused internally on his thoughts or feelings, she begins to read concern, worry, or confusion as anger. Now I want to see what she experiences when Paul's face appears still and dissociative.

"Oh, God!" Jane exclaims with a startle.

"What?" both Paul and I ask in unison.

"Oh, that's really awful, that look. That look is what I see so many times when you're making love to me, Paul. Remember how many arguments we've had over this? Remember?"

"I remember," he replies with a sigh.

"That look," Jane continues, "is just so creepy to me; it's like I don't exist . . . or like you're not there, you're not Paul somehow." She shivers as if chilled. "I'm sorry," she says, reaching over to grab his hands. "I don't mean to make you feel bad, I really don't. It really bothers me, Paul, when you look at me and you're not there."

"Do you know what she's talking about?" I ask him.

"Yeah, I think I do," he replies. "I think I space out sometimes, and she sees it in my eyes."

"But when we're making love?" she asks him.

"I know that I sometimes look at you while fantasizing," he responds. "It's really hard sometimes to concentrate on myself when we're looking at each other." He turns to me and continues, "But then she'll get freaked out, and we just stop having sex and it just all goes downhill from there. I *hate* that she thinks I'm a creep."

"She doesn't think you're a creep," I say, "look at her. Is she looking at you like you're a creep?"

"No," he responds quietly, "she looking at me sweetly."

"I think she's misreading you sometimes and feeling threatened by your voice, perhaps, but more strongly by what she perceives sometimes as anger in your face, and definitely when your eyes are fixed or distant. Let's see what happens when you look at me for a moment."

My intention here is to provide an experience for Paul of what it is like being on the receiving end of a still face. Jane seems to have had disturbing experiences from early childhood of looking into a still face.

The still face has been extensively studied in mother–infant research which has found that unresolved or disorganized caregivers tend to dissociate, leading to still faces (Beebe, 2003; Beebe & Lachmann, 1998; Crandell et al., 2003; Frick & Adamson, 2003; Haley & Stansbury, 2003; Rosario et al., 2004; Tronick, 2003b). This unresponsiveness is highly disturbing to infants, who rely on active interaction, or interactive regulation, with their caregiver. Much attention has been given to the early infant experience with the still face but not with the effects of early still-face experiences on the adult primary attachment relationship.

"I want you to get a feel for this. Right now, I'm looking into your eyes, right?"

"Right," Paul replies.

"Okay, notice what happens to your body when I do this." I begin to stare through Paul, expressionless. He starts to smile and wriggle, but I continue to stare, keeping my face still and motionless.

"Right," Paul says, breaking eye contact and laughing. "I get your point. That *is* creepy."

"That's what she sees when you're making love to her," I say.

He reaches over to her and says, "Oh, honey, I'm so sorry. I didn't know I was doing that. Honestly, I didn't."

"Okay," I say, "here's what I'd like us to do next."

At this point we want to move to an action orientation to pre-empt the despair people often feel when they become aware of a new problem to resolve.

"Jane," I say, "he doesn't know when he's doing that, so expecting him to be on top of this isn't going to work. He needs you to help him with this. That's why you guys are together; you need each other to do things you can't do on your own. He needs to help you do things you can't do alone too. Okay?"

This teaching moment becomes an opportunity to introduce psychobiological principles of interactive regulation and the regulatory advantages of being able to capture shifts and changes in the other's nervous system ahead of the other's awareness.

Jane nods in agreement. I look to Paul, who also nods.

"When Paul worries, his eyebrows furrow. He has deep-set eyes, so I can understand why you might be seeing him as intense at times. I think there's more to this than that, by the way, and we'll get to that later, but for now, he can't tell what his face is doing without you. Okay?"

"Okay," she responds.

"Right," I continue, "so here is what you can do, *sometimes*, not all the time, but sometimes." I instruct Jane to move close to Paul and hold his face in her hands. "I want you to touch the spots where you see anger or tension in his face and eyes. Just gently touch those areas. Inspect his face like a child would. I'm sure your children have explored your face with their hands before, right?"

"Yes," she says, smiling.

"It's very sweet, isn't it?"

"Yes, it is," she replies.

"Well, that's what you're going to do," I say. "You're going to meet your fear of Paul's face by moving forward, not backward. You're going to move forward and use your hands to explore and relax his face."

If Jane's body reacts to Paul as to a threat, even when she consciously believes he wishes her no harm, we must encourage her to move counter to her impulse to create a new experience that supplants the old model; otherwise, we can offer no prospect for change. In this case, she must move forward and physically make contact with what frightens her.

Most psychobiological interventions will seem counterintuitive because the reflex to move toward or away is embedded in procedural memory and influenced by repeated early attachment experiences. The adult primary attachment relationship offers opportunities not otherwise afforded to partners outside of the relationship to explore and heal themselves through the other.

As she touches his face and around his eyes, Paul begins to smile warmly with tears beginning to appear. Jane's face is also smiling warmly. "I like your face right now," she says to Paul.

"I like what you're doing to my face right now," Paul says in return.

"You like his face," I say, "because you're helping him be aware of the tension in his face. Your move forward is an act of friendliness that brings about an immediate shift in both him and you. You see that?"

"Yes, that's incredible. It wouldn't occur to me to do this," Jane says. "This is the last thing I would want to do."

"That's right," I say. "That's why I'm asking you to do this at least once or twice on your own and see what happens."

"Paul," I ask, directing myself to him, "do you know when Jane reacts to your face?"

"I'm not sure what you mean," he replies.

"How do you know if Jane is having a problem with you?" I say, rephrasing the question.

"She'll get angry and tell me to tone it down and not yell or something like that," he says.

"And what do you do when she says that?" I ask.

"I get defensive and angry back."

"I want you to try something like this." I go near Paul's face with a wide, silly smile, and both he and Jane laugh.

"You want me to do that?" Paul asks.

"It would definitely make me laugh if you did that," says Jane.

"Do something different," I say, "it doesn't matter what so long as it reads as friendly to Jane. You guys want something that works quickly to shift each other's states, hopefully toward the positive, but you'll have to experiment here a little. The thing is, your wife at times feels threatened by you, and I don't think you're wanting to threaten her. I don't believe that's what you want. I don't think that you want her to feel frightened. Am I right?"

I want to separate Paul's intent from Jane's perception of his intent and bypass any defensiveness he may experience with the implication that he's doing it purposely or that he is a perpetrator. In this way, I can better get Paul on-board with the idea of his helping her with a past injury instead of feeling like a perpetrator.

"Yes, you're right," Paul replies, "I don't want her to be frightened."

"Then you're going to have to use her reactions as your cue to do something friendly as soon as possible. Learn how to calm her down quickly, and you will calm down with her."

Again, I am using this opportunity to introduce the basics involved in the psychobiological management of two connected nervous systems and the most efficient manner of mutual regulation. The idea here is that the quickest and best way of altering one's state is to affect the partner's state. In other words, I want to encourage the use of interactive regulation.

"If you focus solely on yourself during these moments, matters will become worse. Your job is to help relieve her distress," I say to Paul, "and your job is to relieve his distress," I say to Jane, "and to do it as quickly as possible." I explain simply that couples who relieve distress quickly tend to be more stable and secure.

Noting that they both like this idea, I take the opportunity to restage the morning scene with their daughter.

Jane once again elevates her energy to the point of yelling at Dina. Paul's body reacts once again, and this time I tell him to go instead to Jane and kiss her on the head and leave the room. Both immediately respond with relief and start to laugh.

"That would be so good!" Jane says. Paul, still laughing, "You mean that's all I should do?"

"Yes!" I say emphatically. "Look at what just happened? You did that, and it threw her completely and she relaxed. What effect do you think that will have on Dina? What effect did it have on you?"

"Wow," Paul says. "I don't know."

"You're going to the wrong person when you address Dina," I say to him. The two of you are the master regulators of the household, not Dina or Sam."

Parents should function as master regulators; in that capacity they should manage the collective family arousal by taking proper care of one another. I want to reframe this couple's notion of partnership to include the primacy of their coregulatory responsibilities.

I continue addressing Paul. "Jane initially complained that your voice was boomy, but the sound of your voice quickly took a back seat to the look in your eyes. It's actually you, Paul, who has the stronger reaction to sound here, and it's the sound of Jane's distress that sets you off. Your heart starts racing, and you drop everything just to respond to her distress call. I want to find out more about that later because it's a strong reaction, but for the moment I'm glad that you want to respond to the call."

I turn my attention to Jane and continue. "There are many partners who react quite differently to these distress calls and compared to what some of these people do, you are lucky to have Paul."

Turning back to him, I continue, "Jane does need your help, Paul, but not in the way you think. She doesn't need you to take over, she needs you to help regulate her so that she can continue doing her job with Dina."

The psychobiological principle I introduce here is that of "regulating the regulator." If in the moment Jane's job is to regulate Dina, then Paul's job is to help regulate Jane in a manner that works for her. The same is true when Paul takes the lead as regulator for the children.

I continue. "I want you guys to feel like you are on each other's side when it comes to anything difficult, and parenting is difficult. Remember, you are both generals and as such you both must always convey confidence in one another's competence. Your jobs are to help regulate one another so that you can be more available to your children."

After a short bathroom break we reconvene to do an AAI. I strongly suspect that we will find reasons for Jane's hypersensitivity to both an angry and still face, and for Paul's strong reactions to vocal distress.

Paul and Jane sit next to one another on the long couch. We complete the AAI, and I go over the results with them. Jane's anxiety-filled relationships with her angry, preoccupied mother and her alcoholic, distant father provide insight into her hypervigilance, her overly developed sense of shame and guilt, her reaction to a still face, and her sensitivity to intrusiveness. Jane's protests would result in feeling punished and abandoned, a consequence she would continue to anticipate in her adult relationships. Paul's relationship with his overwhelmed, angry, and preoccupied mother seemed strikingly similar to Jane's. Similarities such as these are common finds in couple AAIs. His role-reversing mother often enlisted his help when overwhelmed by yelling for him to come to her aid. That history accounted for his sensitivity to vocal patterns of distress.

At one point I notice that Jane is leaning away from Paul. I see many shifts and changes in her facial expression while Paul speaks to me, and I interrupt.

"You know," I say to them both, "I keep seeing all these changes in Jane's face, but you, Paul, are not seeing them. That's a problem."

"Oh," responds Paul, who immediately twists his body around to face Jane. In an instant, I see Jane's face turn sour as she backs slightly away. Instantly, Paul turns his face back toward me as Jane then leans toward him and puts her hand on his leg. Paul puts his hand on her hand and then starts to explain to me how he didn't mean to lose track of Jane when he did. He then removes his hand and continues to talk. Jane lowers her head and her arousal begins to drop.

"Did you see what just happened?" I ask them both.

Both respond, "No."

"I'd like to play that back on the video monitor and show you. Would you like that?" I ask.

"Sure," they both agree.

Because I use digital video, I am able to quickly return to the exact moment. I have a large, high-definition monitor in my office that shows detail very well. I replay the moment for them, and they still look confused.

"It happened too fast, didn't it?" I ask.

This time I play the event in slow motion and narrate. I say to Paul that I'm noticing changes in Jane's face, and he's not seeing them—"Right?" I continue, noting that Jane is leaning slightly away from him. As Paul turns to face her, I say, "Watch what her face does."

"Ew," says Jane, "I look so angry."

"Yes!" I respond, freezing the frame. Her face displays a micro-expression, that is, a full facial expression of anger that passes in an instant (Ekman, 1973, 1982, 1993; Ekman & Rosenberg, 2005). "Now watch as Paul sees it and immediately turns away."

"I felt angry at Paul when you pointed out that he wasn't noticing the changes in my face," Jane explains, "and then I felt that he turned to me only because you told him to, and I didn't like that either."

"I know that look that she had on her face," Paul takes Jane's comment further. "It's an awful face, and I can't stand it when she looks at me that way."

I continue to move through the video, frame by frame. "And then what happens?" I ask. "Paul turns away and what happens?"

"I feel bad and guilty whenever I feel angry," says Jane. "I feel like I've done something wrong, and so I put my hand on his leg to fix it . . ."

". . . which I liked, by the way . . . her hand on my leg," Paul quickly adds.

". . . and then he just gave up on me," Jane says in conclusion.

"What do you mean?" I ask her.

"Continue the video and I'll show you," she replies. I move the video forward again, frame by frame. After Jane puts her hand onto Paul's leg, he puts his hand on hers. A moment later he withdraws his hand. She reads this as a reaction to her anger and moving away from him.

"Amazing!" I say. "Paul, were you aware of 'giving up' on Jane when you moved your hand?"

"No!" he exclaims. "No, not at all. I was aware of what I said about her face, but I didn't feel like going away or rejecting her or anything like that." He turns to Jane and says, "I really didn't feel like giving up on you."

Jane considers this and looks bewildered. "I guess that's what I just thought. . . ."

"And your energy seems to drop right after," I said to her. "Paul, watch what she does right after you withdraw your hand. She lowers her head, and you can feel her energy begin to plummet with it. Can you see that?"

"Yeah," he says, "I do . . . and I see that a lot, but I never know what it is."

Paul seems to confirm that Jane tends to go into energy conservation withdrawal—that is, she is prone to overrespond parasympathetically to relational threat.

Energy conservation withdrawal: *The parasympathetic branch of the ANS is largely influenced by the vagus cranial nerve, which is located in the brainstem. The vagus nerve enervates the heart, lungs, pharynx, larynx, and gut. The vagus nerve has two tracks, one that is phylogenetically reptilian and the other that is mammalian. The former, referred to as the* dorsal motor vagal complex, *is responsible for the vasovagal response, commonly experienced as the fainting response to the sight of blood. The dorsal vagal system is always engaged, to some degree, but in certain circumstances it can overengage; our heart rate decreases (bradychardia), our blood pressure drops (hypotension), and we may become nauseous, sweaty, dizzy, and pale. We may develop ringing in the ears, tunnel vision, and may even faint (syncope). Though syncope and vasovagal reactions may be due to medical causes, dorsal vagal "drops" can also occur under extreme conditions of threat where one feels helpless and hopeless about escaping. We see this in the animal world when a small animal is trapped and about to be eaten by a predator. The animal prey becomes limp and lifeless, as if leaving its body. Children and adults who have experienced threatening situations from which they could not escape will either fight, try to flee, or drop parasympathetically into a lifeless, massively down-regulated state, dissociated, numbed by a dumping of beta-endorphins (opioids) into the bloodstream.*

Energy conservation withdrawal is as it sounds: a psychobiological state of withdrawal intended to conserve energy until one can again return to a more physiologically balanced state. The young child left by Mother or Father, if only momentarily, may go into energy conservation withdrawal while waiting for the lost parent to return. This pulling inside allows the child to utilize internal soothing mechanisms such as dissociation or mental imaging of the missing attachment figure. At-

tempts to engage such a child lead to rebuff because outside interaction interferes with the child's attempts at autoregulation and his or her psychic call for the missing figure to return. This dorsal vagal reaction to abandonment and loss is akin to the anaclitic depression that sometimes follows protest and precedes giving up

Underresponders, or those individuals given to dorsal vagal drops rather than to hypersympathetic spikes, tend to be more difficult to work with, given the fact that less of them are actually online. Their recovery rates are also slower than overresponders because the dorsal vagal motor complex tends to shut down everything, and a good deal of energy is required to fire things up again with adrenaline and movement.

"In Jane's AAI, she told us how both parents neglected her and how she would feel guilty for feeling angry or disgusted with them. She believed that she was doing something wrong and that she was responsible for her own neglect. Her mother would 'give up' on her many times in frustration or to punish her. It could very well be that when she drops down like that Jane is reacting to feeling punished or abandoned by you, even though that may not be your intention."

"So what do I do?" Paul asks.

"You could turn to her and make a guess as to what just happened," I say back. "Don't you think you could guess correctly?"

Paul turns to Jane and asks, "Would it help you if I asked what's wrong?"

"Perhaps we can think about it together," I say. "Since you know her, rather than ask her 'What's wrong?', why not just guess? How many things could it be? If you ask your partner 'what's wrong' too often, she might rightfully wonder if you understand her. With what we've done today, don't you have an idea of what bothers her?"

"Yeah," Paul responds. "She tends to feel guilty a lot, like she's doing something wrong or like she's done something to hurt the relationship."

"Right," I say.

Paul continues, "And then she feels like she's going to get punished by being left."

"Right," I say.

"So I can ask you if I just ignored you or withdrew from you," he

173

says to Jane, who is now crying. He reaches for her, and she collapses into his arms.

CONCLUSION

Jane's worry that she was "messing up the marriage" was a *tell* that telegraphed her early attachment history. The couple's parenting struggles led to psychobiological issues around vocal prosody and facial expression that caused dysregulation within and between them. Their ideas about parenting also revealed misunderstanding about their proper roles as coregulators.

We used content material to guide the psychobiological interventions that followed, including exercises that revealed and help parse the partners' various implicit reactions to one another. If we had gone with the content material alone, we would never have been able to intervene on the noncontent level to assess and address the regulatory problems Paul and Jane's collective nervous system encountered every day of their married lives. Neither would we have discovered nor been able to work with the pervasive, fast-acting psychobiological forces that drive a couple to war.

Chapter 13

SIBYL AND ARTHUR

Taking Care of Each Other

Change happens. It happens with individuals, it happens with couples, and it happens in the ways therapists treat their patients. In each case, change does not come easily, or quickly. Methods that enable couples to heal each other and heal themselves are still in the process of development. As Heinz Kohut said about his model of Self Psychology, "First they say it is totally wrong, then they say that some of it isn't too bad, and finally they say, 'What's new, we've been doing it this way all the time'" (personal communication, March 15, 1978)

When I (M.S.) began my clinical training in the 1960s, there was no model of couple therapy. I was taught that a psychotherapist's job, when working with a couple, was to help each partner develop an autonomous self, and that then they could decide whether their marriage was meeting their needs. In *Culture of Narcissism*, (Lasch, 1979), the personal fulfillment of each individual was primary, while the dependence of one person on another to fill emotional needs was seen as co-dependence. Therapist training programs all taught that we should not expect another person to fill our needs. We must each function as mature adults, autonomous and independent. "We must learn to love ourselves before we can love another," was the mantra of that era.

What was less clear was how to love ourselves if we had no early models of secure attachment bonds. As I listened to patients describe their lives and developmental traumas, I recognized the protective defenses that seemed to reemerge repeatedly in adult relationships. I wondered how we could ever learn to love ourselves if we had not experienced love, or felt lovable, in our formative years. As I searched for solutions to this dilemma, in the process writing two books and many articles on treating couples, I found answers that I wanted to share with others. I found colleagues who added greatly to my understanding of how attachment, mind, brain and body influence intimate connections. My goal has been to integrate research in attachment, sensorimotor psychotherapy, interpersonal neurobiology, and the psychobiological approach to see what treatments best help couples. From every perspective I find that the best way for people to meet their own needs is by taking care of each other.

What happens, then, that makes mutual caretaking and interdependence so difficult in modern love relationships? No one who falls in love enters the relationship with a conscious intent to hurt the other and themselves. Few make commitments to a relationship for the purpose of causing pain. But painful patterns of interaction frequently develop. Love turns to war between intimate partners through a series of psychological and physiological interactions that are outside conscious awareness. This raises the infinite question[1] (Bollas, 1989) of cause and cure of emotional suffering in relationships. When a couple seeks the help of a therapist, they have been unable to resolve problems to the satisfaction of both partners. They generally have developed entrenched patterns of behavior that they need help to disrupt. Change requires a healing experience.

For several years the authors of this book have been trying different techniques to learn what best facilitates change in relationships. Our ideas are based on the working hypothesis that people unconsciously recreate early interactional patterns in their adult relationships (Hendrix, 1986). For example, when early bonds are secure, adult relationships tend to be experienced as safe. There is a high probability that two people with histories of secure attachment are likely to find in each other a loving, accepting partner, and through their partnership achieve an inner sense of integration. Although they may have differences, they are capable of maintaining con-

---

1. Questions that invariably lead to other questions.

scious awareness of their feelings and experiences even during an argument.

On the other hand, when early caretakers have not met primary attachment needs, the child develops an expectation that love and attunement will be precarious. Adult partners with insecure attachment patterns tend to test out and often confirm their beliefs that all relationships will disappoint. When people have experienced early traumas and traumatic attachments, there will inevitably be times when new situations trigger the pain of old wounds. What each needs is a different response from the current partner than the one they got in their early years. Mary Main has cited research showing that five years in a securely attached adult relationship can modify an insecure early learned attachment pattern to an earned secure one (Main, 2002)[2]

Although people in relationships do not consciously think about it, each thrives when the other's availability and attunement lead to a calming of the nervous system and facilitate integration. Intimate partners respond to each other nonverbally and automatically, in ways that do not involve conscious thought. When we feel a threat, we protect ourselves. When we feel supported and nurtured in times of stress, we relax. New research showing the connections between brain, mind, and body clarifies how our physical and emotional health is often determined by the calming effect of a loving, accepting other. Intimate partners are in the best position to meet these life-affirming needs. Thus, when two people in a committed relationship modify their beliefs from "take care of yourself first" to "take care of each other," both the relationship and the individuals are likely to grow. As in childhood, movement toward secure development requires a loving other to safely witness and applaud signs of the emerging self.

Earlier chapters demonstrated a number of ways to help partners be there to connect deeply, heal wounds, give and receive affirmation. First, the Adult Attachment Interview (George et al., 1984, 1985, 1996) is a surprisingly effective clinical tool. Although the AAI was developed as a research instrument, its ability to "surprise the unconscious" (George et al., 1985) also helps therapists elucidate the

2. Main, M., Presentation at March 9–10, 2002 UCLA Conference, "Attachment: From Early Childhood Through The Lifespan."

roots of partners' reactions to each other. Once partners recognize their patterns and yearnings, many of the exercises presented in this book can help them respond to and meet each others' needs in profound, often overlooked ways that may be significant enough to change an insecure attachment into an earned secure attachment.

Our ideas are rooted in the reality that in a relationship, the best way to meet one's own needs is to take care of the other. Using mindsight (Siegel, 2010a, 2010b), and being able to hear what the other needs, who the other is, and how the other feels, is what enables a transformation. But change is not necessarily easy. Because transformation of attachment patterns requires not only a shift in thoughts and beliefs, but also an alteration of subcortical neuronal connections, experience itself must shift. That is why therapeutic enactments that mobilize action between partners can be helpful: they help partners listen for messages that are not said in words; understand that everyone hides things from the self and from others; and learn to accept and empathize with the shame, guilt and pain of the other, without judgment. These enactments also allow the partner to experience attunement. This is what happened, gradually at first, with a couple that I finished working with recently.

SIBYL AND ARTHUR

Sibyl and Arthur come in full of fury and on the brink of divorce. Neither understands the person they married, and both are constantly finding fault with the other. Sibyl contacted me (M.S.), saying her individual therapist referred them, and they needed an appointment quickly as she was on the verge of calling her lawyer.

They arrive together, although they have traveled in separate cars. When I open my waiting room door I find a tall, stately woman, carefully groomed and elegantly dressed for a daytime meeting. With her is her husband, a very thin man of indeterminate age, dressed in jeans and a sweater, with hair that looks as though it has a mind of its own. He seems considerably younger than she is, but I learn quickly that they were classmates in the same elementary school.

They report having very similar backgrounds and upbringings. Indeed, they grew up in the same neighborhood and played together until third grade, "at the point where all the boys in class wanted nothing to do with the girls," Sibyl says. They laughed and began telling some entertaining stories about schoolmates and teachers. They lost track of each other in seventh grade when they went to different junior high schools and on to college. They reconnected forty years later, when she was a widow and he had been long divorced. From the beginning, both agree, they felt that they were kindred spirits, since they grew up "in each other's backyards." Marriage followed shortly after friends reintroduced them. They both indicate that for the first two years they did everything together, and were extremely happy.

By the third year of marriage, Sibyl says, the relationship had begun to deteriorate. She complains that Arthur drinks excessively, objects to her having friends, and spends all of his time and money building elaborate model railroads. She sits erect, her body motionless and her voice carefully modulated. Arthur leans forward and cuts her off, saying that he likes her friends, but she gives all of her attention to them. They begin to argue about how he treats her friends and how she wastes her time with hangers-on. "I hear what you think is the problem, Sibyl," I interject. "What about you Arthur? Why do you think the two of you are here?"

"We're really happy most of the time. We have a good life together," he says, denying the reality that she is threatening divorce. I gently encourage him to look at anything that might be making her or them unhappy.

"Sibyl is always entertaining, or going out shopping. Couples should spend their time with each other."

"I like to be with you, but not twenty-four hours a day," she retorts. "I feel smothered sometimes."

Defensively, he responds, "She is busy with her social life. She loves to be with her friends, especially this gay couple. We all go out together to these big social events, and no one talks to me." They start presenting their arguments about whether or not Arthur is prejudiced against gays and whether he wants her to give up all her friends and just be with him. "I like to be with him, but I have a big social life also," Sibyl says. Both direct their comments toward me, giving me the uncomfortable feeling that they expect me to judge whose version of the relationship problems is right.

I ask Arthur and Sibyl to address one another instead of me. "I can't possibly be a referee about who is right; I only know what hap-pens *inside* this office," I say. "What matters here is that you are able to hear and respond to your partner. Can you look at each other, and talk directly about what you each wish for in the relationship?"

Sibyl nods, turns to Arthur, and says, "My biggest complaint is that you have a drinking problem. You get drunk at events that we go to with my friends, and I feel embarrassed to be with you. I saw you go off to the bar with your drinking friends, and told you to come back to the table with me. You just refused, told me that you were with *your* friends and wouldn't leave. When you came back to the table, I felt humiliated."

Arthur stiffens, and denies that he drinks to excess. He says, "It only happened a couple of times," and "I only had three drinks. Usually I have one glass of wine."

"It was three times, and you kept drinking the wine until you began saying things that embarrassed me in front of my friends."

"I just told her," he says to me, "that I'll be with whatever friends I want."

"I told you the last time that if you don't solve your drinking problem, I'm getting a divorce," Sibyl says. Arthur takes a deep breath, but doesn't seem to know what to say. She looks at him, waiting for a response. "It's no use," she says to him, "I cannot live with you." Arthur begins to defend—"Everything is good between us, we'll be fine"—and I intervene.

I say, "Let's try something. Sibyl, tell Arthur that you want a di-vorce. Just look at Arthur right now and tell him, 'I want a divorce.'" As often happens with this kind of intervention, this stops the talk-ing. She shakes her head. "No, I want to make our relationship work." Sibyl has threatened divorce often, but does not actually want to end the marriage.

The threat of divorce hanging over a relationship creates the kind of anxiety that distances partners. We can only make progress after we defuse it. If people want to work on their relationship, there must be a commitment of no exit (Hendrix, 1986). When faced with a real turning point, Sibyl demonstrates this commitment by her ac-tions. She may complain and threaten, but she will not initiate di-vorce. Arthur clearly indicates his desire for the relationship to con-tinue.

"Then let's talk about what is going on in your relationship now, and how to do something different in the future," I say. Offering some psycho-education about the interdependency that partners need to make a relationship work, I point out that their pattern of complaint and defense has been filling all the space in their marriage.

"Your problem may not have anything to do with your social life, Sibyl, or your drinking, Arthur. Your arguments about friends, shopping, and model railroads are merely the surface issues, the top layer of troubles that are interfering with a satisfying relationship. Underneath lie deeper needs and desires for acceptance. When these are not met, patterns of attack and defense emerge. People often have narrative explanations of what is wrong, and of what events or behaviors are causing the problem. But more often the real problem is the repetitive dialogues that keep taking place where neither of you feel listened to, understood, accepted, known, or loved.

"When that begins to happen is that each of you finds a way to ward off the hurt. One way is to distance from each other because the arguments feel too painful. Another is to try to control each other, or blow up in anger. You've talked about the surface problems. What is going on underneath that you don't talk about? You won't be able to solve the problem if you stay with verbal scenarios of specific incidents."

When we are in an attack-and-defend, reactive state, our entire focus is on survival. Our brainstems send us into fight-flight-freeze, and even neutral comments can metamorphose in our brains into fighting words. We can only truly listen when we are in a neurologically receptive state, feeling safe. The first step towards warding off reactivity is to recognize it.

I ask Sibyl and Arthur if they are willing to do an exercise here in the office. When they agree, I give Sibyl a rope and ask her to lay it out in a circle around her in a way that demonstrates to Arthur how close she wants him to come. Sibyl uses the entire rope, keeping Arthur quite distant. Arthur, when it's his turn, wraps the rope around himself twice so Sibyl can come as close as possible. We play with increasing and decreasing the size of the circle, and I ask each to try different approaches, with the other giving feedback about how close is comfortable. We then lay the rope out straight, identifying it as a boundary line. I ask each to take a turn walking across the rope and invading the territory of the other. Sibyl never steps over the "boundary." Arthur asks if he can sit near the rope. Following this, he slowly puts his fingers on the other side of the rope. They begin to laugh, breaking the tension between them for a moment. I ask if they learned anything from the experiment with the rope. Arthur said, "I like to play more than she does." Sibyl added, "You keep crossing my boundaries, same as in our life." Arthur replied, "And you keep pulling away. It's what I keep complaining about."

I ask Arthur and Sibyl to take a minute and check their bodies. "Notice any areas of tension when he crosses the boundary, or when she pulls away. These are the reactive sensations that keep you from being receptive to new information and to each other. Remember how this feels, so that when you notice it, you have a choice to continue or to stop.

"Now take a few minutes to breathe, focusing into any parts of your body that feel tense. Some of the tension may lift, some may not; what is important is awareness. Just continue the breathing until you both tell me that you are ready to go on. I suggest that at home you can do this breathing exercise at times when you feel you cannot take in information. Either of you can ask for a time out to calm yourself and down-regulate, and say that you will be back in ten or fifteen minutes. Then make sure to return to finish the conversation."

Our time is almost up. The next session with this couple will be a good time to look deeper into their histories and expectations, using the modified Adult Attachment Interview. We agree to a three hour session the following week in order to have enough time to do an AAI with each of them listening to the other, and to go over the findings and their meaning.

THE ADULT ATTACHMENT INTERVIEW WITH SIBYL AND ARTHUR

We begin the following session with some playful banter between them. "Last week we spent a lot more time together," Arthur says. "Things are going really well. Maybe we don't need any more sessions."

"I'm still afraid you'll start drinking again, and I worry about it," Sibyl says.

"What are you talking about? We had a lovely week, and now you are starting again," Arthur says.

"You have a problem, and I won't live with it," she shoots back immediately.

"I don't have a problem," he insists. "Everything would be fine if I just had my wife with me instead of running around all day." The two of them sound just as they did the week before.

"Here you are," I say, "Doing it again. You come in feeling pretty good, and drop into your old patterns in the blink of an eye. You've gotten pretty used to it in the last couple of years. Do you want to go with that, or try something new?"

They stop and laugh. "Caught again," said Arthur. "OK. Let's move on." Sibyl smiles.

Sibyl and Arthur's bickering indicates that they want to engage with each other, but at this point, don't know how. The job of the couple therapist is to give the partners the tools to be able to hear what is said and felt by the other, and to learn more about what the other needs. I suggest that if they want to make this relationship work, we begin with an instrument that gives all of us a rapid trip to the past and back, and some awareness of old wounds. "No one escapes childhood without some wounds," I add. "We just need to find out yours."

As previously described, I begin the AAI by explaining that I will be asking a series of questions about their families and their relationship with each of their parents in their early lives, when they were under twelve years old. I tell them that I will do the interview one at a time, but we will later talk together about it. "Who would like to begin?" I ask, and Sibyl volunteers.

"Who was in your family when you were very young?" I begin. Followed by, "What are your earliest memories of the family?"

Both Arthur and I listen to Sibyl talk about her large extended family, with her mother as the matriarch, inviting all the relatives to their home for holidays and birthdays. Sibyl had one older sister who she says is her best friend. I ask her a series of questions in the AAI, and then ask for five words describing her relationship with her mother between the ages of five and twelve. She says, "Exciting," "Protective," "Fun," "Happy," "Serious." I then ask for examples of each word. For "Exciting" she says, "My mother took me to France when I was five, and when I asked to visit Euro Disney, she took me. My sister was at camp, and I was too young to go to camp; mom and I had so much fun." For protective, she says, "In fourth grade my teacher accused me of copying on a test. My mother came to school and demanded we take this up with the principal. She backed me up all the way." Sibyl is clear, concise and on target with each of her descriptions. To the other questions, Sibyl says that her mother took care of her when she was sick or if she hurt herself. She was put to bed by her mom or dad almost every night until she was fourteen, when they stopped.

We also learn that she lost both of her grandparents at age eleven, when her grandfather drove while intoxicated and got into a fatal car crash. Sibyl says she never drinks. "My first husband was an alcoholic when we met, and I told him I would not marry him unless he went to AA and was completely sober. He did and I married him. We had twenty-two happy years together until he died of a heart attack."

Then we go on to the AAI with Arthur. He, too, describes a secure upbringing, as the only child of a traveling salesman and a stay-at-home mother. I begin by asking for five words describing his relationship with his mother before the age of twelve. "Nurturing," "Available," "Playful," "Helpful," "Concerned." Arthur puts a positive spin on everything he describes about his mother. For "Available" he says he recalls at age three being home on a Saturday morning and asking her to read to him. She stopped her housework and sat with him reading for a long time. For the word "playful," he remembers her pitching balls to him when his father was on one of his trips. When he comes to the word "helpful," he uses the same example, her playing ball with him, elaborating that she invited his friends to join them. The first three answers, which relate to ages four and five, seem clear. After that he just repeats, "Everything was good." He says he was sad sometimes, and she was always there. For "concerned" he could give no example and says he doesn't know why he used that word. I notice that his body is tense, and say, "There is something difficult about this for you, isn't there." He nods, catching my eye for a moment and looking sad, but says nothing. I can feel the contact, and I don't push him further at this moment.

I then ask him for five words that describe his relationship with his father before age twelve. The words are, "Kidding," "Playful," "Sports lover," "High expectations," "Absent."

As Arthur gives examples of the first four, there seems to be a lot that he forgets. Each of his examples describes a time when they went to a sporting event, or his dad taught him football and basketball. For "sports lover," he remembers the day when his father brought home a baseball glove and said, "OK, let's play ball." To the word "absent," however, he thinks for a long time. I feel his internal pull to speak or withdraw. We sit silently. Sibyl looks as if she is about to begin speaking; I motion her with my hand to wait.

After a few moments, he sits up straight and says, "When I was twelve, my mother died suddenly. My father took her body to the town in Virginia where she was born and where her family lived."

"Did you go?"

"No, I stayed home with a neighbor."

"And how long was he away?" I ask.

"He didn't come back," Arthur replies quietly.

"Where was he?"

"I don't know," he says.

There is sadness and fear in his eyes. "This must have been so painful," I say. Sibyl reaches over and puts her hand on his knee. He is fighting back the tears and finally lets them flow. He cries for several minutes. He then describes being virtually alone from ages twelve to sixteen. His neighbor looked in on him and a housekeeper came three days a week. He didn't know how she got paid or where money for food came from.

Sibyl says, "My God, you never told me about that. I knew your mother died, but not that your dad abandoned you. How awful it must have been. I know some of the kids who were your friends. They never said anything about it. I thought I knew you so well."

"I never talked to anyone about it. I went to school but I felt kind of frozen and didn't say anything to anyone." Arthur looks a bit dazed as he speaks now, as if he is surprised that he is talking to us.

The Adult Attachment Interview is a fast path to "unthought knowns" (Bollas, 1989). Arthur has suppressed for years his feelings about losing both his mother and father suddenly. Once he begins talking, he doesn't want to stop.

"There was no one to talk to. I remember one of my teachers getting angry with me, asking why I didn't have my mother sign a release so I could go on a school trip. I didn't answer her. I stayed in the school office while my friends spent the day on the trip."

Arthur goes on to describe how he began going with a fast crowd who got in lots of trouble. "Some of them are in jail now," he says. "I could have really messed up my life, but instead I joined the Marines when I was seventeen. Best thing I ever did. They gave me structure, and an education. I went to college when I got out. And I decided I was going to always think positive, and to keep happy. I don't let anything get me down."

A year after Sibyl was widowed, a friend wanted to introduce her to someone from their old neighborhood. She agreed to a blind date and was very pleased to see how much they had in common. They reminisced about the old neighborhood and old friends, and became close very quickly. Arthur says that he never expected that someone like her, so beautiful and talented, could be interested in him. He says, "It was the happiest time of my life."

Sibyl seems truly touched by what she is hearing. She says to him, "So you were completely alone, and had no one to talk about your loss. I didn't understand. When I'm upset, I talk a lot. I want my friends to know how I am feeling. With you . . . you go quiet and seem to go somewhere else. I can't get you to talk. Now I think I know why."

The traumatic experiences during Arthur's twelfth through seventeenth years were more than he could tolerate. He developed a pattern of silently withdrawing from others under times of stress, and his brain became wired to turn to social isolation as a protection from overwhelming emotions. He becomes emotionally and physically rigid whenever strong feelings emerge. The security that Sibyl grew up with, on the other hand, allowed her the freedom to try new things, new friends, and new experiences, with her parents' support and help when she asked for it. As a result, she feels much less anxiety at separation than Arthur does, and expects him to react as she does.

I notice Arthur beginning to tear up again.

"No wonder you drink when we go to parties," Sibyl says, more gently this time. "You feel like I'm leaving you whenever I talk to my friends."

When the time is up, they walk out of my office. Arthur still looks dazed, but he takes Sibyl's hand when she reaches out.

THE WELCOME HOME EXERCISE

The following week Arthur reports that he went to see an addiction therapist after Sibyl made an appointment for him. The therapist said he did not seem to be an alcoholic, but recommended a limit of one glass of wine each night, and referred Arthur to someone to help him with the traumatic loss of his parents.

In order to help them overcome Arthur's difficulties with separation and reunion, I offer Sibyl and Arthur a psychobiological exercise developed by Stan Tatkin, called the Welcome Home Exercise. Partners are instructed to greet one another whenever reuniting after separation, even if that separation only spans the time it would take to run to the market and back. The partner returning home signals that he or she is home. The "home" partner drops whatever he or she is doing (bathroom exempted) and greets the returning partner as near to the entrance as possible. This is done without interruption; that means pets or children cannot intrude, though they may try. The partners commit themselves to reunite first before doing anything else. Instead of a kiss, the couple embraces fully, stomach-to-stomach, hip-to-hip, with face folded in towards the other's shoulders, eyes closed. The therapist should examine couples in the session, preferably with video camera recording[3], to both observe the couple's ease or difficulty folding in to one another and to facilitate proper technique.

The Welcome Home Exercise simulates the strange situation reunion scene (Ainsworth, 1978) between the secure baby and the secure/autonomous caregiver, so folding in with stomach-to-stomach contact is critical. Partners are further instructed to remain in this position until each feels the other relax completely.

---

3. We ask couples for permission to videotape at the beginning of treatment. They are advised that it is for the therapist's later reference, and sometimes for the couples to view in session. Subtle physical changes may be missed while they are happening, and instant playback can help partners observe and appreciate the nonverbal dimension of their relationship.

Sibyl, Arthur, and I agree that they should try this exercise often as a way to see what changes occur in the relationship. I encourage them to share any awareness of how it feels in their bodies as they begin and end the exercise, as they hug closely and then separate from each other. Is there calmness, numbness, a wish to move away, or be closer? Is there an ambivalent, come-close-but-stay-away feeling for either? I reiterate that whatever their feelings, it is not simply an indication of the state of their present relationship. It is an accumulation of old patterns of relating to important figures in each of their lives. The more they can share their moment-to-moment feelings with each other, the more they will understand the way the other operates, and the more power they will have to do small things to improve their relationship. They agree to continue the exercise and see what comes up.

COMMUNICATION AND ATTUNEMENT

In the next session we practice communication skills. I suggest that Sibyl and Arthur have a conversation about one particular problem they are experiencing in their relationship right now. We are not trying to solve the problem in this session, although we may make use of what comes up in a communication exercise in later sessions. What is important is to see how they deal with problems that they want to resolve. The goal is to develop the capacity for attunement to the underlying emotional messages in their communication with each other.

I ask who wants to start, and Sibyl volunteers. I then give the instructions.

"What I want you to do is listen carefully to what Arthur says, and before you respond, reflect back to him in your own words what you heard. He then reports on whether you got him right, partly right, or not at all. If you miss a part, or all, keep trying until you understand what he is trying to tell you. Only after he says you got what he told you completely, can you respond. Then he has to reflect back what you say before he gets another turn." We practice for the rest of the session, and I suggest that at home, they each write down on a file card one thing they wish to work on, and use the communication skills they are learning to move forward with a solution to the issues written on each file card.

By our fifth session they both come in saying things have greatly improved between them, and they are ready to take a break from therapy, they say. They continue to talk about emotions that come up when there are reminders of the past. Sibyl describes again her shock at losing her beloved grandparents to alcohol, and Arthur acknowledges the sense of loss and aloneness that he has been trying to fill ever since his mother and father disappeared. Arthur seems pleased that Sibyl wants to listen to him. She understands why he gets upset when they go to parties, and is now more gentle when she talks to him about it. He recognizes that her grandparents' alcohol-related deaths made her especially reactive to drinking, and now has no more than one glass of wine with dinner. Each is developing a clearer idea of who their partner is and how best to minister to them.

Sibyl and Arthur are becoming increasingly good at listening to each other rather than simply assuming that their ostensibly shared backgrounds make them the same. They are able to recognize and hold their reactivity, and they understand each other's fears and vulnerabilities. As they come to feel safe in the relationship, we see the beginning of an upward spiral. They talk endlessly. They have had sex twice in the past five weeks.

"And to think I came this close to getting a divorce," Sibyl says, putting her thumb and index fingers close together.

We decide to have one more session to discuss the future and what they can do to maintain the relationship in its positive arc, and we end with the understanding that they can return for tune-ups as needed. Their problems are not all resolved, but they have the tools they need to solve them on their own. Sibyl and Arthur are self-aware enough to recognize when they can't hear each other, and attuned enough to become advocates for each other's inner worlds (Siegel, 2010a, 2010b). They always had this ability for attunement and understanding, and used it in many of their relationships with friends. But they shut down with each other when their expectations led to disappointment, causing them to build defensive walls to protect themselves in the relationship. With the awareness that the behaviors they complain about in each other have deeper meanings, they are beginning to find ways to connect as the other wants—addressing not their own, but their partner's needs. This is what makes the difference. When partners take care of each other, both of their needs are met.

DISCUSSION

Every couple who comes to therapy arrives at the first session with a mixture of anxiety and hope. Each partner presents the most pressing problems, hoping the therapist will understand and side with their version of what is wrong with the relationship. Almost always, beneath the surface of the presenting problem are misattunements and unmet needs. The treatment is designed to help the partners become aware of the meaning of their reactivity to one another, and assist them in learning to respond to each others' core issues and vulnerabilities.

When Sibyl and Arthur entered therapy, she was furious and threatening divorce, while he was in denial about the problems and defensive about her complaints. Sibyl felt attacked by Arthur's mild drinking, and Arthur felt wrongly accused and abandoned by Sibyl. Neither was paying attention to what was going on inside the other because both had too much going on within themselves.

The treatment included questions from the Adult Attachment Interview that gave rapid access to their histories as well as to some of their unconscious processes, providing information about precursors to their current distress. Psychoeducation and exercises helped them to see how their wired-in experiences from the past were being played out in the present relationship, leading to cycles of attack and defense.

Such cycles can become a downward spiral that leads ultimately to divorce. But they do not have to. Throughout this book, the authors have shown how important changes can occur in a relatively short time. We have presented a new view of how humans relate: mind to mind, with high and low arousal levels, securely and insecurely attached, and in need of safe attachments in order to develop to full potential. Applying current research in neuroscience, attachment theory, and mindfulness as integrative factors in the psychodynamic treatment of couples can develop healthier interactions.

The work continues to evolve; there are many ways to practice these principles. Each of us brings our own temperament, our own history of relationships, our own training and experience to our work with individuals and couples. Our physical circumstances are different, too. We may or may not have rolling chairs, offices big enough to move people around in, or video recording equipment. Each therapist will end up applying the model in his or her own distinctive way. Still, one theme holds across all the cases presented in this book: The therapist's role is to help partners become aware of the roots of their seemingly unreasonable reactivity to one another, and help them learn to respond in ways that make each feel attuned to, understood, and nurtured.

Current neuroscience research shows that our brains are wired in such a way that there is a strong tendency to recreate old attachment patterns in each new relationship, but those patterns are not fixed in stone. We know now that the brain is mutable (Schore, 2004). While there is an expectation that each new scenario will play out as the oldest one did, there is simultaneously a wish that this time things will be different, that this partner will respond not as our caregivers of the past did, not abusive or abandoning, but in ways that are attuned to our signals of distress and our needs for safety and security. If partners are educated to value those needs, they can—with their commitment to one another as a foundation—influence their rote reactions and move towards a more secure and nurturing partnership.

EPILOGUE

Therapist Self-Care

We have examined over the course of this book many ways to encourage and teach partners to take care of each other. In this chapter we focus on taking care of the other important participant in these interactions, ourselves. How we regulate ourselves depends upon our own personal histories, our innate resources, and whatever growth and healing work we've done over the years. We must balance the needs and protective defenses of the couple with our own resources and self-care.

It is impossible for an outsider to move into the most intimate relationship between husband and wife without being personally affected. This engagement can be a goldmine or a minefield. Ideally we learn to use who we are—our own histories and backgrounds—to provide new experiences, insight, and empathy to those with whom we work therapeutically. In the intimacy of our clinical sessions, a greater sense of self-knowledge and self-care is essential for attaining optimum treatment goals and outcome. As we learn more about our own needs, we can look for ways to enhance our lives, which in turn facilitates our ability to summon the energy and empathy needed to support our patients.

It is very gratifying to feel needed and appreciated, and to see growth and change in the people with whom we work. However, some therapists find such satisfaction through their work that it becomes the center of their lives, and they fill their own needs and yearnings through relationships with their patients. When this is the case, concomitant disappointment, frustration, and other feelings may arise in the therapeutic enactment, particularly when patients fail to change, express upset with the therapist, or decide to terminate prematurely. For example, when the therapist yearns for closer contact to fill an internal void, he or she may have particular difficulty working with the many transferences that arise in couples therapy.

Much of what happens in therapy is below the surface of conscious awareness. Sometimes it is at the "tip of the mind," quickly recognized when it comes up in discussion with peers or in supervision. Other times it is hidden deeply below the surface. The reality is that we experience many of the same emotions as the people with whom we work. As the late Harry Stack Sullivan wrote (1953, p. 7), "In most general terms, we are all much more simply human than otherwise, be we happy and successful, contented, detached, miserable and mentally disordered, or whatever."

Ideally, with the training we receive, our own therapeutic work, the books we read, and the sharing of our difficult patients with peers and in supervision, we continue to expand our ability to help others. Still, we find ourselves in situations that constrict our own self-care, making it difficult to be of help to patients.

If we find ourselves spending hours each day engaged with intense, emotionally charged dialogue, we may look at our schedule in the morning and wish we were somewhere, anywhere else that day. It's hard not to be affected by what comes up in sessions. At times it feels draining. When we experience compassion fatigue (Figley, 1995) it may affect our lives as well as our clinical sessions.

Sometimes we will feel hopeless, angry, or exhausted in response to stressful encounters with couples. This is particularly true when we are working with couples in which one or both partners have experienced severe trauma. Those of us who work with traumatized patients and their partners may also experience vicarious traumatization (McCann & Pearlman, 1990; Courtois, 1993). We must be particularly careful to avoid reactions that affect our ability to be open to engaging with the internal world of these patients. Such feelings may turn chronic and disabling if we attempt to repress them or avoid seeking help when the work begins to feel overwhelming. When sessions with a couple are taking too great a toll, it may require making use of external regulation by calling upon outside resources.

A colleague described her work with a patient whose husband left the marriage soon after her first meeting with them. The patient clung to the therapist in the months that followed. "I have no one else," she said, "I'm all alone in the world. I can't trust anybody else." This highly intuitive therapist, having great compassion for her patient's suffering, worked with her through several suicide attempts, repeated nighttime telephone calls, and two hospitalizations. One day the patient called before her appointment and said, "I can't take it anymore, I want to die." The therapist, fearing that this time the patient might succeed in killing herself, arranged for paramedics to be at her office to take the patient back to the hospital. At her first visit to the hospital, the patient said, "I hate you, I will never trust you again, or anyone with initials after their name, to help me." She followed this with a wrathful letter cancelling all future appointments. Several years later the therapist related this experience in a discussion about countertransference. She said that she was really shaken by what had happened with this patient. "Her neediness, constant state of being upset, the intensity of her anger, was really disturbing my equilibrium." She added, "I didn't know how to help her. It was affecting my time with my husband and my five-year-old child, and I was relieved to be finished with her. But I still feel upset when I think about what happened." This therapist, now a training and supervising analyst at her institute, said that she is now much more careful who she takes into her practice.

How many in the "helping professions" have memories of patients who consumed their lives, had intense rage that made them feel uncomfortable, or caused them to feel sleepy, bored or distant in sessions? Sometimes, deep core problems are worked through and both therapist and patient grow from the mutual engagement in the dark parts of the psyche. This kind of deep interpersonal engagement is enhanced by a collegial relationship where discussion occurs around what is happening in difficult encounters between patient and therapist. The best way to get this kind of help and support is to be part of a peer study group, or an ongoing supervision group. Recognizing what part of the difficulty is based on what the patient brings in, what part belongs with the therapist, and how the two interact in the intersubjective field. It is the same process used in understanding the dynamics of couples with whom we work. Learning how to understand this process is also an important part of self-care. Some examples follow.

EXPERIENCES IN SUPERVISION

In a supervision group focused on couple therapy, a therapist who was truly receptive and engaged deeply with patients asked for help with a couple that she had recently started to see. The therapist had been trained to carefully track for body position, physical responses, and emotions that came up both with patients and with herself. She reported that she had a tension headache following the first session with this couple, and now felt a knot in her stomach every time they came in. She also felt relieved when they had a problem with their babysitter and cancelled their last appointment. She decided it was time to bring it up in supervision.

As she described her difficulty, it became clear to her that listening to the couple argue and talk over each other in the sessions brought up memories of her parents' marriage shortly before they divorced. The image that came up for her was looking through the keyhole of her parent's bedroom door as they fought. As an eight-year-old, she felt that she could do nothing to save their marriage. In the sessions with the couple, each time they said things that hurt each other, it triggered this old pain. Understanding what was precipitating her distress was an important step. She recognized an underlying belief: that it is her job to keep this couple (her parents) from divorcing. This belief was interfering with her ability to attune to the pain felt by each of the partners, and to provide appropriate treatment.

In another instance, a long-time therapist, having difficulty maintaining his full practice, said of a couple he was working with, "They're complaining about unruly kids, about the arguments they get into while traveling, and whether or not to buy their own jet. Here I am, a single father of a kid with ADHD, and a mortgage that I can't pay. Sometimes I'd like to say to them, 'You think you have problems, let me tell you what real problems are.' If it's so hard just to listen to them, how can I help them?"

Our clients stir up our emotions on a regular basis, and even if we choose not to reveal it, it takes a toll. To do effective therapy, we must not only be able to take care of the couples we're treating; we must also be able to take care of ourselves. In the office and in our lives, therapists need to keep self-care in mind.

Unlike the focus on patients' pathologies so common in past training, we now recognize that success in treatment is affected by the therapist's own history, character traits, fulfillment in current life, and the dyadic fit or misalliance in the treatment. All of these things affect the process of therapy. Being mindful of what is happening during sessions is one of the best ways to familiarize ourselves with how we operate in sessions with a couple. We need to become more knowledgeable about our own physical sensations and somatic signs of dysregulation, tiredness, difficulty keeping track of relevant information, and strong emotions toward patients. Also, it is important to expand our ability of self-regulation and widen our own window of tolerance (Siegel, 2010a, 2010b) when we sense that our ability to help is blocked.

SELF-REGULATION

Just as partners fail to hear each other's true messages when they are outside the window of tolerance, so do therapists. When our arousal spikes or drops, we become vulnerable to the very same misapprais-als that occur within couples during periods of distress. For this reason, our own comfort and relaxation are essential to providing a safe milieu for patients, especially the times when we employ pro-vocative interventions intended to stir up discomfort during key moments in the treatment.[1]

Constantly monitoring our bodies makes it possible to calm the self in moments of high reactivity. Unmonitored tightening of the muscles—whether in the arms, legs, shoulders, and neck, or deep in the gut—can often lead to numbing and distancing. In the sessions and on our own, we repeatedly scan for tension, and practice letting it go. This is an important skill to learn because as tension rises in the body, so does arousal level, which interferes with our ability to focus on what is happening in the moment. Conscious breathing can be a useful technique for self-regulating; a long, slow exhalation lowers the heart rate and tempers arousal. It is important to take time prac-ticing this and noticing the effects on the body and mind.

Studies have shown that when clinicians use mindfulness (Kabat-Zinn, 2009; Kornfield, 2009; Siegel, 2010b) they experience de-creased burnout and can maintain higher degrees of empathy with

---

1. See Part II.

patients. Books by Kabat-Zinn (1994), Kornfield (2009), Stahl and Goldstein (2010), and Siegel (2010a, 2010b) are excellent guides to mindfulness practice. Exercising mindfulness can help therapists develop resilience, self-compassion, and self-care in their lives and with their patients. For those not familiar with mindfulness practice, it may feel uncomfortable or unproductive to slow down, breathe deeply, and practice mindful awareness. Clinical studies indicate that the opposite is true, and that mindfulness has profound effects that are both valuable for the therapist, and a good tool to apply with individuals and couples (van der Kolk et al., 1996, 2006).

Noticing and regulating our own internal world is an important part of self-care. We must be aware of how comfortable we are with anger that arises in couple sessions; how attuned we generally are to signs of others' distress; how avoidant or ambivalent we may be about intimacy; and how much we may want to be liked and admired by people who seek our help. It is also important to acknowledge our own values and beliefs about topics such as gender roles, the arousal of sexual feelings, the ethics of extramarital affairs, and divorce. We don't often recognize our own biases, but it is imperative that we do; otherwise, it becomes easy to unconsciously side with the partner who shares our biases. This often happened during the early years of the feminist movement; the unfamiliarity of many men with the language of emotions and greater difficulty showing neediness caused many therapists to see the problems of relationships as caused by male defects.

If a therapist feels bored or sleepy, it may be a sign that something in the session is being put to sleep that needs to come to the surface. When this occurs, it can be helpful to comment on the sleepiness or sense of distance. The partners are as likely as the therapist to be aware of what is happening, or more likely not happening, at that moment. However, it is necessary for the therapist to be self-aware enough to know the unconscious causes of the sleepiness. It is important to come to sessions rested, well nourished and relaxed. If there is a lot of stress in your life, your work as a therapist begins by reducing the noise in your system. If that is the case, and you find yourself getting too relaxed or sleepy, you can up-regulate by moving forward and interacting. A position close enough that the near senses are engaged reduces the sense of boredom and disconnection. If you are not afraid to talk about feeling drowsy or the sense of being distant, it may open a discussion of what the individual or couple is trying to avoid, or keep asleep.

Videotaping clients provides a wonderful opportunity to learn about the clinical session, and offers even more insight about ourselves, as with a videotape, not only are we able to see signs of partners' connections and disconnections, but also, our own. Watching ourselves with our patients—sometimes slowing down the tape to see subtle clues such as the tilt of the head, eyes darting toward or away from one of the partners, or muscles tightening—can help us develop awareness of our part in the interactions. Videotaping can also help us learn to recognize the biases we bring into clinical sessions, by showing us whether we tend to side with one partner over another.

There will be times when we watch ourselves on tape, or discuss our work with peers, that we may feel incompetent. Be assured that even the most experienced therapists feel this way at times. Sometimes we do not have a clear understanding of what is happening in the present moment of the session, and this too gives us important information. By remaining open to others while at the same time being open to ourselves, we may find that we can expand our tolerance for uncertainty. Remaining present through uncertainty and vulnerability can help us expand our ability to contain intense emotions ourselves, and be receptive to our clients' struggles, fears, and guardedness.

One way to be open to the true experience of another person is to relinquish control of our own internal state (Bollas, 1989, Bromberg, 1998, 2006). In order to help our clients attune to themselves and each other without trying to control the outcome, as they go on a journey of discovery, we must be able to do the same. The journey takes us in directions that no one can predict, into realms that may sometimes feel uncomfortable or out of control.

IMMERSION INTO THE DARKNESS

In Plato's[2] metaphor, a group of people who have lived chained in a cave all of their lives, seeing only shadows projected on the wall, begin to ascribe form and meaning to these shadows (Bloom, 1968).

2. In Bloom, A. (1968). *The republic of plato*. New York: Basic Books.

In the cave of our souls we may experience loneliness, anger, erotic or other such feelings, which may immobilize us, or interfere with our ability to feel curious, open, aware and loving. The latter qualities are imperative to living a mindful life (Siegel, 2007). As we gain experience by visiting areas of our own dark shadows, we develop the ability to remain in this unknowing state, advancing forward into the shadowy corners of the psyche, knowing that we will be able to safely emerge.

Sometimes the best thing we can offer the people with whom we work is to go into the darkness together, armed with the knowledge that we have survived the darkness before and can help them find their way out of the cave. We can convey our confidence that we both will come up into the daylight, perhaps initially blinded by the brightness, certainly wary and tired, yet safely armed with new skills for traversing outside the familiarity of the dark cave. As Siegel notes, "There's a gold mine of internal education in learning the art of self-awareness and inter- and intrapersonal attunement" (2010b, p. 43). Acknowledging the not-knowing may be one of the most important keys to supporting others with care and compassion.

THERAPISTS' CONNECTIONS OUTSIDE THE THERAPY SESSIONS

We have found that couple therapists have an easier time in the complexities of the work when they themselves have the support of a stable and secure primary attachment relationship operating according to principles we have discussed in this book. This should include dependable access, good interactive skills, quick repair, like-mindedness, and mutual positive regard. If not currently in a secure primary relationship, there are alternative ways to meet many of these needs in significant other relationships. It is vital to have someone to turn to, whether a close friend, supervisor, peer therapist, parent, or religious leader. In addition, seeking help from established professionals, joining support groups, and sharing one's feelings with family, close friends, and trusted coworkers can be excellent ways to foster self-care.

One of the best ways to develop new skills, recognize our biases, share truths about ourselves, and avoid burnout is to become involved in study groups, or small peer consultation groups, where both the therapist's internal experiences in sessions and the relationship with patients are safe to discuss. Professional "burnout" can come from learning a model of treatment and applying it to everyone, doing the same thing over and over without sufficient gratification, and not knowing how to correct for errors. Depletion and burnout should be discussed openly as common risk factors for all therapists.

Workplace supervision is a helpful way to avoid the sense of isolation and depletion. It is often convenient and free in agency settings. Some agencies offer superb peer group supervision and consultation that give the therapist an opportunity to share common experiences. However, some workplace settings have clear requirements and rules about the number of sessions and type of treatment expected that make depth supervision unavailable; if this is the case, it is important for therapists to find other sources of collegial connection and self-care.

If no supervision group is available, it is possible to create one by organizing a discussion group around a specific theme, such as treatment of unresolved loss and grief in couple therapy or, for those willing to take a risk, transference and countertransference. It can be very helpful to hold weekly meetings and share the cost of hiring a senior clinician to oversee the group. With enhanced communication, group supervision by telephone or Internet is entirely feasible. Even if there are no like-minded clinicians in the area in which you practice, you still have access through the Web to training and supervision with leading teachers from all over the world.

LIFELONG LEARNING

Solid training in one modality of treatment at the onset of our clinical careers can form a foundation for continued learning, as we gain knowledge and perspective throughout our careers. The field of psychotherapy offers many ways of working, and those who are well-versed in several clinical models can draw from different approaches for different patient needs.

Lifelong learning includes staying in touch with the literature in books and journals to learn about cutting-edge research and treatment modalities, which we can then assimilate into our clinical practice. It also includes finding access to the many continuing education programs available, which are designed by professional organizations for every level of mental health practice. Many organizations offer regularly scheduled meetings to discuss current treatment approaches and skills. Universities and institutes provide lectures and ongoing courses in the application of new research in attachment, neuroscience, mindfulness, couple therapy, and many other subjects, providing a solid understanding of various treatment models.

PERSONAL EMPOWERMENT

Many clinicians will experience isolation, feel overwhelmed by personal issues, or be unable to cope with the combined pressures of work and home life at some point in their career. Such feelings can be addressed by considering one or more of the following recommendations.

For Your Work

- Set up strong boundaries regarding work hours and availability for after-hour telephone sessions.
- Become aware of the type of people with whom you work best, and those that create the most difficulty for you.
- Using mindfulness, maintain a state of observation of what goes on in each partner, in the couple, and in you.
- Be aware your own body and how it speaks to you.
- Stay present with your own sensations and movement. Your reactions may give you important information about what is happening between the partners and within each of them.
- Learn when your reactions are appropriate to bring to the couple's attention.
- Collaborate with agency supervisors and colleagues to offer yourself as a resource for those with whom you work best.
- Form groups with colleagues where the subject can be therapeutic failures rather than successes. Remember that the best learning comes from recognizing our mistakes. Giving supervision and feedback to others is as much of a learning experience as receiving supervision.

For Yourself

- Take a relaxing vacation to replenish your energy and vitality.
- Develop interests and hobbies outside the therapy field. Take classes, go to concerts, and attend conferences to meet new people who share your interests.
- Stop for a moment to examine priorities, change personal and professional habits, and find avenues of self-replenishment.
- Seek help for any addictions and/or unresolved psychological issues that may be impeding personal and professional well-being.
- Exercise and practice deep breathing for your health.

CONCLUSION

A sense of internal gratification is essential for clinicians, particularly at times when they may receive little affirmation or appreciation for their work. The demands on the therapist may strain the ability to consistently uphold the standards set by our profession. Moreover, no one can sustain an optimum level of functioning all the time. We have personal lives, family struggles, illnesses, as well as unresolved issues from our past experiences. Why then do we therapists seem so prepared to expect this level of excellence from ourselves? There is a persistence of unrealistic and unrealizable ideals that continue to influence theory and aspirations.

Early in our careers, all of us are convinced that if we only knew more, learned more, and felt more secure with our training, we would be quite comfortable handling whatever comes up in session. Yet no matter how experienced, every one of us at times has felt a lack of competence in certain therapeutic situations. Every mind is a different world, and every couple is a unique coming together of two different worlds. We can't possibly know how to handle every situation. That is what keeps us studying and learning.

There will be times when we must accept our limitations, even if we are experienced practitioners with highly developed skills of attunement to the physical and emotional states of those with whom we work. There will be people whom we cannot help, and things that will impinge on the treatment, such as temperamental issues, unresolved trauma or loss, and significant psychological defenses—

not to mention deaths in the family or financial struggles. Some of these problems lie in our patients, some lie within ourselves, and some are entirely out of our control.

Some aspects of our own personalities have taken years to develop and may not be so open to major transformation. Sometimes we must have the courage to acknowledge that we cannot help a patient or a couple. Other times, we must have the wisdom to recognize that our beliefs about what a person needs from us are very different from what that person hopes to get from us.

We should not assume that treatment problems are caused by patient resistance rather than the intersubjectivity of the relationship. If we find that we cannot alter our way of working to fit the personality of a particular patient or couple, we may need to discuss the situation with someone we trust, and if necessary make a referral. If we find that we have similar reactions with a number of people with whom we are working, it is up to us to make use of supervision and our own therapy to help illuminate our part in therapeutic impasses.

One thing is certain: We will be affected by the people with whom we work. Rather than trying to avoid this by building a shield around ourselves, we can learn, as we have advocated throughout this book, to trust ourselves and others enough to let down our defenses, open ourselves to deep connections, to expand our windows of tolerance, and help develop interdependent relationships that enhance the life of each partner. This is a recipe for success in our lives and in our work.

APPENDIX A

A Neurobiological Vocabulary

SOCIAL–EMOTIONAL SKILLS
AND DEFICITS

No brain is perfect. We all have deficits, and most of the time we can get around them. It's in the context of intimate relationships—when we really need all oars in the water—that deficits in social–emotional functioning are largely revealed. Two people in a primary attachment relationship depend on one another to regulate each other's nervous systems through close interaction; any social–emotional deficits can rapidly lead to misattunement, poor error correction, dysregulation, misappraisal, and eventually to a psychobiological threat response that anticipates trauma.

In Appendix A we define the neurological deficits a therapist can learn to spot, the underlying anatomy of these deficits, and the physiological systems that can make moments of social misattunement feel like life-threatening experiences.

Most of the problems couples face involve failures of interactive regulation. Signals cross in ways that partners may not even register. It's the therapist's job to recognize when these crossed signals reflect some developmental neurological deficit in social–emotional functioning and then, by engaging the other partner, begin to overcome them.

We may see deficits arise in a partner's ability to attend to detail, read interoceptive and exteroceptive cues, experience empathy, detect shifts in affect and arousal, name feelings and emotions, identify body sensations, and so on. We may notice one partner paying exclusive attention to his or her partner's mouth instead of the eyes. We may notice that a partner is continuously unable to wait his or her turn to speak or makes too many misappraisals of the other partner's motives and intentions. These are but a few examples of signs and symptoms that may be signals of developmental or other neurological deficits affecting social–emotional acumen.

EMOTIONAL IQ

What we ordinarily regard as "intelligence" is left-brain, verbal, logistic–sequencing–organizing capacities. An individual who is intellectually brilliant in the working world may not be as successful in the loving world because the required skill set is different. In fact, those with good right-brain development and social–emotional acumen—high emotional IQ (Goleman, 1996)—combined with measurable attachment security do better in all relationships, work and love, regardless of education and socioeconomic status (Carlson et al., 2003, 2004; Sroufe, 2003; Tronick, 2003a).

The first 18 months of postnatal development contain highly critical periods for the growth of structures and neuropathways that are integral to our basic social–emotional acuity (empathic attunement and the ability to read facial cues, vocal tones, and body posture). A *critical period* is like a one-time super sale—you can get a lot of stuff while it's available, but when that sale is over, it's on to the next. Right-brain development depends on our experience with another person; opportunities are abundantly available for skin-to-skin, face-to-face interactions with a psychologically available primary caregiver. Without such interaction the child's right hemisphere fails to set up properly, resulting in greater than usual apoptotic events (cell death) and impoverished neural connectivity. The left hemisphere may be able to compensate for missed critical periods of right-hemisphere development and perform certain of the right's social–emotional functions, but it is not likely to do so as fast or as well. Right-hemisphere deficits will show up in primary adult romantic relationships when appropriate and timely responses to novel social and emotional cues are critical.

READING FACIAL CUES

The ability to read facial cues is particularly important to attunement and interactive regulation. Humans are primarily visual animals and, although other sensory perceptions (auditory, tactile, olfactory, and gustatory) exert a strong influence in close interactions with others, near vision is the strongest player in the multimodal sensory orchestration of attunement and interactive regulation. A partner's failures to quickly read, interpret, and respond to facial cues will likely result in misattunements and mutual dysregulation.

Significant facial cues come in the form of sudden changes in skin coloration; tightening or relaxing of the orbicular muscles around the eyes, corrugated muscles of the forehead, zygomatic muscles around the mouth, and buccinator muscles of the cheeks; gaze aversion; and pupil dilation. Accurate receiving, perceiving, and interpreting of these cues primarily depends on the right-limbic and frontal cortical areas.

Difficulty reading faces could be a sign of autism or Asperger's or could simply be a symptom of someone who is avoidantly attached. Lack of sensitive or enriched interactive play during critical periods of social–emotional development prevents children from building an extensive lexicon of facial and vocal expressions vital to reading the complexity of another person. A tendency to focus on the mouth instead of the eyes may also account for problems in picking up facial cues.

EMPATHIC ATTUNEMENT

Empathy, the distinctly human expression of *sharing* another's experience, is different from sympathy, which is a *recognition* of another's pain. Empathy can be viewed on two levels: cognitive and somatoaffective. On the cognitive level, empathy is similar to sympathy, which is a kind of mental recognition of another's situation or condition expressed either verbally or nonverbally. An individual with a basically intact left hemisphere is equipped with the requisite understanding of human relations and social expectations needed to express cognitive empathy. On the somatoaffective level, however, empathy is the real-time experiencing of another's sorrow, anguish, or pain as if it were happening to oneself. Experiencing another's pain requires the ability to (1) put oneself in another's shoes (a function of ventromedial and orbitofrontal cortices), (2) process interoceptive (bodily) cues (a function of the amygdala, anterior cingulate, and insula), and (3) grasp the other's reality (an intuitive function of a well-integrated right hemisphere). Integrating the functions of these structures—the orbitofrontal cortex, amygdala, hippocampus, anterior cingulate, insula, right and left hemispheres—facilitates the empathic functions of theory of mind; somatosensory awareness; attachment; sequencing, detailing, tracking time and space; holding and waiting; and understanding the most essential part of some idea or experience (getting the gist).

AFFECT BLINDNESS AND ALEXITHYMIA

Affect blindness and alexithymia are developmental deficits with regard to empathy. *Focal affective blindness* refers to an inability to discern subtle shades of emotion in other people, whereas *alexithymia* refers to an inability to detect and/or name internal somatoaffective states in oneself (Moriguchi, Orishi, Lane, Maeda et al., 2006).

A person with affect blindness may be "blind" to mild anger or to sadness that's not fully expressed, picking up on emotions if their partner shows obvious, broad signs but failing to detect smaller shifts. Positive emotional expressions can be as troublesome as negative ones. This problem might show up, say, with one partner not recognizing expressions of sexual excitement or love from the other. An affectively blind partner may not detect a full pallet of emotions, or may pick up on primary but not blended affects, which requires more social–emotional complexity.

The alexithymic person who does not know what he or she is feeling has an impaired ability to "read" his or her own somatoaffective, interoceptive cues and thus is also affectively blind. An alexithymic partner will obviously have a difficult time reading and responding to the other's affective states and state shifts. Organic causes (e.g., stroke, dementia, traumatic brain damage, pervasive developmental disorder) aside, alexithymia has been described as a functional, and sometimes structural, deficit in right-brain, frontolimbic circuits (Larsen, Brand, Bermond & Hijman, 2003; Henry, 1997).

AFFECT CONTAGION AND OVERRESPONSE

Affect contagion describes what's going on when individuals who have "thin boundaries" complain they "feel too much" in the company of others whom they judge to be in pain; they find themselves overempathizing or "catching" the affective state of the other. These individuals will often overrespond to emotional cues, leading to intrusiveness and dysregulation. Some suggest that overresponders may have overactive amygdalae and insulae as well as poor ventromedial prefrontal regulatory command over these areas, particularly when affect contagion appears undifferentiated (Coates & Moore, 1997; Coates, 1998).

THEORY OF MIND

Our curiosity about ourselves and others is a function of theory of mind. As children, we develop an appreciation for our own mind and the minds of others. This appreciation contributes to our developing differentiation ("We have separate minds") and individuation ("My mind is unique, and so is yours"). Theory of mind also implies an ability to reflect on the self with a partner, in a diary, or in therapy. Theory of mind is most connected with the right orbitofrontal cortex, which develops around 10–18 months.

SOMATOSENSORY AWARENESS

Social skills that employ empathy, attunement, and self- and interactive regulation rely on the ability to read and respond to bodily cues in both self and other. Such somatosensory awareness requires good vertical integration between the body and subcortical structures such as the amygdala and higher right-hemisphere regions such as the insula, anterior cingulate, and orbitofrontal cortex to organize and interpret sensory information into emotional meaning and differentiation between self and other. It is not enough for me to simply know what is going on in my body and in my mind; I also must be able to know the difference between what's going on in me and what's going on in you.

ATTACHMENT

We come into this world with the drive to form emotional bonds with others; however, environment and constitution can cause deficits in this area. Many antisocial individuals come from highly neglectful or abusive childhoods. Some individuals may have constitutional or developmental neurological deficits that affect their ability to attach. Both the amygdala and the insula, as well as several neurotransmitters and hormones, have been implicated in attachment/bonding experiences and behaviors. Individuals with low attachment drive may also display problems with theory of mind, somatosensory awareness, and empathy.

SEQUENCING, DETAILING, AND TRACKING TIME AND SPACE

Interactive regulation requires more than simply being able to read internal and external cues. If one partner has difficulty tracking time and space—that is, he or she continually loses track of time or is unaware of his or her surroundings—the result could be dysregulating for both partners. The "spacy" or "distracted" partner is likely reliant upon autoregulation for stimulation and soothing but may be dealing with a true deficit involving any one or more of a number of areas (e.g., attention, dissociation, chronic sleep deprivation, issues with medications, substance abuse).

In general, when under too much stress or when recalling a very upsetting event, both partners will have difficulty in this area because the hippocampus goes offline under such conditions. Discussed in greater detail below, the hippocampus is largely responsible for short-term memory, establishing place and context, and sequencing. The left hemisphere is also involved in these tasks, particularly with regard to sequencing and detailing.

Verbal precision is another sequencing and detailing skill; partners who ramble may dysregulate their distressed loved ones who require a concise, well-organized narrative. Left-leaning partners who are strong on precision are sometimes weak in the opposite arena: They have trouble grasping the bigger picture, or gist. Their overfocus on detail will dysregulate their distressed partner, who is waiting for the relief that comes from understanding the overall problem.

HOLDING AND WAITING

Our ability to control our impulses is an essential social skill. Partners who have difficulty with holding and waiting continually cut each other off, jump to conclusions, or react nonverbally (e.g., deep sighing, eye rolling, grimacing) too soon. Sometimes this behavior is simply an issue of impoliteness or a reaction to heightened threat. Other times it may be a real deficit involving poor self-regulation and may even be a sign of organic or neurological issues concerning the frontal lobes. High-arousal couples often have difficulty in this area of holding and waiting.

CONCLUSION

Interactive regulatory problems naturally arise from deficits in all these areas, which cause partners to fail to detect or respond to injuries and attunement errors either quickly enough or at all. These empathic failures, or misattuned moments, cause a disturbance in the couple's intersubjective field, leading at least one partner to feel attacked. This momentary breach in the safety and security system can quickly escalate into dysregulation of the ANS and activation of the HPA axis, which begins to ready the body for fight–flight–freeze or collapse. Repeated, unrepaired instances of misattunement will lead to a kindling of the arousal system, with each familiar encounter becoming more of a threat. Misappraisals of intent are very common, even inevitable, in these situations, which adds to the mess.

The couple therapist will have to examine this dynamic between partners closely to find the likely source of the repeated misattunements. Such an examination may lead to discoveries of deficits in either or both partners. While working to shore up developmental delays or deficits in one partner, the therapist may simultaneously need to bolster the other partner's self-regulatory capacity in the face of an under- or overresponsive partner.

THE THREAT RESPONSE NETWORK

The dance of attunement during interactive regulation is exquisite and moves back and forth before words can be thought or spoken. But attunement is never continuous or perfect—good interactive regulation also means good error correction and repair. Without quick and frequent repair, the glitches begin to be "felt" in the body and "thought" in the mind as stress. This experience of stress disrupts (if even momentarily) the couple's sense of safety and security and engages the threat response network. The four main systems involved in the threat response network relevant to our work with couples are the autonomic nervous system (ANS), the limbic–hypothalamic–pituitary–adrenal axis (LHPA), the vagal motor complex, and memory.

THE AUTONOMIC NERVOUS SYSTEM

The ANS is the meat and potatoes of the psychobiological approach to couple therapy. (Unless otherwise indicated, the ANS is what we mean when we say, simply, *nervous system*.) Every romance is a relationship between two nervous systems, interacting both chemically and electrically with one another. Excitement, attraction, relaxation, fight and flight responses are all mediated by the ANS, which has two primary branches: the sympathetic (emergency response, controlling excitation) and the parasympathetic (calming response, controlling relaxation). The energy-expending sympathetic component affords us stimulation and vitality; the energy-conserving parasympathetic component affords us relaxation and serenity. The sympathetic nervous system kicks into gear whenever we are faced with something new and exciting—or terrifying and dangerous: heart and breathing rates, blood pressure, and body temperature increase, and the blood supply moves from stomach to limbs in preparation for action. When the parasympathetic system engages, in contrast, we feel calm, serene, and relaxed: heart and breathing rates, blood pressure, and body temperature decrease, and blood moves back into the digestive system in preparation for eating and sleeping. (When warriors go to battle, their sensoria are enlivened; when the battle is over, the warriors calm down, realize how hungry they are, get something to eat, and go off to sleep.)

The sympathetic and parasympathetic systems are like an accelerator and a brake. If moving toward someone or something in an accelerated fashion is vital to self-activation, motivation, success, freedom, surrender, passion, progress, intimacy, and resolution, then moving away from someone or something in a braking fashion is vital to self-control, measured response, discernment or judgment, gratification delay, self-protection, and modulated aggression. Acceleration is a sympathetic function. Some individuals cannot and do not accelerate, tending instead toward the inhibited, careful, slow, and deliberate; theirs is a more halting, avoidant, or ambivalent approach to things and people. The balancing braking mechanism is a parasympathetic function.

The two systems together create a balance, much as do opposing muscles in the arms or legs, where movement and stillness depend upon continuous tension in opposing muscular formations. The tension between the sympathetic and parasympathetic systems is therefore homeostatic. Primary couples, be they parent–child or adult lovers, enjoy a kind of perfect tension (the quiet-alert state) between sympathetic and parasympathetic nervous systems when both partners feel safe and secure.

The ANS plays a large role in love and romance. The in-person courtship process is entirely sympathetically driven, involving both far (vision and sound) and near senses (near vision, sound, smell, touch, taste). The come-hither, vitality aspects (energy, interest, excitement) of the sympathetic nervous system attract and draw two people together like magnets.[1] Later stages of love and romance also depend on the parasympathetic nervous system, which anchors us like a rock tied to a helium balloon and helps us recover from excitement and relax. The quiet-alert state allows us to be in repose with another person, relatively free of anxiety or boredom. Mutually shared parasympathetic states form the basis of long-term romantic relationships and are a hallmark of secure primary attachment relationships.

The ANS can drive us from being lovers to being predators if we feel we are in danger. When we see, hear, or smell danger, the amygdala fires and the ANS mans the battle stations, preparing us to fight, flee, or to be invaded, killed, or eaten (i.e., to disappear psychophysiologically). Fighting or fleeing occurs when the sympathetic branch triggers neurochemical and hormonal reactions that allow us to expend the necessary energy to move and act. If we are trapped and helpless in the face of overwhelming danger, the parasympathetic branch triggers neurochemical and hormonal reactions that allow us to conserve energy, shut down, and become still.

Once we are in predatory mode, we can say and do things that are threatening or warlike; our need for survival seems to overwhelm our need for love and connection. Of course, this goes both ways: Predatory partners also commonly feel like prey, and partners who feel like prey commonly act in a predatory manner. It is because the triggers are immediate and the psychobiological sequelae emerge faster than either can think that both partners can come to represent predation to one another.

THE LIMBIC–HYPOTHALAMIC–PITUITARY–ADRENAL AXIS

At the center of our adaptation to stress and threat is the LHPA. Part brain, part neuroendocrine, the LHPA not only controls reactions to stress but also regulates sexuality, digestion, energy expenditure, and storage, as well as our immune system and emotional states. It is

---

1. Now, with online dating and courtship, the rules are changing: attraction is not visual, at least not in real time; the fantasy of another person, at least on the physical level, is prolonged.

extremely relevant to our work as couple therapists because of its obvious impact on emotions and arousal and its less obvious impact on our physical health and longevity. The LHPA axis has a life-altering effect on our metabolic, immune, inflammation, and cardiovascular systems.

In response to signals of danger, the hypothalamus stimulates production of corticotropin releasing hormone (CRH), which regulates the production of stimulating neurotransmitters and hormones in the sympathetic nervous system, notably noradrenaline, dopamine, and adrenaline. CRH production leads to a stress countermeasure regulated by cortisol (the body's stress hormone) in the parasympathetic nervous system. The LHPA axis is supposed to be engaged on an as-needed basis because the materials it puts out when activated are "expensive": They produce wear and tear on all organs and systems. Cortisol, for example, which decreases inflammation and acts as a counterbalance to adrenaline, is also neurotoxic (kills neurons) and cytotoxic (kills cells). Its continuous presence in our blood and urine represents a less-than-healthy adaptive struggle to maintain homeostasis and points to chronic stress, threat, and a difficult life in general.

In cases of adult-onset PTSD, the LHPA axis remains highly activated due to intense fright (flashbacks), ongoing threat, and other associated problems such as sleep disorders and substance use. The brain, mind, and body just cannot absorb and metabolize the traumatic experience and heal (Briere, 2006). PTSD is sometimes referred to as big "T" trauma, embodying overwhelming episodes of extraordinary danger, threat, or loss. Our couples often come to the table with small "t" trauma, however—early relational trauma, or ambient trauma, so called because the ongoing threat is continuously "in the air," "in the environment," or "in the relationship" and cannot be limited to single or even multiple events (Lieberman et al., 2005; Lyons-Ruth et al., 2006; Schore, 2001; van der Kolk, 1987, 1989; van der Kolk et al., 1996). Relational trauma, too, activates the emergency response system.

The LHPA, which comprises both brain and neuroendocrine components, as noted, is discussed in greater detail below. The brain components include portions of the limbic circuit, most notably the amygdala and the hypothalamus. The neuroendocrine components include the pituitary and adrenal glands and the production of various stimulating and calming neurotransmitters and hormones that act to titrate and balance our arousal and readiness to act.

Emergency Response in the Limbic Brain

The limbic brain, sometimes called the limbic circuit or system, represents our sentient (feeling) heritage. It provides us with memory, appetites, emotions, and senses. It plays a vital regulatory, life-sustaining role that affects all bodily systems and organs, and it includes many structures, most of which reside in the medial (middle) part of the brain. Discussion here is limited to the areas relevant to threat response: the amygdala, hippocampus, cingulate gyrus, hypothalamus, and pituitary gland.

The Amygdala: Threat Scanner

The amygdala, one of our most primitive limbic structures, sits low, embedded in the temporal lobes. It develops around 50 days postconception, about the same time as most reptilian structures. Infamous for its role in mediating the responses of fear, threat, and aggression, the amygdala is a primary warning processor and plays a key role in emotional learning and activation of the sympathetic nervous system (e.g., through excitement and threat response). It continually sweeps the environment for danger in a "down-and-dirty" fashion, indiscriminately grabbing gross perceptual data and sending it upward to higher cortical areas for parsing and error correction. The upward processing of subcortical data requires a certain amount of time and resources, neither of which is in great supply during periods of distress or perceived threat. The amygdalae largely run the threat/response show between partners, which is not a matter of two whole brains at war but a case of two dueling amygdalae. When partners bombard one another with threatening words, phrases, movements, postures, facial expressions, and sounds, the amygdalae leave little or no time for error correction from higher cortical areas. When the amygdala rules, it changes the function and structure of the entire brain: The amygdala actually grows physically larger (hypertrophy) and the hippocampus shrinks (atrophy) (Brambilla et al., 2004; McEwen, 2001; Sala et al., 2004; Schore, 2002d).

The brain reorganizes for war, not love. A warring brain shuts down the production of new brain cells in the dentate gyrus (a minor part of the hippocampus and one of the only known structures that grows new brain cells) and keeps the HPA axis regularly engaged (and maintaining the aforementioned unhealthily high cortisol blood levels). In couples where both partners suffer from unresolved relational trauma, the threatening triggers may come so fast and often that each becomes exhausted and discouraged by intense, long-lasting arguments about misappraised intentions, behavioral and verbal sequences, time and place, and so on. Presentation of high-level threat reaction, misappraisal, disorganization, and disorientation is indicative of a hyperresponsive LHPA system. Hippocampal function is compromised, as is ventromedial prefrontal influence over amygdalar reactivity. The result is an unremitting interpersonal stress that further inhibits hippocampal memory and tracking capacities while galvanizing an already hypertrophic amygdala.

Because our lower limbic structures are primarily survival oriented, we say that they constitute the warring brain. However, they also are responsible for some of our most basic relational impulses. They move us toward others for safety, procreation, warmth, and connection; they drive our hunger, lust, needs, and wants. The amygdala is not simply the fear, threat, and aggression center for which it gets a bad rap; it is also involved in emotional memory and memory consolidation, face recognition, facial expression, gaze monitoring, food selecting, sexuality, and much more. Thus, in adult dyadic relationships, the tension between love and war begins, but does not end, with these survival structures.

The Hippocampus: Location, Location, Location

The hippocampus, which sits above the amygdala within the temporal lobes, is a key primitive structure in the loving–warring brain because of its role in short-term and episodic memory, its control of corticosteroid (antistress hormone) production, and its ability to encode and retrieve information about new surroundings (novelty) and directions. The right hippocampi of London taxi cab drivers, famous for their internal virtual maps that enable them to place things in spatial memory, were larger than those of people who did not drive for a living (Maguire et al., 1997). Hippocampal deficits include directional confusion and continual difficulty with short-term memory, semantic and autobiographical memory, and reconstruction of recent relationship events. Chronic stress commonly leads to hippocampal atrophy and malfunction.

The Cingulate Gyrus: Hurt and Pain

The cingulate gyrus lies atop the hippocampus, amygdala, and corpus callosum (the band of connective fibers that joins the two hemispheres of the brain). It plays an important role in our emotional response to physical and psychological pain, the regulation of aggression, and our ability to shift attention (Bush et al., 2000). It also plays a part in our holding on to, and letting go of, emotional pain, particularly anger and worry (Driessen et al., 2004; Nyberg et al., 2000; Saxena et al., 2004; West & Travers, 2008). Studies have found that the cingulate lights up in the human brain when feelings of rejection are provoked (Eisenberger et al., 2003). Partners who behave addictively, argumentatively, uncooperatively, oppositionally, or obsessively in holding onto past hurts may have cingulate-driven warring brains.

The Hypothalamus: Threat Central Command

The hypothalamus is the primary output gateway of the limbic circuit. It has many important reciprocal connections with the limbic, reptilian, and frontal cortices. Functionally, the hypothalamus affects both warring and loving aspects of the brain, influencing emotions, stress and threat reactions, sexual responsiveness, and emotional and physical hunger and satisfaction. It is the loving–warring brain's central station and is intimately involved in sympathetic (emergency) and parasympathetic (relaxing) activation. It also plays a large role in body temperature and sleep–wake regulation.

The Pituitary Gland: The Juicer

Both a brain structure (about the size of a pea) and a gland that secretes hormones (e.g., adrenocorticotropic hormone [ACTH], endorphins, oxytocin, and vasopressin), the pituitary plays both sides of the warring–loving fence. On the one hand, it sends out activating hormones that lead to war, as when, as part of a warring relay system, it signals the adrenal glands to secrete adrenaline for fighting and fleeing. On the other hand, as part of a loving relay system, the pituitary secretes endorphins, the body's natural opiates, and oxytocin, the human bonding hormone.

Emergency Response in the Neuroendocrine System

When we speak about the neuroendocrine system, we are referring to a combination of the nervous and endocrine systems and to the interactions that take place between them. The key players in these interactions are the hypothalamus, pituitary, adrenal glands, and their associated neurotransmitters and hormones. The neuroendocrine system is responsible for many bodily functions, including reproduction; the body's response to stress and infection; metabolic, electrolyte, and blood pressure regulation; maternal behavior; and mood. Too few or too many endogenous hormones and neurotransmitters can readily disrupt balance (McEwen, 2003). An overabundance or paucity of activating or inhibiting neurotransmitters in the brain can cause anxiety, depression, aggression, impulsivity, obsession, malaise, poor attention or memory, and so on. Likewise, an imbalance of hormones in the blood can cause systemic problems in the autoimmune, cardiovascular, metabolic, and inflammatory systems.

Neurotransmitters relay, modulate, and amplify brain cells. Hormones are chemicals that are released by cells and travel the bloodstream to other cells in the body. Neurotransmitters are "cheaper" to make because of their simplicity and recyclability. They are faster because their only job is to make connections between brain cells. A neurotransmitter can also be a hormone, the difference between them being the method and location of release—brain or bloodstream and neuron to neuron or adrenal gland to organ. For example, adrenaline and noradrenaline are neurotransmitters when released from one presynaptic nerve cell to act on a neighboring postsynaptic nerve cell, and they are hormones when released by the adrenal gland into the blood to act on the heart, lungs, or other organs.

Neurotransmitters cross the synapses, much as ships cross the sea, in little boats called *vesicles*, carrying messages from port to port, only they do so with lightning speed. The vesicle system is ecological because it recycles unused neurotransmitters. The ports in this analogy are dendrites and axon terminals, cell projections that send and receive information, respectively. Neurotransmitters are keys that must fit the locks, called *neuroreceptors*. The key–lock match determines whether action or inaction will occur. When a neurotransmitter is able to bind to a matching receptor, it either stimulates or inhibits an electrical response in the receiving neuron. Some neurotransmitters and hormones are exciting, whereas others are calming in their effect. Exciting neurotransmitters include glutamate, noradrenaline, and dopamine. Noradrenaline and dopamine double as hormones and along with adrenaline form a group of exciting hormones called *catecholamines*. Calming neurotransmitters include gamma-aminobutyric acid (GABA) and serotonin, and calming hormones include oxytocin (Birkmayer & Riederer, 1989; Collu, 1982a, 1982b; Müller & Nisticò, 1989; Törk et al., 1995).

Adrenaline: Action and Memory

Noradrenaline and adrenaline, two catecholamines essential to the sympathetic nervous system, facilitate attention, action, and memory formation. Though part of the fight–flight response, adrenaline is also responsible for come-hither mating responses such as pupil dilation. Adrenaline is necessary for memory formation: Just enough adrenaline is good, but too much can lead to traumatic flashbulb memory in the amygdala. *Flashbulb memory* is a memory created in great detail during a personally significant, emotional event; it has a photographic quality.

Adrenocorticotropic Hormone: Adrenal Messenger

ACTH is an essential hormone released from the pituitary gland to stimulate production of the stress hormone cortisol, which is produced in the cortex portion of the adrenal gland, and of the activating hormones noradrenaline and adrenaline, which are produced in the medulla section of the adrenal gland. ACTH is secreted from the anterior pituitary in response to CRH from the hypothalamus.

Corticotropin-Releasing Hormone: Key Regulator of Stress

Corticotropin-releasing hormone (or *factor*, as it is sometimes called) is the key regulator of the human stress response system. It is released by the hypothalamus and functions as both a hormone and a neurotransmitter; it stimulates the adrenal cortex to produce ACTH, cortisol, and other stress-related hormones, such as beta-endorphins. CRH also is inhibited by cortisol, making it part of a negative feedback loop that provides checks and balances for the entire stress response system. CRH is implicated in a host of autoimmune and psychiatric problems, including Cushing's disease, anorexia nervosa, depression, and anxiety disorders (Dube et al., 2009; Pesce, 2006; Chousos, 2009).

Cortisol: Anti-Inflammation

Glucocorticoids, including cortisol, produce a long-term, slow response to stress by raising blood glucose levels through the breakdown of fats and proteins; they also suppress the immune response and inhibit the inflammatory response. Often referred to as the "stress hormone," cortisol's role is actually *anti*stress: It responds to the action of adrenaline.

Noradrenaline: Attention and Stress

Noradrenaline (or norepinephrine) is related to the hormone adrenaline (or epinephrine). It is the main neurotransmitter for the somatic nervous system and can be considered the neurotransmitter counterpart of adrenaline, a kind of *pre*adrenaline. As with all catecholamines, too much or too little affects energy and attention and therefore love and war between partners.

Vagal Motor Complex

The vagal motor complex plays an enormous role in the self- and interactive regulatory process as a modulator of parasympathetic (also known as vagal) tone. As noted, the parasympathetic branch of the ANS is the relaxing counterpart to the excitable sympathetic branch. Vagal tone slows the breath and lowers heart rate and blood pressure, allowing us to recover from extreme states of arousal.

The vagus nerve is the 10th of 12 cranial nerves and the only one that starts in the brainstem and extends down through the neck, chest, and abdomen. It affects heart rate, visceral (stomach) activities (e.g., peristalsis), sweating, and speech. According to the polyvagal theory (Porges, 1998, 2001), the vagus nerve has two branches: one old—the dorsal (toward the back) vagal, also known as the dumb/reptilian vagal; and one new—the ventral (toward the abdomen) vagal, also known as the smart/social vagal.

Dumb Vagal System: Agent of War

As part of the body's threat response system, the dorsal vagal motor complex (dumb vagal) reacts immediately to stimuli that trigger our basic instinctual drive for survival. It sets off a sequence of neuroendocrine (hormonal) activities that, as a system, protect us from pain and life-threatening danger in a very different way than sympathetic activation does: The whole body shuts down. The dorsal vagal reaction may be an evolutionarily ancient adaptation to surviving major wounds; it is sometimes referred to as "blood-loss phobia." Any threat that is akin to being cut into, penetrated, invaded (physically or psychically), or eaten can induce a shift to an extreme energy-conserving state, which presents as depressed, collapsed, or dissociated. This reaction is extremely important for the therapist to track, as it can point to severe early abuse or trauma (Perry, 2001; Perry et al., 1995; Porges, 1995; Scaer, 2001).

The vasovagal response triggered by our dumb vagal system includes a dramatic drop in blood pressure and heart rate that can leave us feeling faint, nauseous, sweating, and pale. During this state of energy conservation withdrawal the brain uses minimal resources. Blood flow to the limbs is reduced, and the neuroendocrine system pumps beta endorphins—the body's natural opioids to reduce pain—into the blood. Humans in a dorsal vagal state may be subject to periods of syncope (fainting) or even cardiac arrest due to "overdosing" on endogenous opiates. Energy conservation withdrawal is like playing dead when confronted with an insurmountable and imminent predatory threat. Instead of marshaling the fight–flight–freeze (deer in the headlights) response, the "victim" experiences a telescoping down of awareness and perception as everything appears slow, humorless, flat, deadened, or hopeless. The dorsal vagal motor complex mediates shame, which helps explain why shame is such a deeply painful affect to endure and a state from which we are sometimes slow to recover.

Our vagal tone is often set during pre- and postnatal periods of early development. Genetic or congenital factors as well as environmental or relational factors (e.g., our early relationship with a primary caregiver) affect our vagal tone. Some individuals are more prone than others to vasovagal reactions. People who commonly go into parasympathetic energy conservation withdrawal can be termed underresponders (whereas those who tend to go into sympathetic fight–flight–freeze in reaction to threat are termed overresponders); their reaction to threat is biological, reflexive, primitive, and without any conscious choice.

A partner who begins to complain of stomach pain or nausea, sweating, blanching, and psychomotor slowing is signaling enormous distress that must be identified and addressed. The therapist can help the still well partner to regulate the collapsing partner by shifting their physicality and demeanor—having the noncollapsing partner move forward into close visual range of the other, with sustained gaze in close physical proximity, can help stimulate that partner upward. Any movement or muscle tension on the part of the collapsing partner can also help increase blood pressure.

Smart Vagal System: Agent of Love

Both the dumb and smart vagal tracks affect heart rate, blood pressure, and parasympathetic down-regulation. One is rather brutish and the other more refined. The dumb vagal, if in charge, will tend to throw the master switch and collapse the system, whereas the smart vagal is a more nuanced modulator of sympathetic arousal—relaxing the system just enough for it to continue functioning properly.

The smart vagal is a more recent evolutionary addition that is central to human interaction and relationship. It is a critical self-regulatory mechanism beacuse it is partly under the conscious control of higher cortical areas. A deep, diaphragmatic breath can engage the smart vagal system by sending a parasympathetic volley to the heart, thereby helping the entire body to calm down.

If the dumb vagal system is self-survival centered, then the smart vagal system is relationship-centered. Without the ventral (or smart) vagal system, we would be unable to calm ourselves down when frustrated or aroused by another person. Close physical proximity with another human being would be time-limited, at best, and romance would be short-lived.

The therapist can use the smart vagal system as an intervention for teaching self-regulation by coaching partners on diaphragmatic breathing, especially during periods when one partner is under stress. Other methods of self-regulation include the tracking of muscle tension and the conscious, repeated releasing of tension; moving closer to a threatening partner (contrary to impulse) for physical comfort or sustained eye contact; or pulling away from a threatening partner (impulse aligned) and momentarily dropping the gaze.

Memory Systems

Attachment and arousal are, in a very real sense, memory systems. Our earliest experiences are embedded in memory, and these memories are encoded differently depending upon our level of development and the type of experience. Just as the ANS and the LHPA, discussed above, are anticipatory systems, so is memory itself: We anticipate the future in relation to our experiences from the past.

Memory comes in different forms. There's short-, mid-, and long-term memory; there's memory we can experience in our body, through our senses, and in our mind; there's memory that operates below our awareness and memory that is totally conscious. There's memory we can recall with words, and memory where words fail us. These wordless, implicit memories are encoded in the right hemisphere and arise as experiences from the past recognized in the present or anticipated in the future.

Most of what occurs between partners in real time involves implicit, procedural memories which do not have a narrative and therefore cannot be recalled or explained away. In the presence of perceived threat, fast-acting procedural memory spares us from recollection or narratives—time-consuming conscious activities that, if the threat were real, could put our very lives in danger.

Explicit Forms of Memory

Explicit or declarative memory is overt, clear, unambiguous; it is what we can explain, declare, or demonstrate in some self-determined manner, and it engages language of some kind (verbal, written, or signed). Developmentally, explicit memory comes later than implicit memory, usually around the time of language and speech acquisition. Explicit forms of memory encoding and retrieval are commonly, though not unexceptionably, ascribed to the left hemisphere. We generalize here in the direction of explicit systems processed in the left brain.

The hippocampus is critical to explicit short-term memory capture (also known as working memory), without which we would be unable to form new memories or learn new things. Long-term memory formation depends upon hippocampal communication with the prefrontal cortex, much of which occurs during sleep when the brain maps and duplicates memory traces from the day's events (Axmacher et al., 2008). Chronic stress negatively affects hippocampal function, including the storage and retrieval of short-term memory.

Episodic memory, another type of explicit memory, allows us to recall events, times, places, and associated emotions in relation to our experience. Partners under chronic stress will demonstrate continuous problems with short-term memory and with the declarative recollections of events. Acute stress compromises hippocampal capacity to sequence and contextualize experience, thereby causing threatened partners to misreport threatening events. The left hemisphere largely confabulates retrospectively what the hippocampus failed to encode at the time. Thus, partners cannot possibly recall declaratively what occurred during emotionally dysregulating, mutually threatening events. Still, they will try to recruit each other to their way of organizing such events. The psychobiologically aware therapist will understand that such attempts are likely to result in the reenactment of trauma.

Explicit memory forms the content, or explicit aspect, of couple therapy—partners' explanations, descriptions, and complaints. But because chronic activation of threat systems (a brain continually at war) negatively affects hippocampal memory, highly dysregulated partners will frequently misreport events and misappraise one another's intentions, both current and past.

Implicit Forms of Memory

Implicit systems are nonverbal, nonconscious, and embedded in the body. Implicit memory is powerful because it directly involves primitive structures in the right hemisphere. The integrative processing power of the right brain enables it to perform complex data arrays simultaneously, whereas the left brain manages data in detailed sequences.

During infant development, the right brain builds general conceptual frameworks that it will later use "to choreograph the left brain's acquisition of fine discriminations" (Schutz, 2005, p. 13). Basic pre- and postnatal functions and experiences become wired into the system and encoded as procedural memory (below); they cannot be considered "thought" in the cognitive sense. This wiring becomes part of who we are and affects how we move toward and away from others on a moment-to-moment basis. Early encoded implicit systems become automatic, reflexive, and part of our personality structure (Tatkin, 2003a, 2004, 2007a, 2007d).

Implicit memory is nondeclarative and features prominently in the nonverbal aspect of couple therapy, which is procedural, associative, somatic, conditioned, and emotional. Understanding the implicit realm of memory, expression, and interaction is at the very core of the psychobiological approach to couple therapy.

Procedural Memory

Whenever we learn something or encounter novelty, we engage more of our brain to manage and organize the new experience, task, or information. Repetition allows the brain to free up resources by storing learned experience as procedural memory. This is how dancers learn routines, musicians learn songs, basketball players learn to slam-dunk, and so on. It also is how partners learn about each other, especially at the beginning of the relationship.

Early nonverbal experience is stored as procedural memory. Such experience is body based, involving both motor and sensory neuropathways. For example, curling one's hair around a finger during conversations may be a behavior resulting from a procedural memory of finger-curling a blanket as an infant. Similarly, an otherwise inexplicable aversion to the smell of a rose may be connected to a procedural, implicit memory that associates the smell with an emotionally negative experience.

Flashbulb Memory

Those of us who have adopted abused animals understand that startle reflexes never fully vanish. Abuse or trauma becomes stored as flashbulb memory in the amygdala. It is so called because of its immediate, evocative, and utterly preserved nature. Traumatized people fully reexperience, rather than remember, the trauma as if it were occurring in real time, in the form of "flashbacks" via all the senses—a startle, a panic attack, or a full psychotic break. To date, we have not found a way to "reset" the amygdala and clear its memory, although many try through drugs and alcohol.

Autobiographical Memory

Autobiographical memory involves a kind of subjective time travel. It is our memory of "me" in a place, within a context, with feelings, and with or without people and objects. Although autobiographical memory is largely ascribed to the right hemisphere, it generally includes a narrative with which to order and convey the memory (Daselaar et al., 2007; Driessen et al., 2004; Schore, 1994, 2002b, 2002c). The AAI (explained and illustrated in Part II of this book) examines declarative and autobiographical memory in relation to early childhood experience with primary caregivers. This very stressful process challenges neurobiological integration of two different memory systems: explicit left and implicit right.

Memory plays an enormous role in both love and war. The differences between explicit and implicit forms of memory are vital in the psychobiological approach. Couples come to therapy relying upon their narratives, and they expect the therapist to do the same. I hope by now we have convinced the reader that narratives most often contain confabulations and errors, and that the psychobiologically oriented couple therapist must capture implicit forms of memory in the wake of experiences that occur during the therapy session itself. In committing to working in this way, the couple therapist will likely find that the body always remembers—and the body never lies.

CONCLUSION

The ubiquitous, complex, and largely unconscious workings of anticipatory systems are the reason the psychobiological approach to couple therapy focuses on process rather than content. Anticipatory systems include the ANS, the LHPA axis, and implicit memory. The latter focuses our therapy on right-brain bodily experience as evoked during the therapy session.

Implicit, nonconscious systems drive love and war in adult romantic relationships. More than 90% of what goes on between partners at any given time is happening at a nonverbal, procedural, and somatic level (Briñol et al., 2006; Degonda et al., 2005; Habel et al., 2007; Perugini, 2005; Schott et al., 2005; Spiering et al., 2003; Turk-Browne et al., 2006; Winston et al., 2002). This is particularly true under stress because of the rapid activation of subcortically driven survival systems, which "hijack" parts of the brain responsible for full conscious awareness and contingent choice making. The right brain processes experience at lightning speeds using all the sense organs (with vision the most powerful) far more speedily than the left brain translates it into language and speech. Explicit, declarative appraisals and explanations are bound to be imprecise, at best, and completely confabulated, at worst. Thus partners under interpersonal stress rarely know what they are doing, or why (Tatkin, 2006b, 2009a, 2009c). By utilizing experiential techniques and experimentation to expose repeatable implicit patterns of turning toward and away, the psychobiologically oriented couple therapist can bypass verbal content—which is slower by nature and prone to confabulation and distortion—and intervene directly at the level of fast-acting neurobiological systems.

APPENDIX B

The Adult
Attachment Interview

Throughout this volume, both authors have described their use of selected Adult Attachment Interview protocol queries in conjunction with couple therapy. Here, we begin by briefly describing the interview protocol, together with its accompanying scoring and classification system. We then continue to describe some of its uses in studies of couples in interaction.

The Adult Attachment Interview (AAI) consists in a set of 20 questions with accompanying probes and was developed by Mary Main and her students in the Department of Psychology at the University of California, Berkeley (George, Kaplan, & Main, 1984, 1985, 1996). Following a brief introductory set of queries, the interviewer asks for an overall description of the interviewee's relationships with parents in childhood, and then asks for five adjectives to describe the relationship with the "mother" (or other person serving as the primary caregiver) during childhood. Once these adjectives are given, the person being interviewed is asked, adjective by adjective, for any memories they have of incidents or episodes which can show why they have chosen that particular adjective. Five adjectives and probes for memories or incidents showing why the adjective was chosen are then asked for the father. In later questions speakers are asked, for example, which parent they felt closer to in childhood, and how they think their early experiences with their parents may have affected the development of their personality. Other questions focus on experiences such as loss of loved persons through death and what the speaker sees as the after-effects of these experiences. Similar questions are asked regarding abuse.

Within this volume we have made occasional reference to an individual's attachment organization. As identified in the AAI, these estimates of a person's overall "state of mind with respect to attachment," as it is called, are made by trained coders working with verbatim AAI transcripts. A transcript is judged secure (formally, secure-autonomous) when a speaker is judged to be relatively clear, coherent, and collaborative. A widely-replicated finding regarding the AAI has been that speakers whose interview transcripts have been judged secure-autonomous are likely to be sensitive, responsive patients and to have young children whose attachments to them seem secure. There are also four ways of speaking about one's attachment history that indicate "insecure" states of mind. These are associated with less sensitive caregiving of children, and of course correspondingly, with child insecurity. The four insecure classifications assigned to the AAI include insecure-dismissing, insecure-preoccupied, insecure-unresolved with respect to past traumatic experiences, and cannot classify. These have been most recently detailed by Main, Hesse, and Goldwyn (2008).

As the work we have presented in this volume has already suggested, research has consistently shown that persons found secure on the AAI are likely to enjoy the most favorable interactions with—and to be the most supportive to—their romantic partners. For example, a study at the University of Minnesota showed that young people found secure on the AAI at age 19 had more favorable interactions with partners 1 or 2 years later than did young people who had been found insecure on the AAI (Roisman et al., 2001; see also Creasey, 2002). In another study, Judith Crowell and her colleagues at Stony Brook (Crowell et al., 2002), found that, as contrasted with members of insecure couples, members of secure couples were able to use one another as a secure base from which to explore their relationship, and—a critical element which we have emphasized throughout this volume—were able to turn to each other even during conflict. Similarly, Brouthillier and colleagues (2002) found that secure AAI classifications predicted proactive emotion regulation during marital conflict. In a more recent study conducted at Berkeley, women whose language usage on the AAI led to their classification as unresolved with respect to loss showed more anxiety and anger in interactions with their husbands than did other women, although on self-report inventories these same women did not note interactive difficulties (Busch, Cowan, & Cowan, 2008). Most recently—and perhaps especially pertinent to this volume—Crowell and colleagues (Crowell, Treboux, & Brock-meyer, 2009) reported that in a large-scale study of couples, adult children of divorce who had been found secure on the AAI were significantly less likely to have divorced their partners during the early years of marriage than were insecure participants.

REFERENCES

Agudo, J. (2009). Chronic stress. *Neuroendocrine Dysfunction, 500*(2), 4–7.

Ainsworth, M. D. (1978). *Patterns of attachment: A psychological study of the strange situation.* New York: Erlbaum.

Ainsworth, M. D. (1989). Attachments beyond infancy. *American Psychologist, 44*(4), 709–716.

Appelman, E. (2001). Temperament and dyadic contributions to affect regulation: Implications from developmental research for clinical practice. *Psychoanalytic Psychology, 18*(3), 534–559.

Atkinson, L., Leung, E., Goldberg, S., Benoit, D., Poulton, L., Myhal, N., et al. (2009). Attachment and selective attention: Disorganization and emotional stroop reaction time. *Development and Psychopathology, 21*(01), 99–126.

Axmacher, N., Haupt, S., Fernandez, G., Elger, C., & Fell, J. (2008). The role of sleep in declarative memory consolidation—direct evidence by intracranial eeg. *Cerebral Cortex, 18*(3), 500.

Baradon, T., & Steele, M. (2008). Integrating the AAI in the clinical process of psychoanalytic parent-infant psychotherapy in a case of relational trauma. In H. Steele and M. Steele (Eds.), *Clinical Applications of the Adult Attachment Interview* (2008), 195–212. New York: The Guilford Press.

Bartels, A., & Zeki, S. (2000). The neural basis of romantic love. *NeuroReport, 11*(17), 3829–3834.

Beauregard, M., Levesque, J., & Bourgouin, P. (2001). Neural correlates of conscious self-regulation of emotion. *Journal of Neuroscience, 21*(18), 165.

Bechara, A., Damasio, H., & Damasio, A. R. (2000). Emotion, decision making and the orbitofrontal cortex. *Cerebral Cortex, 10*(3), 295–307.

Beebe, B. (2003). Brief mother–infant treatment: Psychoanalytically informed video feedback. *Infant Mental Health Journal, 24*(1), 24–52.

Beebe, B., & Lachmann, F. (1998). Co-constructing inner and relational processes: Self- and mutual regulation in infant research and adult treatment. *Psychoanalytic Psychology, 15*(4), 480–516.

Beer, J. S., Heerey, E. A., Keltner, D., Scabini, D., & Knight, R. T. (2003). The regulatory function of self-conscious emotion: Insights from patients with orbitofrontal damage. *Journal of Personality and Social Psychology, 85*(4), 594–604.

Beneli, I. (1997). *Selective attention and arousal.* Retrieved January 16, 2006 from http://www.csun.edu/~vcpsy00h/students/arousal.htm.

Berlin, H. A., & Rolls, E. T. (2004). Time perception, impulsivity, emotionality, and personality in self-harming borderline personality disorder patients. *Journal of Personality Disorders, 18*(4), 358–378.

Berlin, L., Cassidy, J., & Shaver, P. (1999). *Handbook of attachment: Theory, research, and clinical applications.* New York: Guilford Press.

Birkmayer, W., & Riederer, P. (1989). *Understanding the neurotransmitters: Key to the workings of the brain.* Wein; New York: Springer–Verlag.

Blakemore, S., & Frith, U. (2004). How does the brain deal with the social world? *NeuroReport, 15*(1), 119.

Blanchard, D., & Blanchard, R. (2008). Defensive behaviors, fear, and anxiety. In D. Blanchard, R. Blanchard, G. Griebel & D. Nutt (Eds.), *Handbook of anxiety and fear* (pp. 63–79). Amsterdam, The Netherlands: Academic Press.

Bloom, A. (1968). *The republic of Plato.* New York: Basic Books.

Bollas, C. (1989) *The shadow of the object: Psychoanalysis of the unthought unknown.* New York: Columbia University Press.

Bollas, C. (2010). Manuscript of presentation in Japan, September 26, 2009. Revised for English publication. In press.

Bourne, V. J., & Todd, B. K. (2004). When left means right: An explanation of the left cradling bias in terms of right hemisphere specializations. *Developmental Science, 7*(1), 19–24.

Bouthillier, D., Julien, D., Dubé, M., Bélanger, I., & Harmelin, M. (2002). Predictive validity of adult attachment measures in relation to emotion regulation behaviors in marital interactions. *Journal of Adult Depression, 9*(4), 291–305.

Bowen, M. (1978). *Family therapy in clinical practice.* New York: Aronson.

Bowlby, J. (1969). *Attachment and loss.* New York: Basic Books.

Bowlby, J. (1979a). On knowing what you are not supposed to know and feeling what you are not supposed to feel. *Canadian Journal of Psychiatry, 24*, 403–408.

Bowlby, J. (1979b). *The making and breaking of affectional bonds.* London: Tavistock.

Bowlby, J. (1982). *Attachment.* New York: Basic Books.

Bowlby, J. (1988). *A secure base: Parent–child attachment and healthy human development.* New York: Basic Books.

Bowlby, J., & Ainsworth, M. D. S. (1952). *Maternal care and mental health.* Geneva: World Health Organization.

Brambilla, P., Soloff, P. H., Sala, M., Nicoletti, M. A., Keshavan, M. S., & Soares, J. C. (2004). Anatomical mri study of borderline personality disorder patients. *Psychiatry Research, 131*(2), 125–133.

Briñol, P., Petty, R. E., & Wheeler, S. C. (2006). Discrepancies between explicit and implicit self–concepts: Consequences for information processing. *Journal of Personality and Social Psychology, 91*(1), 154–170.

Bromberg, P.M. (1998). *Standing in the spaces: Essays on clinical process, trauma, and dissociation.* New Jersey: Analytic Press.

Bromberg, P.M. (2006). *Awakening the dreamer: Clinical journeys.* New Jersey: Analytic Press.

Buchholz, E. S., & Helbraun, E. (1999). A psychobiological developmental model for an "alonetime" need in infancy. *Bulletin of the Menninger Clinic, 63*(2), 143–158.

Burleson, M. H., Poehlmann, K. M., Hawkley, L. C., Ernst, J. M., Berntson, G. G., Malarkey, W. B., et al. (2003). Neuroendocrine and cardiovascular reactivity to stress in mid-aged and older women: Long-term temporal consistency of individual differences. *Psychophysiology, 40*(3), 358–369.

Busch, A. L., Cowan, P. A., & Cowan, C. P. (2008). Unresolved loss in the Adult Attachment Interview: Implications for marital and parenting relationships. *Development and Psychopathology, 20*(2), 717–735.

Bush, G., Luu, P., & Posner, M. I. (2000). Cognitive and emotional influences in anterior cingulate cortex. *Trends in Cognitive Sciences, 4*(6), 215–222.

Byng-Hall, J. (1999). Family and couple therapy: Toward greater security. In J. Cassidy & P. Shaver (Eds.), *Handbook of attachment: Theory, research, and clinical applications* (pp. 625–645). New York: Guilford Press.

Camille, N., Coricelli, G., Sallet, J., Pradat-Diehl, P., Duhamel, J.-R., & Sirigu, A. (2004). The involvement of the orbitofrontal cortex in the experience of regret. *Science, 304*(5674), 1167–1170.

Cappas, N. M., Andres-Hyman, R., & Davidson, L. (2005). What psychotherapists can begin to learn from neuroscience: Seven principles of a brain-based psychotherapy. *Psychotherapy: Theory, Research, Practice, Training, 42*(3), 374–383.

Carlson, E. A., Sampson, M. C., & Sroufe, L. A. (2003). Implications of attachment theory and research for developmental-behavioral pediatrics. *Journal of Developmental and Behavioral Pediatrics, 24*(5), 364–379.

Carlson, E. A., Sroufe, L. A., & Egeland, B. (2004). The construction of experience: A longitudinal study of representation and behavior. *Child Development, 75*(1), 66–83.

Carlson, M., Dragomir, C., Earls, F., Farrell, M., Macovei, O., Nystrom, P., et al. (1995). Effects of social deprivation on cortisol regulation in institutionalized Romanian infants. *Society of Neuroscience Abstracts, 21,* 524.

Cassidy, J. (2001). Truth, lies, and intimacy: An attachment perspective. *Attachment and Human Development, 3*(2), 121–155.

Cassidy, J., & Mohr, J. J. (2006). Unsolvable fear, trauma, and psychopathology: Theory, research, and clinical considerations related to disorganized attachment across the life span. *Clinical Psychology: Science and Practice, 8*(3), 275–298.

Cassidy, J., & Shaver, P. R. (1999). *Handbook of attachment: Theory, research, and clinical applications.* New York: Guilford Press.

Chamberlain, S. R., Menzies, L., Hampshire, A., Suckling, J., Fineberg, N. A., del Campo, N., et al. (2008). Orbitofrontal dysfunction in patients with obsessive–compulsive disorder and their unaffected relatives. *Science, 321*(5887), 421–422.

Charney, D. S. (2004). Psychobiological mechanisms of resilience and vulnerability: Implications for successful adaptation to extreme stress. *American Journal of Psychiatry, 161*(2), 195–216.

Chisholm, K., Carter, M. C., Ames, E. W., & Morison, S. J. (1995). Attachment security and indiscriminately friendly behavior in children adopted from Romanian orphanages. *Development and Psychopathology, 7*(2), 283–294.

Chrousos, G. (2009). Stress and disorders of the stress system. *Nature Reviews Endocrinology, 5*(7), 374–381.

Clulow, C. F. (2001). *Adult attachment and couple psychotherapy: The "secure base" in practice and research.* London: Brunner-Routledge.

Cohen, M. X., & Shaver, P. R. (2004). Avoidant attachment and hemispheric lateralisation of the processing of attachment–and emotion–related words. *Cognition & Emotion, 18*(6), 799–813.

Collu, R. (1982). *Brain neurotransmitters and hormones.* New York: Raven Press.

Collu, R. (1982). *Brain peptides and hormones.* New York: Raven Press.

Cottrell, E., & Seckl, J. (2009). Prenatal stress, glucocorticoids and the programming of adult disease. *Front. Behav. Neurosci, 3,* 19.

Cowan, P., & McHale, J. (2006). Coparenting in a family context: Emerging achievements, current dilemmas, and future directions. *New Directions for Child and Adolescent Development, 1996*(74), 93–106.

Cozolino, L. (2006). *The neuroscience of human relationships: Attachment and the developing social brain brain.* New York: Norton.

Crandell, L. E., Patrick, M. P., & Hobson, R. P. (2003). "Still-face" interactions between mothers with borderline personality disorder and their 2–month-old infants. *British Journal of Psychiatry, 183,* 239–247.

Creasey, G., (2002). Association between working models of attachment and conflict management behavior in romantic couples. *Journal of Counseling Psychology, 49*(3), 365–375.

Crittenden, P. (2008). Quality of attachment in the preschool years. *Development and Psychopathology, 4*(2), 209–241.

Crowell, J.A., Treboux, D., & Brockmeyer, S. (2009). Parental divorce and adult children's attachment representations and marital status. *Attachment and Human Development, 11*, 87–101.

Crowell, J. A., Treboux, D., Gao, Y., Fyffe, C., Pan, H. & Waters, E. (2002). Assessing secure-base behavior in adulthood: Development of a measure, links to adult attachment relations, and relations to couples' communication and reports of relationships. *Developmental Psychology, 38*, 679–693.

Damasio, A. R. (1994). *Descartes' error: Emotion, reason, and the human brain.* New York: Putnam.

Daselaar, S. M., Rice, H. J., Greenberg, D. L., Cabeza, R., LaBar, K. S., & Rubin, D. C. (2008). The spatiotemporal dynamics of autobiographical memory: Neural correlates of recall, emotional intensity, and reliving. *Cerebral Cortex, 18*(1), 217–229.

Davidson, R. (2008). Asymmetric brain function, affective style, and psychopathology: The role of early experience and plasticity. *Development and Psychopathology, 6*(04), 741–758.

Degonda, N., Mondadori, C. R. A., Bosshardt, S., Schmidt, C. F., Boesiger, P., Nitsch, R. M., et al. (2005). Implicit associative learning engages the hippocampus and interacts with explicit associative learning. *Neuron, 46*(3), 505–520.

del Amo, E. M., & Urtti, A. (2008). Current and future ophthalamic drug delivery systems: A shift to the posterior segment. *Drug Discovery Today, 13*(3–4), 135–143.

Demos, K. E., Kelley, W. M., Ryan, S. L., Davis, F. C., & Whalen, P. J. (2008). Human Amygdala sensitivity to the pupil size of others. *Cerebral Cortex, 18*(12), 2729–2734.

Dicks, H. V. (1967). *Marital tension: Clinical studies toward a psychological theory of interaction.* London: Routledge & Kegan Paul.

Doi, T. (1971/2002). *The anatomy of dependence.* Tokyo: Kodansha International.

Doidge, N. (2007). *The brain that changes itself.* New York: Viking Press.

Driessen, M., Beblo, T., Mertens, M., Piefke, M., Rullkoetter, N., Silva–Saavedra, A., et al. (2004). Posttraumatic stress disorder and fmri activation patterns of traumatic memory in patients with borderline personality disorder. *Biological Psychiatry, 55*(6), 603–611.

Dube, S., Fairweather, D., Pearson, W., Felitti, V., Anda, R., & Croft, J. (2009). Cumulative childhood stress and autoimmune diseases in adults. *Psychosomatic Medicine, 71*(2), 243.

Eagle, D. M., Baunez, C., Hutcheson, D. M., Lehmann, O., Shah, A. P.,

& Robbins, T. W. (2008). Stop-signal reaction-time task performance: Role of prefrontal cortex and subthalamic nucleus. *Cerebral Cortex, 18*(1), 178.

Eisenberger, N. I., Lieberman, M. D., & Williams, K. D. (2003). Does rejection hurt? An fmri study of social exclusion. *Science, 302*(5643), 290–292.

Ekman, P. (1973). *Darwin and facial expression: A century of research in review.* New York: Academic Press.

Ekman, P. (1982). *Emotion in the human face* (2nd ed.). New York: Cambridge University Press.

Ekman, P. (1993). Facial expression and emotion. *American Psychologist, 48*(4), 384–392.

Ekman, P., & Friesen, W. V. (1984). *Unmasking the face: A guide to recognizing emotions from facial clues.* Palo Alto, CA: Consulting Psychologists Press.

Ekman, P., & Rosenberg, E. L. (2005). *What the face reveals: Basic and applied studies of spontaneous expression using the facial action coding system (FACS)* (2nd ed.). New York: Oxford University Press.

Fairbairn, W. R. D. (1972). *Psychoanalytic studies of the personality.* London: Routledge & Kegan Paul.

Ferrando, S., & Okoli, U. (2009). Personality disorders: Understanding and managing the difficult patient in neurology practice. *Seminars in Neurology, 29*(3), 266–271.

Feeney, B. C. (2007). The dependency paradox in close relationships: Accepting dependence promotes independence. *Journal of Personality and Social Psychology, 92,* 268–285.

Fisher, H. (2004). *Why we love: The nature and chemistry of romantic love.* New York: Holt.

Fonagy, P. (2001). *Attachment theory and psychoanalysis.* London: Other Press.

Fonagy, P., & Target, M. (1997). Attachment and reflective function: Their role in self-organization. *Development and Psychopathology, 9,* 679–700.

Fosha, D. (2000). *The transforming power of affect: A model of accelerated change.* New York: Basic Books.

Fosha, D. (2003). Dyadic regulation and experiential work with emotion and relatedness in trauma and disorganized attachment. In M. F. Solomon & D. J. Siegel (Eds.), *Healing trauma: Attachment, mind, body, and brain* (pp. 221–281). New York: Norton.

Fosha, D., Siegel, D. J., & Solomon, M. F. (Eds.). (2009). *The healing power of emotion: Affective neuroscience, development, and clinical practice.* New York: Norton.

Fraley, R. C., & Waller, N. G. (1998). Adult attachment patterns: A test of the typological model. In J. A. Simpson & W. S. Rholes (Eds.), *Attachment theory and close relationships* (pp. 77–114). New York: Guilford Press.

Frick, J. E., & Adamson, L. B. (2003). One still face, many visions. *Infancy, 4*(4), 499–501.

Fries, A., & Pollak, S. (2007). Emotion processing and the developing brain. In D. Coch, G. Dawson, & K. W. Fischer (Eds.), *Human behavior, learning, and the developing brain: Typical development* (pp. 329–360). New York, NY: Guilford Press.

Galvan, A., Hare, T. A., Parra, C. E., Penn, J., Voss, H., Glover, G., et al. (2006). Earlier development of the accumbens relative to orbitofrontal cortex might underlie risk-taking behavior in adolescents. *Journal of Neuroscience, 26*(25), 6885.

George, C., Kaplan, N., & Main, M. (1984/1985/1996). *The Attachment Interview for Adults*. Unpublished manuscript, Berkeley, CA.

Gillath, O., Selcuk, E., & Shaver, P. R. (2008). Moving toward a secure attachment style: Can repeated security priming help? *Social and Personality Psychology Compass, 2*(4), 1651–1666.

Goleman, D. (1996). *Emotional intelligence: Why it can matter more than IQ*. London: Bloomsbury.

Gottman, J. (1995) *Why marriages succeed or fail . . . and how you can make yours last*. New York: Simon & Schuster.

Gottman, J. (1999). *The marriage clinic: A scientifically based marital therapy*. New York: Norton.

Gottman, J. & Silver, N. (2004). *Seven principles for making marriage work*. New York: Crown Publishers.

Gunnar, M. R., Morison, S. J., Chisholm, K. I. M., & Schuder, M. (2001). Salivary cortisol levels in children adopted from Romanian orphanages. *Development and Psychopathology, 13*(3), 611–628.

Habel, U., Windischberger, C., Derntl, B., Robinson, S., Kryspin–Exner, I., Gur, R. C., et al. (2007). Amygdala activation and facial expressions: Explicit emotion discrimination versus implicit emotion processing. *Neuropsychologia, 45*(10), 2369–2377.

Haley, D. W., & Stansbury, K. (2003). Infant stress and parent responsiveness: Regulation of physiology and behavior during still-face and reunion. *Child Development, 74*(5), 1534–1546.

Haradon, G., Bascom, B., Dragomir, C., & Scripcaru, V. (1994). Sensory functions of institutionalized Romanian infants: A pilot study. *Occupational Therapy International, 1*, 250–260.

Harlow, H. F., & Mears, C. (1979). *The human model: Primate perspectives*. London: Winston.

Harlow, H. F., & Woolsey, C. N. (1958). *Biological and biochemical bases of behavior*. Madison: University of Wisconsin Press.

Hazan, C., & Shaver, P. (1987). Romantic love conceptualized as an attachment process. *Journal of Personality and Social Psychology, 52*(3), 511–524.

Hendrix, H. (1986). *Getting the love you want*. New York: Holt.

Henry, J. P. (1997). Psychological and physiological responses to stress: The right hemisphere and the hypothalamo–pituitary–adrenal axis, an inquiry into problems of human bonding. *Acta Physiological Scandinavia Supplement, 640,* 10–25.

Hesse, E. (1999). The Adult Attachment Interview. In Cassidy & Shaver (Eds.), *Handbook of attachment: Theory, research, and clinical applications* (pp. 395–433). New York: Guilford Press.

Hesse, E., & Main, M. (2006). Frightened, threatening, and dissociative parental behavior in low-risk samples: Description, discussion, and interpretations. *Development and Psychopathology, 18*(2), 309–343.

Hill, A. L., & Braungart-Rieker, J. M. (2002). Four-month attentional regulation and its prediction of three-year compliance. *Infancy, 3*(2), 261–273.

Hofer, M. A. (2005). The psychobiology of early attachment. *Clinical Neuroscience Research, 4*(5–6), 291–300.

Hofer, M. A. (2006). Psychobiological roots of early attachment. *Current Directions in Psychological Science, 15*(2), 84–88.

Holmes, J. (2004). Disorganized attachment and borderline personality disorder: A clinical perspective. *Attachment and Human Development, 6*(2), 181–190.

Horowitz, J., Logsdon, M., & Anderson, J. (2005). Measurement of maternal–infant interaction. *Journal of the American Psychiatric Nurses Association, 11*(3), 164.

Iacobini, M. (2008). *The new science of how we connect with others.* New York: Farrar, Straus and Giroux.

Iacoboni, M., Koski, L. M., Brass, M., Bekkering, H., Woods, R. P., Dubeau, M.-C., et al. (2001). Reafferent copies of imitated actions in the right superior temporal cortex. *Proceedings of the National Academy of Sciences, 98*(24), 13995–13999.

Johnson, S. M. (2003). Introduction to attachment: A therapist's guide to primary relationships and their renewal. In S. M. Johnson & V. E. Whiffen (Eds.), *Attachment processes in couple and family therapy* (pp. 5–17). New York: Gilford Press.

Johnson, S. M. (2004). *The practice of emotionally focused couple therapy: Creating connection* (2nd ed.). New York, NY: Brunner-Routledge.

Johnson, S. M. (2007). A new era for couple therapy: Theory, research, and practice in concert. *Journal of Systemic Therapies, 26*(4), 5–16.

Johnson, S. M. (2008a). Emotionally focused couple therapy. In *Clinical handbook of couple therapy* (pp. 107–XXX). New York: Guilford Press.

Johnson, S. M. (2008b). *Hold me tight: Seven conversations for a lifetime of love.* New York: Little, Brown.

Johnson, S., & Denton, W. (2002). Emotionally focused couple therapy: Creativity connection. *Clinical Handbook of Couple Therapy,* 221–250.

Johnson, S. M., Makinen, J., & Millikin, J. (2001). Attachment injuries in couples relationships: A new perspective on impasses in couples therapy. *Journal of Marital and Family Therapy, 27,* 145–156.

Kabat-Zinn, J. (1994) *Wherever you go, there you are: Mindfulness meditation in everyday life.* New York: Hyperion.

Kahn, M. (1963). Cumulative trauma. *Psychoanalytic Study of the Child, 18,* 286–306.

Khan, R. M., & Sobel, N. (2004). Neural processing at the speed of smell. *Neuron, 44*(5), 744–747.

Kaler, S. R., & Freeman, B. J. (1994). Analysis of environmental deprivation: Cognitive and social development in Romanian orphans. *Journal of Child Psychology and Psychiatry, 35*(4), 769–781.

Kawashima, R., Sugiura, M., Kato, T., Nakamura, A., Hatano, K., Ito, K., et al. (1999). The human amygdala plays an important role in gaze monitoring: A PET study. *Brain, 122*(4), 779.

Kay, R. (2003). "The Chameleon Chronicles: From Background to Foreground," Natura Artis Magistra: (Un)conscious Animals as Teachers of STDP. Proceedings of the Conference (pp. 6–18). Amsterdam: VKDP.

Kochanska, G., & Coy, K. C. (2002). Child emotionality and maternal responsiveness as predictors of reunion behaviors in the strange situation: Links mediated and unmediated by separation distress. *Child Development, 73*(1), 228–240.

Kohut, H. (1984). *How does analysis cure?* Chicago: University of Chicago Press.

Kohut, H. (1971). *The analysis of the self: A systematic approach to the psychoanalytic treatment of narcissistic personality disorders.* New York: International Universities Press.

Kohut, H. (1977). *The restoration of the self.* New York: International Universities Press.

Kornfield, J. (2009) *Wise heart: A guide to the universal teachings of Buddhist psychology.* New York: Hyperion.

Krolak-Salmon, P., Hénaff, M.-A., Isnard, J., Tallon-Baudry, C., Guénot, M., Vighetto, A., et al. (2003). An attention modulated response to disgust in human ventral anterior insula. *Annals of Neurology, 53*(4), 446–453.

Kunert, H. J., Druecke, H. W., Sass, H., & Herpertz, S. C. (2003). Frontal lobe dysfunctions in borderline personality disorder? Neuropsychological findings. *Journal of Personality Disorders, 17*(6), 497–509.

Larsen, J. K., Brand, N., Bermond, B., & Hijman, R. (2003). Cognitive and emotional characteristics of alexithymia: A review of neurobiological studies. *Journal of Psychosomatic Research, 54*(6), 533–541.

Lasch, C. (1977). *Haven in a heartless world.* New York: Basic Books.

Lasch, C. (1979). *Culture of narcissism.* New York: W. W. Norton & Company.

LeDoux, J. E. (1998). *The emotional brain: The mysterious underpinnings of emotional life*. New York: Simon & Schuster.

Lichtenberg, J. D. (1991). What is a selfobject? *Psychoanalytic Dialogues, 1*(4), 455–479.

Lyons-Ruth, K. (2003). The two-person construction of defenses: Disorganized attachment strategies, unintegrated mental states, and hostile/helpless relational processes. *Journal of Infant, Child, and Adolescent Psychotherapy, 2,* 105.

Lyons-Ruth, K., & Spielman, E. (2004). Disorganized infant attachment strategies and helpless-fearful profiles of parenting: Integrating attachment research with clinical intervention. *Infant Mental Health Journal, 25*(4), 318–335.

Maguire, E. A., Frackowiak, R. S. J., & Frith, C. D. (1997). Recalling routes around london: Activation of the right hippocampus in taxi drivers. *The Journal of Neuroscience, 17*(18), 7103–7110.

Mahler, M. S. (1968). *On human symbiosis and the vicissitudes of individuation*. New York: International Universities Press.

Mahler, M. S. (1974). Symbiosis and individuation: The psychological birth of the human infant. *Psychoanalytic Study of the Child, 29,* 89–106.

Mahler, M. S. (1979). *Separation–individuation*. New York: Aronson.

Mahler, M. S., Bergman, A., & Pine, F. (1975). *The psychological birth of the human infant: Symbiosis and individuation*. New York: Basic Books.

Mahler, M. S., Pine, F., & Bergman, A. (2000). *The psychological birth of the human infant: Symbiosis and individuation*. New York: Basic Books.

Main, M. (2000). The organized categories of infant, child, and adult attachment. *Journal of the American Psychoanalytic Association, 48,* 1055–1096.

Main, M. (2002). "Attachment: From early childhood through the lifespan." University of California, Los Angeles, First Annual Attachment Conference.

Main, M., Goldwyn, R., & Hesse, E. (2003). Adult attachment scoring and classification systems (Version no. 7.2) (Unpublished manuscript). Department of Psychology, University of California, Berkeley, CA.

Main, M., Hesse, E., & Goldwyn, R. (2008). Individual differences in language usage in recounting attachment history. In H. Steele and M. Steele (Eds.), *Clinical Applications of the Adult Attachment Interview* (2008). New York: The Guilford Press.

Main, M., & Hesse, E. (1990). Parent's unresolved traumatic experiences are related to infant disorganized attachment status: Is frightened and/or frightening parent behavior the linking mechanism? In M. Greenberg, D. Cicchetti, & E. Cummings (Eds.), *Attachment during the preschool years: Theory, research, and intervention* (pp. 161–182). Chicago: University of Chicago Press.

Main, M., Kaplan, N., & Cassidy, J. (1985). Security in infancy, childhood, and adulthood: A move to the level of representation. *Monographs of the Society for Research in Child Development, 50*(1/2), 66–104.

Main, M., & Solomon, J. (1986). Discovery of a new, insecure–disorganized/disoriented attachment pattern. In T. Brazelton & M. Yogman (Eds.), *Affective development in infancy* (pp. 95–124). Norwood, NJ: Ablex.

Main, M., & Solomon, J. (1993). Procedures for identifying infants as disorganized/disoriented during the ainsworth strange situation. In D. L. Greenberg, D. Cicchetti, & E. Cummings (Eds.), *Attachment in the preschool years: Theory, research, and intervention* (pp. 121–160). Chicago, Il: University of Chicago Press.

Main, M., & Weston, D. (1981). The quality of the toddler's relationship to mother and to father: Related to conflict behavior and the readiness to establish new relationships. *Child Development, 52*(3), 932–940.

Makinen, J., & Johnson, S. M. (2006). Resolving attachment injuries in couples using EFT: Steps towards forgiveness and reconciliation. *Journal of Consulting and Clinical Psychology, 74*, 1055–1064.

Manning, J. T., Trivers, R. L., Thorhill, R., Singh, D., Denman, J., Eklo, M. H., et al. (1997). Ear asymmetry and left-side cradling. *Evolution and Human Behavior, 18*(5), 327–340.

Masterson, J. F. (1981). *The narcissistic and borderline disorders: An integrated developmental approach.* Larchmont, NY: Brunner/Mazel.

Maville, J., Bowen, J., & Benham, G. (2008). Effect of healing touch on stress perception and biological correlates. *Holistic Nursing Practice, 22*(2), 103.

McCullough Vaillant, L. (1997). *Changing character.* New York: Basic Books.

McEwen, B. (2003). Mood disorders and allostatic load. *Biological Psychiatry, 54*(3), 200–207.

McEwen, B. S. (2000). The neurobiology of stress: From serendipity to clinical relevance. *Brain Research, 886*(1–2), 172–189.

McEwen, B. S. (2001). Plasticity of the hippocampus: Adaptation to chronic stress and allostatic load. *Annual New York Academy of Sciences, 933*, 265–277.

McGoldrick, M., Gerson, R., & Petry, S. (1999). *Genograms: Assessment and intervention* (3rd ed.). New York: Norton.

Minzenberg, M., Poole, J., & Vinogradov, S. (2008). A neurocognitive model of borderline personality disorder: Effects of childhood sexual abuse and relationship to adult social attachment disturbance. *Development and Psychopathology, 20*(1), 341–368.

Montirosso, R., Borgatti, R., Premoli, B., Cozzi, P., & Tronick, E. Z. (2007). Emotional regulation in early infancy: Evidence from expressive gestures during the still–face procedure. *Giornale italiano di psicologia, 1*(1), 193–222.

Montirosso, R., Premoli, B., Cozzi, P., Borgatti, R., & Tronick, E. (2007). Regolazione emozionale in bambini tra i 3 ei 6 mesi: Applicazione del paradigma still–face. *Giornale italiano di psicologia, 1*(1), 193–222.

Moriguchi, Y., Ohnishi, T., Lane, R., Maeda, M., Mori, T., Nemoto, K., et al. (2006). Impaired self–awareness and theory of mind: An fmri study of mentalizing in alexithymia. *Neuroimage, 32*(3), 1472–1482.

Morris, J. S., Öhman, A., & Dolan, R. J. (1998). Conscious and unconscious emotional learning in the human amygdala. *Nature, 393*(6684), 467–470.

Morris, J. S., Ohman, A., & Dolan, R. J. (1999). A subcortical pathway to the right amygdala mediating "unseen" fear. *PNAS, 96*(4), 1680–1685.

Müller, E. E., & Nisticò, G. (1989). *Brain messengers and the pituitary*. San Diego, CA: Academic Press.

Narvaez, D. (2008). Triune ethics: The neurobiological roots of our multiple moralities. *New Ideas in Psychology, 26*(1), 95–119.

Neborsky, R., & Solomon, M. F. (2001). Attachment bonds and intimacy: Can the primary imprint of love change? In M. F. Solomon, R. J. Neborsky, & L. McCullough (Eds.), *Short-term therapy for long-term change* (pp. 155–185). New York: Norton.

Nelson, E. E., & Panksepp, J. (1998). Brain substrates of infant–mother attachment: Contributions of opioids, oxytocin, and norepinephrine. *Neuroscience and Biobehavioral Reviews, 22*(3), 437–452.

Nicholls, M., Clode, D., Wood, S., & Wood, A. (1999). Laterality of expression in portraiture: Putting your best cheek forward. *Proceedings of the Royal Society of London-B-Biological Sciences, 266*(1428), 1517–1522.

Nyberg, L., Habib, R., & Herlitz, A. (2000). Brain activation during episodic memory retrieval: Sex differences. *Acta Psychologica, 105*(2–3), 181–194.

Oberndorf, C. P. (1938). Psychoanalysis of married couples. *Psychoanalytic Review, 25*, 435–475.

Ogden, P., & Minton, K. (2000). Sensorimotor psychotherapy: One method for processing traumatic memory. *Traumatology, 6*(3), 149–173.

Ogden, P., Minton, K., & Pain, C. (XXXX). *Trauma and the body: A sensorimotor approach to psychotherapy*. New York: W. W. Norton & Company.

Oitzl, M., Champagne, D., van der Veen, R., & de Kloet, E. (2009). Brain development under stress: Hypotheses of glucocorticoid actions revisited. *Neuroscience and Biobehavioral Reviews.*

Oliver, M. (1998). *West wind: Poems and prose poems.* New York: Mariner Books.

Panksepp, J. (2005). *Affective Neuroscience: The Foundations of Human and Animal Emotions.* Oxford: Oxford University Press.

Pardon, M., & Marsden, C. (2008). The long–term impact of stress on brain function: From adaptation to mental diseases. *Neuroscience and Biobehavioral Reviews, 32*(6), 1071–1072.

Perry, B. D. (2001). Violence and childhood: How persisting fear can alter the developing child's brain. In D. Schetky & E. Benedek (Eds.), *Textbook of child and adolescent forensic psychiatry* (pp. 221–238). Washington DC: American Psychiatric Press.

Perry, B. D., Pollard, R. A., Blakley, T. L., Baker, W. L., & Vigilante, D. (1995). Childhood trauma, the neurobiology of adaptation and use–dependent development of the brain: How states become traits. *Infant Mental Health Journal, 16* (4), 271–291.

Perry, C. T., Oum, P., & Gray, S. H. (2007). The body remembers: Somatic symptoms in traumatized Khmer. *Journal of the American Academy of Psychoanalysis and Dynamic Psychiatry, 35*(1), 77–84.

Perugini, M. (2005). Predictive models of implicit and explicit attitudes. *British Journal of Social Psychology, 44*(1), 29–45.

Pesce, M. (2006). Stress and autoimmune thyroid diseases. *Neuroimmunomodulation, 13*, 309–317.

Piaget, J. (1999). *The moral judgment of the child.* London: Routledge.

Piaget, J. (2001). *The psychology of intelligence.* London: Routledge.

Porges, S. W. (1995). Orienting in a defensive world—Mammalian modifications of our evolutionary heritage—A polyvagal theory. *Psychophysiology, 32*(4), 301–318.

Porges, S. W. (1998). Love: An emergent property of the mammalian autonomic nervous system. *Psychoneuroendocrinology, 23*(8), 837–861.

Porges, S. W. (2001). The polyvagal theory: Phylogenetic substrates of a social nervous system. *International Journal of Psychophysiology, 42*(2), 123–146.

Porges, S. W. (2003). The polyvagal theory: Phylogenetic contributions to social behavior. *Physiology and Behavior, 79*(3), 503–513.

Prescott, J. W. (1975). Body pleasure and the origins of violence. *The Futurist, 9*(2), 64–74.

Roisman, G. I., Madsen, S. D., Henninghausen, K. H., Stroufe, L. A., & Collins, W. A. (2001). The coherence of dyadic behavior across parent–child and romantic relationships as mediated by the internalized representation of experience. *Attachment and Human Development, 3*, 156–172.

Rolls, E. T., McCabe, C., & Redoute, J. (2007). Expected value, reward outcome, and temporal difference error representations in a probabilistic decision task. *Cerebral Cortex, 18*(3), 652–663.

Rothschild, B. (2003). *The body remembers casebook: Unifying methods and models in the treatment of trauma and PTSD.* New York: Norton.

Sala, M., Perez, J., Soloff, P., Ucelli di Nemi, S., Caverzasi, E., Soares, J. C., et al. (2004). Stress and hippocampal abnormalities in psychiatric disorders. *European Neuropsychopharmacology, 14*(5), 393–405.

Saxena, S., Brody, A. L., Maidment, K. M., Smith, E. C., Zohrabi, N., Katz, E., et al. (2004). Cerebral glucose metabolism in obsessive-compulsive hoarding. *American Journal of Psychiatry, 161*(6), 1038–1048.

Scaer, R. C. (2001). The neurophysiology of dissociation and chronic disease. *Applied Psychophysiology and Biofeedback, 26*(1), 73–91.

Schacter, D. L. (2000). *Memory, brain, and belief.* Cambridge, MA.: Harvard University Press.

Schoenbaum, G. (2004). Affect, action, and ambiguity and the amygdala–orbitofrontal circuit. Focus on "combined unilateral lesions of the amygdala and orbital prefrontal cortex impair affective processing in rhesus monkeys." *Journal of Neurophysiology, 91*(5), 1938–1939.

Schore, A. N. (1994). *Affect regulation and the origin of the self: The neurobiology of emotional development.* Hillsdale, NJ: Erlbaum.

Schore, A. N. (1997). Early organization of the nonlinear right brain and development of a predisposition to psychiatric disorders. *Development and Psychopathology, 9*, 595–631.

Schore, A. N. (2000). Attachment and the regulation of the right brain. *Attachment and Human Development 1*(2), 23–47.

Schore, A. N. (2001a). Effects of a secure attachment relationship on right brain development, affect regulation, and infant mental health. *Infant Mental Health Journal, 22*(1–2), 7–66.

Schore, A. N. (2001b). The effects of early relational trauma on right brain development, affect regulation, and infant mental health. *Infant Mental Health Journal, 22*(1–2), 201–269.

Schore, A. N. (2001c). Minds in the making: Attachment, The self-organizing brain, and developmentally-oriented psychoanalytic psychotherapy. *British Journal of Psychotherapy, 17*(3), 299–328.

Schore, A. N. (2002a). Advances in neuropsychoanalysis, attachment theory, and trauma research: Implications for self-psychology [Research article]. *Psychoanalytic Inquiry, 22*(3), 433–484.

Schore, A. N. (2002b). *Affect dysregulation and disorders of the self.* New York: Norton.

Schore, A. N. (2002c). *Affect regulation and repair of the self.* New York: Norton.

Schore, A. N. (2002d). Dysregulation of the right brain: A fundamental mechanism of traumatic attachment and the psychopathogenesis of posttraumatic stress disorder. *Australian and New Zealand Journal of Psychiatry, 36*(1), 9–30.

Schore, A. N. (2005). Attachment trauma and the developing right brain: Origins of pathological dissociation. In A. N. Schore (Ed.), *Attachment trauma and the developing right brain* (pp. 1–36). New York: Norton.

Schott, B. H., Henson, R. N., Richardson–Klavehn, A., Becker, C., Thoma, V., Heinze, H. J., et al. (2005). Redefining implicit and explicit memory: The functional neuroanatomy of priming, remembering, and control of retrieval. *Proceedings of the National Academy of Sciences, 102*(4), 1257.

Schutz, L. E. (2005). Broad–perspective perceptual disorder of the right hemisphere. *Neuropsychology Review, 15*(1), 11–27.

Shaver, P. R., Belsky, J., & Brennan, K. A. (2000). The Adult Attachment Interview and self-reports of romantic attachment: Associations across domains and methods. *Personal Relationships, 7*(1), 25–43.

Shibata, K., Yamagishi, N., Goda, N., Yoshioka, T., Yamashita, O., Sato, M.-A., et al. (2008). The effects of feature attention on prestimulus cortical activity in the human visual system. *Cerebral Cortex, 18*(7), 1664–1675.

Siegal, M., & Varley, R. (2002). Neural systems involved in "theory of mind." *Nature Reviews Neuroscience, 3*(6), 463–471.

Siegel, D. J. (1999). *The developing mind: Toward a neurobiology of interpersonal experience.* New York: Guilford Press.

Siegel, D. J. (2006). An interpersonal neurobiology approach to psychotherapy: awareness, mirror neurons, and neural plasticity in the development of well-being. *Psychiatric Annals, 36*(4), 248.

Siegel, D. J. (2010a). *Mindsight: The new science of personal transformation.* New York: Bantam.

Siegel, D. (2010b). *The mindful therapist: A clinician's guide to mindsight and neural integration.* New York: W. W. Norton.

Siegel, D. J., & Hartzell, M. (2003). *Parenting from the inside out: How a deeper self-understanding can help you raise children who thrive.* New York: Tarcher/Putnam.

Sieratzki, J. S., & Woll, B. (1996). Why do mothers cradle babies on their left? *Lancet, 347*(9017), 1746–1748.

Slade, A. (2000). The development and organization of attachment: Implications for psychoanalysis. *Journal of the American Psychoanalytic Association, 48*(4), 1147–1174.

Soloff, P. H., Meltzer, C. C., Becker, C., Greer, P. J., Kelly, T. M., & Constantine, D. (2003). Impulsivity and prefrontal hypometabolism in borderline personality disorder. *Psychiatry Research, 123*(3), 153–163.

Solomon, M. F. (1989). *Narcissism and intimacy: Love and marriage in an age of confusion.* New York: Norton.

Solomon, M.F. (1994). *Lean on Me: The power of positive dependency in intimate relationships.* New York: Simon & Schuster.

Solomon, M. F. (2009). "Emotion in romantic partners: Intimacy found, intimacy lost, intimacy reclaimed In D. Fosha, D. J. Siegel, M. F. & Solomon (Eds.), *The healing power of emotion: Affective neuroscience, development, and clinical practice.* New York: Norton.

Spiering, M., Everaerd, W., & Janssen, E. (2003). Priming the sexual system: Implicit versus explicit activation. *The Journal of Sex Research, 40*(2), 134–146.

Sroufe, L. A. (1985). Attachment classification from the perspective of infant–caregiver relationships and infant temperament. *Child Development, 56*(1), 1–14.

Sroufe, L. A. (2003). Attachment categories as reflections of multiple dimensions: Comment on Fraley and Spieker (2003). *Developmental Psychology, 39*(3), 413–416; discussion 423–419.

Stahl, B., & Goldstein, E. (2010). A mindfulness-based stress reduction workbook. Oakland, CA: New Harbinger Publications.

Steele, M., Hodges, J., Kaniuk, J., Steele, H., Hillman, S., & Asquith, K. (2008). Forecasting outcomes in previously maltreated children: The use of the AAI in a longitudinal adoption study. In H. Steele and M. Steele (Eds), *Clinical applications of the adult attachment interview* (2008).

Steele, H., Steele, M., Croft, C., & Fonagy, P. (1999). Infant–mother attachment at one year predicts children's understanding of mixed emotions at six years. *Social Development, 8*(2), 161–178.

Steele, H., & Steele, M. (2008a). *Clinical applications of the adult attachment interview.* New York: The Guilford Press.

Steele, H., & Steele, M. (2008b). On the origins of reflective functioning. In F. Busch (Ed.), *Mentalization: Theoretical considerations, research findings, and clinical implications* (p. 133–156). New York: Analytic Press.

Stern, D. N. (1985). *The interpersonal world of the infant: A view from psychoanalysis and developmental psychology.* New York: Basic Books.

Sullivan, H. S. (1953). *The interpersonal theory of psychiatry.* New York: W. W. Norton & Company.

Tatkin, S. (2003a). Marital therapy and the psychobiology of turning toward and turning away: Part 1. *The Therapist, 75*(5), 75–78.

Tatkin, S. (2003b). "Marriage and the mother-infant dyad: Relational trauma and its effects on the success and failure of both." Paper presented at *From Neurons to neighborhoods: The neurobiology of emotional trauma; Innovative methods for healing children and adults,* conference, May 17, Los Angeles, CA.

Tatkin, S. (2004). A developmental psychobiological approach to therapy. *Psychologist–Psychoanalyst, 23*(4), 20–22.

Tatkin, S. (2006a). *Partner Attachment Inventory.* Unpublished manuscript,

University of California at Los Angeles, Department of Family Medicine.

Tatkin, S. (2006b). A synopsis of my approach to couples therapy. *The Therapist, 17*(5), 50–57.

Tatkin, S. (2007). Pseudo-secure couples. *The Therapist, 19*(1).

Tatkin, S. (2009a). Addiction to "alone time": Avoidant attachment, narcissism, and a one-person psychology within a two-person psychological system. *The Therapist, 57*(00), 37–45.

Tatkin, S. (2009b). A psychobiological approach to couple therapy: Integrating attachment and personality theory as interchangeable structural components. *Psychologist–Psychoanalyst: Division 39 of the American Psychological Association, 29*(3), 7–15.

Tatkin, S. (2009c). I want you in the house, just not in my room . . . unless I ask you: The plight of the avoidantly attached partner in couples therapy. *New Therapist Magazine, 62*, 37–45.

Tebartz van Elst, L., Hesslinger, B., Thiel, T., Geiger, E., Haegele, K., Lemieux, L., et al. (2003). Frontolimbic brain abnormalities in patients with borderline personality disorder: A volumetric magnetic resonance imaging study. *Biol Psychiatry, 54*(2), 163–171.

Tebartz van Elst, L., Woermann, F., Lemieux, L., & Trimble, M. (2000). Increased amygdala volumes in female and depressed humans. A quantitative magnetic resonance imaging study. *Neuroscience Letters, 281*(2–3), 103–106.

Teicher, M. H., Andersen, S. L., Polcari, A., Anderson, C. M., & Navalta, C. P. (2002). Developmental neurobiology of childhood stress and trauma. *Psychiatric Clinics of North America, 25*(2), 397–426, vii–viii.

Törk, I., Tracey, D. J., Paxinos, G., & Stone, J. (1995). *Neurotransmitters in the human brain*. New York: Plenum Press.

Trevarthen, C. (2001). Intrinsic motives for companionship in understanding: Their origin, development, and significance for infant mental health. *Infant Mental Health Journal, 22*(1–2), 95–131.

Trevarthen, C., & Aitken, K. J. (2001). Infant intersubjectivity: Research, theory, and clinical applications. *Journal of Child Psychology and Psychiatry and Allied Disciplines, 42*(1), 3–48.

Tronick, E. Z. (2003a). "Of course all relationships are unique": How co-creative processes generate unique mother–infant and patient–therapist relationships and change other relationships. *Psychoanalytic Inquiry, 23*(3), 473–491.

Tronick, E. Z. (2003b). Things still to be done on the still-face effect. *Infancy, 4*(4), 475–482.

Troxel, W., Robles, T., Hall, M., & Buysse, D. (2007). Marital quality and the marital bed: Examining the covariation between relationship quality and sleep. *Sleep Medicine Reviews, 11*(5), 389–404.

Tulving, E. (2001). The origin of autonoesis in episodic memory. In H.

Roediger, J. Nairne, I. Neath & A. Surprenant (Eds.), *The nature of remembering: Essays in honor of Robert g. Crowder* (pp. 17–34). Washington, DC: American Psychological Association.

Tulving, E. (2005). Episodic memory and autonoesis: Uniquely human. In H. Terrace & J. Metcalfe (Eds.), *The missing link in cognition: Origins of self-reflective consciousness* (pp. 3–56). New York: Oxford University Press.

Turk–Browne, N. B., Yi, D. J., & Chun, M. M. (2006). Linking implicit and explicit memory: Common encoding factors and shared representations. *Neuron, 49*(6), 917–927.

van der Kolk, B. A., Pelcovitz, D., Roth, S., & Mandel, F. S. (1996). Dissociation, somatization, and affect dysregulation: The complexity of adaption to trauma. *American Journal of Psychiatry, 153*, 83–93.

van der Kolk, B. A., Weisaeth, L., & McFarlane, A. (Eds) (2006). *Traumatic stress: The effects of overwhelming experience on mind, body, and society.* New York: Guilford Press

van Ijzendoorn, M. H. (1995). Adult attachment representations, parental responsiveness, and infant attachment: A meta-analysis on the predictive validity of the adult attachment interview. *Psychological Bulletin, 117*(3), 387–403.

Volling, B. L., McElwain, N. L., Notaro, P. C., & Herrera, C. (2002). Parents' emotional availability and infant emotional competence: Predictors of parent–infant attachment and emerging self-regulation. *Journal of Family Psychology, 16*(4), 447–465.

von Grünau, M., & Anston, C. (1995). The detection of gaze direction: A stare-in-the-crowd effect. *Perception, 24*(11), 1297.

Vyas, A., Bernal, S., & Chattarji, S. (2003). Effects of chronic stress on dendritic arborization in the central and extended amygdala. *Brain Research, 965*(1–2), 290–294.

Vyas, A., Jadhav, S., & Chattarji, S. (2006). Prolonged behavioral stress enhances synaptic connectivity in the basolateral amygdala. *Neuroscience, 143*(2), 387–393.

Vyas, A., Mitra, R., Shankaranarayana Rao, B., & Chattarji, S. (2002). Chronic stress induces contrasting patterns of dendritic remodeling in hippocampal and amygdaloid neurons. *Journal of Neuroscience, 22*(15), 6810.

Waters, E., & Cummings, E. M. (2000). A secure base from which to explore close relationships. *Child Development, 71*(1), 164–172.

Waters, E., Merrick, S., Treboux, D., Crowell, J., & Albersheim, L. (2000). Attachment security in infancy and early adulthood: A twenty-year longitudinal study. *Child Development, 71*(3), 684–689.

West, R., & Travers, S. (2008). Tracking the temporal dynamics of updating cognitive control: An examination of error processing. *Cerebral Cortex, 18*(5), 1112–1124.

Wicker, B., Perrett, D. I., Baron-Cohen, S., & Decety, J. (2003). Being the target of another's emotion: a PET study. *Neuropsychologia, 41*(2), 139–146.

Wilkins, W., & Wakefield, J. (1995). Brain evolution and neurolinguistic preconditions. *Behavioral and Brain Sciences, 18*(1), 161–181.

Winnicott, D. W. (1957). *The child and the outside world: Studies in developing relationships.* London: Tavistock.

Winnicott, D. W. (1965). *The maturational process and the facilitating environment: Studies in the theory of emotional development.* New York: International University Press.

Winnicott, D. W. (1969). The use of an object. *International Journal of Psycho-Analysis, 50,* 711–716.

Winston, J. S., Strange, B. A., O'Doherty, J., & Dolan, R. J. (2002). Automatic and intentional brain responses during evaluation of trustworthiness of faces. *Nature Neuroscience, 5*(3), 277–283.

Zimmermann, P. (1999). Structure and functions of internal working models of attachment and their role for emotion regulation. *Attachment and Human Development, 1*(3), 291–306.

INDEX

Index